Cultural Practices of Vic

Cultural Practices of Victimhood aims to set the agenda for a cultural study of victimhood. Words such as 'victim' and 'victimhood' represent shifting cultural signifiers, their meaning depending on the cultural context of their usage. Using case studies and through a practice-based approach, questions are asked about how victimhood is defined and constructed, whether in the ritual commemoration of refugees on Lampedusa, the artistic practices of an Aboriginal artist such as Richard Bell, or the media practices associated with police violence.

Consisting of contributions by cultural studies experts with an interest in victim studies, this book seeks a double readership. On the one hand, it intends to break new ground with regards to a 'cultural turn' in the field of criminology, in particular victimology. On the other hand, it also seeks to open up discussions about a 'victimological turn' in culture studies. The volume invites scholars and advanced students active in both domains to reflect on victimhood in cultural practices.

Martin Hoondert studied musicology and theology and is specialized in music and rituals. Since 2007 he has been (associate) professor of Music, Religion and Ritual at the Department of Culture Studies of Tilburg University. His research focuses on 'music and death' and 'practices of memorialization'.

Paul Mutsaers studied cultural anthropology at Utrecht University and works as a police anthropologist for the Department of Culture Studies, Tilburg University, where he is employed as a postdoctoral researcher. He has previously worked at the Police Academy of the Netherlands, where he carried out his PhD research on police discrimination.

William Arfman has a background in the archaeology and anthropology of Central America, as well as the comparative study of religion. Currently, he is a postdoctoral associate and lecturer in the field of ritual studies at Tilburg University. Favouring an interdisciplinary approach, his main research interests are late modern ritual dynamics, ritual innovation and traditionality, ritual and (community) art, and ritual commemoration.

Victims, Culture and Society

Edited by:
Sandra Walklate
University of Liverpool, UK and Monash University, Australia
Kerry Carrington
Queensland University of Technology, Australia

Concerns about victimisation have multiplied over the last 50 years. *Victims, Culture and Society* explores the major concepts, debates and controversies that this concern has generated across a range of disciplines but particularly within criminology and victimology. As the impact of globalisation, the movement of peoples, the divergences between the global north and the global south have become ever more apparent, this series provides an authoritative space for original contributions in making sense of these far-reaching changes on individuals, localities and nationalities. These issues in their very nature demand an interdisciplinary approach and an interdisciplinary voice outside conventional conceptual boundaries. *Victims, Culture and Society* offers the space for that voice.

Each author will adopt a strong personal view and offer a lively and agenda-setting treatment of their subject matter. The monographs will encompass a transnational, global or comparative approach to the issues they address. Examining new areas of both empirical and theoretical inquiry the series offers the opportunity for innovative and progressive thinking about the relationship between victims, culture and society. The books will be useful and thought-provoking resources for the international community of undergraduates, post-graduates, researchers and policy makers working within the broad field of victimisation.

Governing Child Abuse, Voices and Victimisation
The Use of the Public Inquiry into Child Sexual Abuse in Christian Institutions
Jodi Death

Cultural Practices of Victimhood
Edited by Martin Hoondert, Paul Mutsaers and William Arfman

For more information about this series, please visit: www.routledge.com/Victims-Culture-and-Society/book-series/VICS

Cultural Practices of Victimhood

Edited by
Martin Hoondert,
Paul Mutsaers and
William Arfman

Routledge
Taylor & Francis Group

LONDON AND NEW YORK

First published 2019 by Routledge

2 Park Square, Milton Park, Abingdon, Oxon OX14 4RN

605 Third Avenue, New York, NY 10017

Routledge is an imprint of the Taylor & Francis Group, an informa business

First issued in paperback 2021

British Library Cataloguing-in-Publication Data
A catalogue record for this book is available from the British Library

Library of Congress Cataloging-in-Publication Data
Names: Hoondert, Martin J. M., 1967- editor. | Mutsaers, Paul, editor. | Arfman, William R., editor.
Title: Cultural practices of victimhood / edited by Martin Hoondert, Paul Mutsaers and William Arfman.
Description: Abingdon, Oxon ; New York, NY : Routledge, 2018.
| Series: Victims, culture and society | Includes bibliographical references and index.
Identifiers: LCCN 2018010967| ISBN 9781138552814 (hardback) | ISBN 9781315148335 (ebook)
Subjects: LCSH: Victims of crimes–Cross-cultural studies. | Victims–Cross-cultural studies.
Classification: LCC HV6250.25 .C85 2018 | DDC 362.88–dc23
LC record available at https://lccn.loc.gov/2018010967

ISBN: 978-1-138-55281-4 (hbk)
ISBN: 978-0-367-48348-7 (pbk)

Typeset in Sabon
by Wearset Ltd, Boldon, Tyne and Wear

MIX
Paper from
responsible sources
FSC   FSC® C013985
www.fsc.org

Printed in the United Kingdom
by Henry Ling Limited

Contents

Figures

Introduction

Cultural practices of victimhood

*Martin Hoondert, Paul Mutsaers
and William Arfman*

Opening up victimology

Victims are of all times and places. Even the shortest of excursions into a
field like legal anthropology will bring it home to us that, despite its many
variations, victimhood has chronotopic stability: it exists in societies and
communities across time and space. Skimming through the pages of clas-
sics, such as Malinowski's *Crime and Custom in Savage Society* (1926),
Hoebel's *The Law of Primitive Man* (1954) or Gluckman's *The Judicial
Process among the Barotse of Northern Rhodesia* (1955), we may conclude that the commonalities that characterize humankind are, for a large
part, due to the fact that law is inherent to social organization itself. Laws
of one kind or another exist everywhere because crimes do, and where
crimes occur people usually suffer at the hands of others.

Stating that victimhood is a global and timeless phenomenon may be a
truism, but victimology as a distinct intellectual speciality was added to the
ranks of academia not so long ago. To our knowledge, the term victimology was first used by Mendelsohn in 1947 to describe the scientific study
of crime victims, but the discipline only really matured with the establishment of journals such as *Victimology* (1976) and the *International Review
of Victimology* (1989) as well as the *World Society of Victimology* (1979)
and the attendant proliferation of studies and publications (Kirchhoff,
2010). Interestingly, even before it had put itself on the map, the discipline
was already criticized from within. Quinney (1972) for instance, wrote in
his seminal article 'Who is the Victim?' that the dominant image held of
the victim by victimologists is that of a passive victim of 'conventional'
crime, meaning normal, routine, ordinary crime usually occurring in public
(cf. Walklate, 2012). This orientation, characteristic of positivist victimology, is individualistic, passive and static and has kept other categories and
relationships hidden from view.

This remains the case and Quinney's points of critique are as relevant
today as they were at the time he uttered them (cf. Walklate, 2012). For
instance, with respect to the passivity assigned to victims, victimologist

Van Dijk (2009) has argued that victims are still generally considered to be the 'sacrificed ones' who lack any kind of agency (in this volume, see also Lieke Wijnia, Chapter 5, for the notion of sacrifice in early definitions of victimhood and Paul Post, Chapter 3, on sacrifice rituals). Some years later, Van Dijk's colleague Pemberton at the International Victimology Institute Tilburg argued that we therefore need to embrace a radical victimology that engages 'with victims as social actors able to wield agency and shape how they experience victimization rather than just as people who have had things done to them' (Green & Pemberton, 2018, n.p.). Such a victimology understands victims as sovereigns rather than subjects.

Similarly, Quinney's concern with the simplistic definition of crime is equally relevant today. He challenged his readers to 'conceive of the victims of police force, the victims of war, the victims of the correctional system, the victim of state violence, the victims of oppression of any sort' as legitimate areas of concern (Quinney, 1972, p. 321; Walklate, 2012, p. 175). More recently, these areas have indeed been explored by victimologists – e.g. the work of Kauzlarich, Matthews and Miller (2001) on state crime or the various contributions in Letschert and Van Dijk (2011) on victims of environmental pollution, privatized war, and in international criminal courts – but they remain marginal, unless the broader literature regarding transitional justice, peace-building and post-conflict management is drawn into the field (e.g. Hayner, 2011; McEvoy & McConnachie, 2012).

These and other limitations may be due to the fact that victimology has sprung from criminology and has been more isolated from perhaps less obvious but adjacent fields nonetheless. After all, many other scholars have worked on and with victims of various kinds. A casual and random scan of our book shelves draws our attention to, for instance, (critical) race and (post) colonial studies (Bulmer & Solomos, 1999; Essed & Goldberg, 2002; Fanon, 1961; Gilroy, 1987; Merry, 2000; Miles, 1993), literature on migration control and the 'deportation regime' (Andersson, 2014; Blommaert, 2009; Bosworth, 2014; De Genova & Peutz, 2010; Peutz, 2006), studies of neoliberal punishment (Rosas, 2012; Wacquant, 2009), and ethnographies of police violence (Beek, Göpfert, Owen, & Steinberg, 2017; Denyer Willis, 2015; Feldman, 2015; Robb Larkins, 2015). This is not to argue in any way that these studies and approaches should be given priority; we simply want to convey that victimhood has been studied from many different angles and that the incorporation of these studies and approaches may enrich victimology. Opening up the field, as we demonstrate in this book, yields new and surprising insights with respect to victimhood and its narratives, scales, representations, mediatizations, twists, memorializations, complexities, absences and inversions.

The authors in this book are ideally suited to open up the field, as they come from various corners of the social sciences and humanities: ritual studies, sociolinguistics, anthropology, literary studies, victimology, and museum studies. Our paths crossed because of our joint interest in culture studies more generally, and more specifically because we all participated in a conference on the cultural practices of victimhood, held in May/June 2016 at Tilburg University by the Department of Culture Studies in cooperation with the Institute for Ritual and Liturgical Studies. We came together because our common and convergent interests lay in the ways victimhood is culturally constructed and practised; hence the current division of the book into ritual, artistic and media practices (more below). From the very outset we turned away from the narrowness of positivist victimological definitions of victims as individualistic, passive and static. Rather, we took our inspiration from ideas that circulate within cultural victimology: 'Being or becoming a victim is not a neat or absolute journey. Acquiring the status of victim involves being party to a range of interactions and processes, including identification, labelling and recognition' (Mythen, 2007, p. 466).

Cultural practices of victimhood

Focusing squarely on how victimhood is *culturally practised* is a highly effective manner to discredit positivist, mainstream definitions of victim(hood). The practice-part automatically means that passive notions are substituted by active ones. It starts from the idea that victims do not simply have things done to them – an idea that is firmly corroborated in these chapters. Victims have agency, they often have a political will and they actively give meaning to victimhood through various practices. Whether they do so as sovereigns, subalterns, or something in-between has to be investigated on a case-to-case basis, but in the various studies that are documented in this book, we never encountered victims who only passively suffer. What's more, looking at how victimhood is practised means that it is understood not as a natural but a social fact, insofar as it needs to be explained by the sociality through which it is given meaning and the social structure in which such meaning is inscribed and encoded.

Taking practice as one of the key concepts in this volume brings performance theory into our research. The broad field of performance studies gives us at least two important tools for analysis. First, performance studies help us to analyse the 'doing' with simple but useful questions such as: what kind of action takes place, who acts, what materials are used, what roles can be distinguished, who is the public, what are the purposes or functions etc. (Grimes, 2014; Schechner, 2006)? Second, 'performance' points at the concept of 'performativity', which allows us to ask how the performance affects participants, audiences and institutional contexts. Performativity is more than functional efficacy; it points at effects of a performance beyond intentions and expectations. Practices of victimhood might both inscribe victimhood into the bodies of people and release them from the burden of being a victim. The concept of performativity focuses our minds on the impression of practices and leads us away from predefined definitions of victim and victimhood.

All these practices can, to a certain extent, be characterized as practices of memorialization. They implicitly or explicitly deal with the recent or distant past. A refugee who writes a novel in which he uses his experiences as a refugee, deals with his or her past (Rigney, 2010). A Sinti composer who writes a Requiem to commemorate the Sinti and Roma, killed during the Second World War, deals with the past (Polak, 2013). A government that commissions a design of a memorial to commemorate the victims of a terrorist attack, deals with the past (Foote, 2003). In focusing on what people *do* to grapple with and give meaning to their suffering we take on part of the agenda as delineated by Gabe Mythen in his already mentioned chapter on cultural victimology: 'a cultural inflection within victimology might encourage research into representations of crime victims in popular culture, forms of cultural resistance to victim categorization, the discursive deconstruction of the language of victimization and the symbolic production of the victim' (Mythen, 2007, pp. 479–480).

This brings us to the culture-part. One very obvious part of the social structure that shapes victims and the experience of victimhood in a significant way is, of course, the law. Law and the various legal categories and concepts that come along with it – such as blame, wrongdoing, rights, victim, offender, culpability and crime – tell us something about a society and the way it gives order and meaning to relationships (see Paul Mutsaers, Chapter 8, this volume). Victims have to find their way through a legal system and the various legal practices involved. In contrast to more conventional studies of law, we can understand it as a part of culture and, by extension, the legal entanglements of victims can be understood as entanglements in cultural practices. In fact, law does the work of culture: it offers a vision of society, categories of identity, a framework for ordered relationships and it is an important force in shaping human behaviour and lending significance to it; in other words, it is a constructive element within culture (Geertz, 1983; cf. Mutsaers, this volume; Rosen, 2006, 2017). So, when victims go to court they enter a cultural domain and face the 'cultural power of law' (Merry, 2000).

And yet, legal practice (as cultural practice) is not our prime concern. In fact, as the reader will find out between the covers of this book, victims sometimes actively oppose the justice system exactly because it contributes to the individualization of their problems (and thus reinforces positivist notions of victimhood). Western-dominated theories and practices of justice are often of a liberal bent (e.g. Goodale, 2017; Peterson, 2010; Rosen, 2006), giving priority to individual rights and freedoms. This is a cultural precept in and of itself, one that makes it very hard for victims to gain recognition for the collective aspects of victimhood or the structural aspects of crime (e.g. state crime), because there often is no place for groups as distinct legal entities in Western legal systems. So, if we want to study the cultural representations of and by victims, the different contestations and negotiations of victim categorizations, the language of victimization, and the symbolic production of the victim (cf. Mythen, 2007) – in other words, the 'social' in victimhood – we thus better turn to other kinds of cultural practices than legal ones. So we ask: how is victimhood experienced and imbued with meaning beyond the bounds (and constraints) of the legal system?

As stated, this book is centred on ritual, artistic and media practices and deals with a wide range of subjects: rituals and counter-rituals after Srebrenica (Hoondert), a monument for refugees and the diverse attitudes towards victims (Arfman), the ritual repertoire of victimhood in the context of Fortress Europe and the refugee crisis (Post), the contested representation of victim experiences at the Berlin Wall Memorial Museum (Clarke), the reversal of victimhood in Aboriginal art (Wijnia), artistic practices of memorialization for victims of terrorism and abuse of power in the Basque Country (Varona), fictional literature as crucial social knowledge about migrant victims in Europe (Heynders), 'masculine victimhood' in the online Manosphere and cultural templates for violence (Blommaert), victimhood and digital protest in the context of police violence and racism in the United States (Mutsaers) and, finally, the semiotics of the 2016 Cologne sexual assaults and their media representations (Kroon). Through the lens of various cultural practices, we study how victims are represented and talked about, how dead bodies are transformed into political capital, how victimhood relates to moral panic, how killers appropriate the status of victim in online media, how victim categorizations are resisted, stretched and transformed, and much more. The chapters are diverse and each one has its own qualities, but they all have at least one thing in common: all show that being or becoming a victim is not a neat or absolute journey (to refer, once again, to Mythen, 2007). Let us consider the chapters in more depth.

Structure of the book: rituals, arts and media

Before we continue, however, a caveat should be lodged: the distinction between ritual, artistic and media practices is not as strict as the section outline suggests. It has come about in a rather organic way, due to the various areas of expertise and interest of the authors, and mainly serves an organizational purpose. It goes without saying that the overlap between these practices is substantial. In times of global communication, many ritual and artistic practices are widely mediatized; media activities are often ritualistically performed; and rituals and art are sometimes deliberately performed in the vicinity of each other. We use the three categories to underscore different features rather than essential differences and we will pay more attention to their intertwinement below.

At this point it is important to repeat, however, that we think of all three as *cultural* practices. In the most general sense of the world 'culture', it can be argued that – just like the law – rituals, art and media give meaning to life. They offer a framework for ordered relationships and experiences, they shape human behaviour and lend significance to it, they stimulate social imagination, and they help people to make sense of the world. The authors in this book have developed their own approaches to culture and how it relates to victimhood. Some have done so more explicitly than others. Heynders understands novels as an important form of social knowledge about refugees and migrants and their victimization. Relatedly, Blommaert approaches the darkest corners of the internet as a learning environment (for better or worse) that offers cultural templates for 'abnormal' victim identities and violent behaviour. Hoondert, Arfman, Clarke, Post and Varona study rituals and art to understand how people deal with past experiences of pain and anguish. Wijnia investigates how victimhood is culturally constructed in the Aboriginal art of Richard Bell, who deploys it to challenge projections and normative expectations regarding Aboriginal art in an art world dominated by the West. Kroon turns to the cultural power of media frames and takes the interpretations of the Cologne translation note as a microcosm of a more general trend to frame cultural others as perpetrators even before conviction. Finally, Mutsaers looks at digital protests of Black Lives Matter activists against police as cultural practices that challenge the conventional ways in which victims, offenders and the state are socially constructed in a legal culture. Together, they make a very strong case for the contribution of cultural studies to our understanding of victimhood as dynamic, social and actively (re)lived.

Ritual practices

In the first section of this book we present ritual practices as a lens to study the construction of victimhood. In the tradition of the Tilburg 'Ritual in Society' research group, we use an open and broad approach to ritual. Ritual as a concept has become obsolete in day-to-day practices, although these practices actually show a lot of what, from a scholarly perspective, can be called 'ritual'. Yet, also from an analytical and scholarly perspective the definition of what a ritual is, is not very clear; if there is a definition, it primarily depends on the context in which research has taken place. However, this does not imply that the conceptual work around ritual is or should be completely arbitrary. What we need is a so-called polythetic definition, which, in contrast to a monothetic definition that relies on exclusive criteria that have to be part of all the phenomena referred to as ritual, works with a set of characteristics that *may* be applied (Snoek, 2006). One way of working out the main characteristics of a polythetic definition of ritual is the application of a wide range of theoretic concepts that shed light on several aspects of rituals, e.g. performance, gender, agency, embodiment, efficacy. In 1990, Ronald Grimes presented a list of characteristics of a ritual that will help us to analyse cultural practices of victimhood from the perspective of ritual theory (Grimes, 1990, p. 14). Using Grimes' list implies that often used characteristics to define rituals, such as 'invariant', 'traditional', 'community-based', might not apply.

Studying rituals using this open and broad perspective points at several cultural domains or fields where rituals can be traced. Traditionally, rituals are linked to the domain of religion. However, with the waning influence of religion since the 1960s, at least in Western Europe, rituals have been transferred to, and new rituals have emerged in, other cultural domains, such as the domain of leisure and sport, art and wellness (Post, 2011, 2015). A dominant and very much visible ritual repertoire in our culture is linked to the domain of memory and dealing with the past. These practices of memorialization cover a range of activities, performances, processes, narratives, organizations and material objects. Besides memorials and remembrance days, museums, online memorial websites, documentaries, movies, books, politics of burial, truth seeking mechanisms, judicial processes and apologies also contain practices of memorialization and are ways of dealing with the past (Erll & Nünning, 2010; Plate & Smelik, 2013). Some of these practices are culturally accepted as ritual, others can be studied *as* ritual, using the already mentioned open perspective and making use of concepts from ritual studies, such as transformation, repetition, tradition and, once again, performance. Looking at these practices through the lens of ritual gives insight into the performance of commemorative rituals, the material culture, the landscape of commemoration, and the way these practices construct and define victimhood.

In the first chapter, Martin Hoondert analyses the rituals and 'counter-rituals' related to the 1995 genocide in Srebrenica. Hoondert describes the ritual complexity to give insight into the cultural representations of suffering as expressed by Bosniaks and Bosnian Serbs. He then gives an argument for ritual criticism: these rituals turn Bosnians into prisoners of their own history. They re-enact the war and reinforce ethno-religious boundaries. In order to truly achieve a post-war situation, those involved in the rituals need to abandon the claim of a monopoly on truth and search for shared narratives. Ritual criticism, as such, is criticism that starts from a contextual analysis and does not shy away from formulating a new normative framework.

Next, William Arfman presents a community artwork by a refugee artist, entitled *Monument for Boat Refugees*. In this chapter we come across the close links between ritual, art and memory practices. Arfman analyses the monument for boat refugees both as ritual, so using ritual theory, and from a philosophical-victimological angle. The artwork/ monument is playful and serious at the same time and invites passers-by to engage. In offering people a moment to reflect, the monument relies on the ritual-like elements of repetition, performativity, symbolism and liminality. This liminality is not confined to the artwork itself: participants deciding to enter the limited liminal arena of the art installation, enter the much larger liminal arena of the European refugee crisis as well. In a second round of analysis, Arfman uses Trudy Govier's philosophical discussion of four attitudes towards victims and explores how the monument for boat refugees goes against attitudes towards victimhood that are dominated by either silence or blame, and promotes attitudes of deference and victims' agency.

In the last chapter of the ritual section, Paul Post studies refugees' travels from Africa via the island of Lampedusa (Italy) to West-European host countries. He describes the individual and collective rituals that are performed during this journey. His chapter is a sequel to a previous project on rituals after disasters, one of the projects of the Tilburg 'Ritual in Society' research group (Post, Grimes, Nugteren, Pettersson, & Zondag, 2003), and is linked to ongoing research on practices of memorialization after atrocities and large-scale human rights violations. Post explores the refugees' ritual repertoire and in doing this he describes a ritual repertoire of victimhood, which is characterized by several, sometimes contrasting themes, such as mourning, burying, healing, coping with trauma, commemoration, doing justice, restoration, reconciliation, protest, starting a new life. The ritual repertoire of victimhood seems to identify, construct and resist victimhood.

Artistic practices

In Part II we explore victimhood through the lens of artistic practices. These practices are materialized, embodied meanings (Danto, 2013), challenging the spectator, reader or listener to unravel their meanings. Like ritual practices, artistic practices in relation to victimhood are also closely linked to memory. Art mediates and remediates memories, but, referring to MacLuhan's famous catchword (MacLuhan, 1964), the artwork or performance is also a way of memory making. Two characteristics of 'memory artwork' distinguish artistic practices from other practices related to victims, victimhood and memory (Erll, 2011, pp. 144–153). First, art has what we may call 'fictional privileges', i.e. the possibility to imagine alternative realities. Artworks are perceived *as* art, thus as polyvalent forms of representation which can also integrate imagined elements into their version of the past, e.g. in telling the victim's life-story. As such, artworks and performances are memory-reflexive and memory-productive. Second, art constructs versions of the past, both affirmative and subversive, traditional and new ones, and makes this process of construction observable, and thus also criticisable. In constructing a narrative of the past, artwork has the ability to refer to the forgotten and repressed, as well as the unnoticed, unconscious and unintentional aspects of our dealing with the past. As such, artworks can be critical to both victims and perpetrators, blurring the boundaries between perpetrators and victims, and nuancing the often one-sided versions of the 'truth' about the past.

In this book, several 'loci' related to artistic practices come to the fore: the museum, theatre and literature. David Clarke details in his chapter the complicated development of the Berlin Wall Memorial Museum at Bernauer Straße in Berlin. Drawing on Luhmann's system theory, he analyses the dynamics and conflicts between professional heritage organizations and victims' organizations, that is, between the 'system of science' and the 'system of protest'. On top of that, there is another system (the 'political system') that persistently seizes upon this conflict for its own purpose. Clarke offers a nuanced discussion of the trajectory that led to the museum, giving a voice to all the actors and interest groups involved. In his conclusion he points at the political system's possibility and responsibility to recognize the victims' voice as a way of successful management of disputes regarding the museum as a practice of both memorialization and transitional justice.

Lieke Wijnia also positions the topic of her chapter in the museum, in this case the Stedelijk Museum Bureau Amsterdam (SMBA) which hosted an exhibition by the Aboriginal artist Richard Bell (1953) and invited colleagues. Wijnia explores the exhibition by means of the notion of victimhood. Her analysis leads to an exploration of the questions of who we are talking about when using the concept of victimhood, what it means to be a victim, and how visual art offers strategies to express (and upset) the cultural boundaries of victimhood that are present in the relationship between artist and audience. By means of Bell's and his colleagues' artworks, the self-evident, unquestioned character of living a comfortable life is turned into a discomfort for a part of the audience. This has been analysed in terms of the reversal of victimhood; that is, in his work Bell does not emphasize how Aboriginals feel inferior and less worthy as a result of the imposition of western values and social structures upon them. Rather, he turns this process around, by pointing out how those doing the projecting should question their own cultural, moral and normative frameworks.

Gema Varona deals with the current struggle in the practices of memorialization for victims of terrorism and abuse of power in the Basque Country, using new perspectives in victimology. Her perspective of critical victimology meets the above-mentioned critique on positivist victimology, taking a non-essentialist, non-antagonist and non-pathological vision of the processes of victimization. Varona describes and evaluates an ephemeral public theatre production performed in 2016, remembering victims through music, words and pictures or videos. The theatre production emancipated the victims from their invisibility and vulnerability and turned them into a visible presence, and as such the staged memory was restorative. Moreover, the project broke with the stereotyped image of victims whose entire life is dominated by their victimization and who are isolated from other life dimensions and people. The audience invited to this theatre production recognized the individualized memories as something of the past, but referring to the future. The project made the darkness of victimization visible and, as such, it was prospective, aiming at future generations.

Odile Heynders connects to the strong tradition of dealing with victims in literature, particularly migrant and refugee literature (e.g. Burns, 2013; Jin, 2008; Ponzanesi & Merolla, 2005). A good example of this genre is the novel *African Titanics*, written by Abu Bakr Kahhāl (2014), which tells the story of Kahhāl's alter ego, a refugee who left Eritrea for Denmark, as an 'Odyssean adventure'. This book, and there are many others to be mentioned, helps us to understand what refugees go through and gives refugees a voice in the public domain as victims of war or other causes of forced migration. Marcia Lynx Qualey, an expert in Arab literature, qualified Kahhāl's novel from a cultural and social perspective:

> [...] it is equally wrong to read Kahhāl's book only for its aesthetic value – which is just as possible. The novel is a lovely piece of craftsmanship [...]. Yet the book doesn't want to be read that way, either. In the end, it insists on this: that we remember these 'migrants' as we go about our day. It insists that these individuals *deserve* their space in the larger stream of human stories. [Emphasis in original.]

In a similar vein, Heynders deals in her chapter with migration in the context of Europe. She builds a very strong case for the importance of literature (and the study thereof) in the context of (irregular) migration and the complex configuration of victims, survivors, bystanders, border officials and law keepers that comes with it. Focusing on two contemporary novels, she analyses the knowledge on migrant experiences that is provided by these novels and how this knowledge contributes to the societal reframing of migrants in making an affective request to human solidarity and awareness. Heynders presents literature as a sort of hermeneutic warning system that produces social knowledge that allows readers to develop interpretations and imaginations which differ significantly from the hyperhermeneutics that is forced on people on an almost daily basis by the hysterical media and politics on migration and asylum.

Media practices

In Part III we turn to media practices as a vehicle through which victims and processes of victimization are rendered visible (e.g. Tulloch, 2006). Media practices are obviously characterized by the involvement of media such as television and radio, and social media such as Twitter and Facebook. Here, we are not primarily interested in the technologies of media, but in the communicative effects. Through our practice approach, we are drawn to the influence of media on the ideas people have or gain regarding victims and victimhood. Lisa Gitelman's definition of media aligns well with our approach:

> [Media are] socially realized structures of communication, where structures include both technological forms and their associated protocols, and where communication is a cultural practice, a ritualized collocation of different people on the same mental map, sharing or engaged with particular ontologies of representation.
>
> (Gitelman, 2008, p. 7)

One of the key issues in studying media practices related to victimhood is the selectivity of media. The newsworthiness of events determines the visibility and creates a hierarchy of victims (Landau, 2006) and the presence of victims in the media might serve other goals, such as presenting a moral compass or a political statement (Crumbaugh, 2007). As Landau stated, 'images of victimhood are a product of a variety of processes that reflect the social location of individuals and groups in society' (Landau, 2006, p. 22). The attention paid to the connection between media, victims and (the construction of) victimhood has increased over the past few decades due to what Furedi (1998) has called 'the culture of victimhood'. We believe that a critical review of the selection processes by both the traditional and social media is needed.

Two of the three chapters in this section deal with online media, the third chapter focuses mainly on newspapers. Paul Mutsaers analyses the Black Lives Matter movement in the US, which is present and visible on Facebook and Twitter. Through these online media anti-police protests and concomitant victimhood-claiming are expressed and shared. The Black Lives Matter movement challenges the position of the individual in legal processes by exposing police violence against Black Americans as a form of structural violence amounting to state crime, rather than incidents involving individuals. As such, digital activism can help to gain recognition for victimhood as a form of collective suffering, because social media do the work of the public. That is to say, they can bring together a multitude of strangers around a public issue, an online public in which victims can directly participate as sovereigns, who do not merely suffer from but also subvert the social structures that work at their disadvantage.

Jan Blommaert presents a rather confusing chapter. Confusing because it invites the reader to the less commonly visited fringes of the Web 2.0, a space called the 'Manosphere'. And confusing because a reversal of victimhood seems to take place. In the Manosphere, men gather to exchange experiences and views on the oppressive role and position of women in their worlds, and often do so by means of misogynist, sexist, (often) racist and (sometimes) violent discourse. Although the Manosphere is very much an online zone of social activity operating in the shadows of the Web, there are some moments of public, offline visibility. Blommaert starts from one such moment, the killing of six people by Elliot Rodger, in May 2014, California. Blommaert explores how the online infrastructures of the Manosphere provide affordances for constructing a logic of action, strengthening Rodger's sense of victimhood and providing rationalizations for the murders he committed. The analysis shows how this remarkable case of victimhood and the experiences of victimization are rendered 'normal' and how the victim becomes, in the end, a perpetrator.

In the last chapter of this section, Sjaak Kroon analyses the newspaper reporting of the wave of sexual assaults that allegedly took place on New Year's Eve 2015/2016 in the German city of Cologne. The starting point of his chapter is a small note, a snippet of paper. This note contains Arabic words and expressions with a German translation, some of which have a sexual connotation. In newspapers, this note was presented as 'proof' of the intention of immigrants/refugees to seduce and abuse German women. According to the newspapers, the note suggests that the men who committed the crimes of robbery, theft, groping, sexual harassment and rape on New Year's Eve 2015/2016 in Cologne were of North African or Arab origin. This suggestion was however quickly transformed into an almost general public consensus that the Cologne perpetrators belonged to a community of (mainly) newly arrived refugees and asylum seekers in Germany. As such, the note led to the construction of (unproven) perpetratorship. In this way the alleged perpetrators ended up as nothing more or less than victims, victims of popular sentiment created by the media. Kroon's analysis shows the reversal, not, as we have seen, from innocent audience to witness and perpetrator (Wijnia) or from victim to perpetrator (Blommaert), but from perpetrator to victim.

An invitation

The chapters in this book confirm that what Furedi (1998) proclaimed two decades ago is still very much true: the attention for victimhood is at its zenith. It has been so for a long time, and rightfully so. In times of rugged and unapologetic individualism and shattered communities, suffering and mourning are social acts that bring people together and assist them in (re)building communities, societies, publics and nations. That these social forms can be very dark (see Blommaert in Chapter 9) or stand in the way of peacebuilding (see Hoondert in Chapter 1) is another matter, but the 'social' in victimhood ought to be recognized as a legitimate area of study in the humanities and social sciences concerned with victims. It is in this light that we proposed to open up victimology and let other disciplines in, and we hope that this book builds a strong case for culture studies as a suitable candidate (and for the focus on cultural practices of victimhood as deep social activities in particular).

But the invitation goes both ways. Just as much as we advocate the embrace of cultural studies by victimologists, we seek to open up discussions about a 'victimological turn' in culture studies. By no means do we want to argue that culture studies has never been preoccupied with victims. The work of prominent scholars in the field such as Stuart Hall (e.g. Hall, 2002; Hall, Critcher, Jefferson, Clarke, & Roberts, 1978) and Paul Gilroy (e.g. Gilroy, 1987) would render such an argument absurd, as would the unwavering focus on the 'suffering subject' by one of the mother disciplines of culture studies – anthropology (e.g. Karpiak, 2016; Robbins, 2013). But victim studies could be incorporated in a more systematic and programmatic way, in order to make sure that it stays on our radar. This book should therefore be read as an invitation to both sides and we look forward to responses from colleagues in the fields of victimology *and* culture studies who wish to contribute to the synergy.

At the end of this Introduction we express our gratitude to Sandra Walklate for her encouragement to publish our research on cultural practices of victimhood, and to Carine Zebedee of the Tilburg School of Humanities for her great support in preparing the texts and images for publication.

References

Andersson, R. (2014). *Illegality, Inc: Clandestine migration and the business of bordering Europe*. Oakland: University of California Press.

Beek, J., Göpfert, M., Owen, O., & Steinberg, J. (Eds.). (2017). *Police in Africa: The street level view*. London: Hurst & Company.

Blommaert, J. (2009). Language, asylum and the national order. *Current Anthropology, 50*(4): 415–441.

Bosworth, M. (2014). *Inside immigration detention*. Oxford: Oxford University Press.

Bulmer, M., & Solomos, J. (1999). *Racism*. Oxford: Oxford University Press.

Burns, J. (2013). *Migrant imaginaries: Figures in Italian migration literature*. Oxford: Peter Lang.

Crumbaugh, J. (2007). Are we all (still) Miguel Ángel Blanco? Victimhood, the media afterlife, and the challenge for historical memory. *Hispanic Review, 75*(4), 365–384.

Danto, A. C. (2013). *What art is*. New Haven: Yale University Press.

De Genova, N., & Peutz, N. (Eds.). (2010). *The deportation regime: Sovereignty, space and the freedom of movement*. Durham, NC: Duke University Press.

Denyer Willis, G. (2015). *The killing consensus: Police, organized crime, and the regulation of life and death in urban Brazil*. Oakland: University of California Press.

Erll, A. (2011). *Memory in culture*. Basingstoke: Palgrave Macmillan.

Erll, A., & Nünning, A. (2010). *A companion to cultural memory studies*. Berlin/New York: De Gruyter.

Essed, Ph., & Goldberg, D. T. (Eds.). (2002). *Race critical theories*. Oxford: Blackwell Publishers.

Fanon, F. (1961). *The wretched of the earth*. London: Penguin Books.

Feldman, I. (2015). *Police encounters: Security and surveillance in Gaza under Egyptian rule*. Stanford, CA: Stanford University Press.

Foote, K. E. (2003). *Shadowed ground: America's landscapes of violence and tragedy* (revised and updated edition). Austin: University of Texas Press.

Furedi, F. (1998). New Britain: A nation of victims. *Society*, *35*(3), 80–84.

Geertz, C. (1983). *Local knowledge: Further essays in interpretive anthropology*. New York: Basic Books.

Gilroy, P. (1987). *There ain't no black in the Union Jack*. Chicago: The University of Chicago Press.

Gitelman, L. (2008). *Always already new: Media, history and the data of culture* (1st paperback edition). Cambridge, MA: MIT.

Gluckman, M. (1955). *The judicial process among the Barotse of Northern Rhodesia*. Manchester: Manchester University Press.

Goodale, M. (2017). *Anthropology and law: A critical introduction*. New York: New York University Press.

Green, S., & Pemberton, A. (2018). The impact of crime: Victimisation, harm and resilience. In S. Walklate (Ed.), *Handbook of victims and victimology* (2nd edition). London: Routledge.

Grimes, R. L. (1990). *Ritual criticism: Case studies in its practice, essays on its theory*. Columbia, SC: University of South Carolina Press.

Grimes, R. L. (2014). *The craft of ritual studies*. Oxford: Oxford University Press.

Hall, S. (2002). Race, articulation, and societies structured in dominance. In Ph. Essed & D. T. Goldberg (Eds.), *Race critical theories* (pp. 38–68). Oxford: Blackwell Publishers.

Hall, S., Critcher, C., Jefferson, T., Clarke, J., & Roberts, B. (1978). *Policing the crisis: Mugging, the state, and law and order*. London: Palgrave Macmillan.

Hayner, P. B. (2011). *Unspeakable truths: Transitional justice and the challenge of truth commissions* (2nd edition). New York: Routledge.

Hoebel, E. A. (1954). *The law of primitive man: A study in comparative legal dynamics*. Cambridge, MA: Harvard University Press.

Jin, H. (2008). *The writer as migrant*. Chicago: University of Chicago Press.

Kahhāl, A. B. H. (2014). *African Titanics*. London: Darf Publishers.

Karpiak, K. (2016). The anthropology of police. In B. Bradford, B. Jauregui, I. Loader, & J. Steinberg (Eds.), *The Sage handbook of global policing*. Los Angeles: Sage.

Kauzlarich, D., Matthews, R. A., & Miller, W. J. (2001). Toward a victimology of state crime. *Critical Criminology, 10*(3), 173–194.

Kirchhoff, G. F. (2010). History and a theoretical structure of victimology. In S. G. Shoham, P. Knepper, & M. Kett (Eds.), *International handbook of victimology* (pp. 95–126). Boca Raton: CRC Press.

Landau, T. (2006). *Challenging notions: Critical victimology in Canada.* Toronto: Canadian Scholars' Press.

Letschert, R., & Van Dijk, J. (Eds.). (2011). *The new faces of victimhood: Globalization, transnational crimes, and victim rights.* Dordrecht: Springer.

MacLuhan, M. (1964). *Understanding media: The extensions of man.* Bergenfield, NJ: New American Library.

Malinowski, B. (1926). *Crime and custom in savage society.* London: Kegan Paul, Trench, Trubner.

McEvoy, K., & McConnachie, K. (2012). Victimology in transitional justice: Victimhood, innocence and hierarchy. *European Journal of Criminology, 9*(5), 527–538.

Merry, S. E. (2000). *Colonizing Hawai'i: The cultural power of law.* Princeton, NJ: Princeton University Press.

Miles, R. (1993). *Racism after 'race relations'.* London: Routledge.

Mythen, G. (2007). Cultural victimology: Are we all victims now? In S. Walklate (Ed.), *Handbook of victims and victimology* (pp. 464–483). Cullompton, UK: Willan.

Peterson, J. H. (2010). 'Rule of Law' initiatives and the liberal peace: The impact of politicised reform in post-conflict states. *Disasters, 34*(supplement 1), 15–39.

Peutz, N. (2006). Embarking on an anthropology of removal. *Current Anthropology, 47*(2): 217–241.

Plate, L., & Smelik, A. (2013). Performing memory in art and popular culture: An introduction. In L. Plate & A. Smelik (Eds.), *Performing memory in art and popular culture* (pp. 1–22). New York: Routledge.

Polak, K. (2013). Teaching about the Genocide of the Roma and Sinti during the Holocaust: Chances and challenges in Europe today. *Intercultural Education, 24*(1–2), 79–92.

Ponzanesi, S., & Merolla, D. (2005). *Migrant cartographies: New cultural and literary spaces in post-colonial Europe.* Lanham, MD: Lexington Books.

Post, P. (2011). Fields of the sacred: Reframing identities of sacred places. In P. Post, A. L. Molendijk, & J. Kroesen (Eds.), *Sacred places in modern western culture* (pp. 13–59). Leuven: Peeters.

Post, P. (2015). Ritual studies. *Oxford research encyclopedia of religion.* Oxford: Oxford University Press. Retrieved from https://pure.uvt.nl/portal/en/publications/ritual-studies(53922eba-41ab-4c03-adad-535d1a6a4fc5).html.

Post, P., Grimes, R., Nugteren, A., Pettersson, P., & Zondag, H. (2003). *Disaster ritual: Explorations of an emerging ritual repertoire* (Volume 15). Leuven: Peeters.

Quinney, R. (1972). Who is the victim? *Criminology, 10*(3), 314–323.

Rigney, A. (2010). The dynamics of remembrance: Texts between monumentality and morphing. In A. Erll & A. Nunning (Eds.), *A companion to cultural memory studies* (pp. 345–353). Berlin/New York: De Gruyter.

Robb Larkins, E. (2015). *The spectacular Favela: Violence in modern Brazil.* Oakland: University of California Press.

Robbins, J. (2013). Beyond the suffering subject: Toward an anthropology of the good. *Journal of the Royal Anthropological Institute*, 19(3), 447–462.

Rosas, G. (2012). *Barrio libre: Criminalizing states and delinquent refusals of the New Frontier*. Durham/London: Duke University Press.

Rosen, L. (2006). *Law as culture: An invitation*. Princeton: Princeton University Press.

Rosen, L. (2017). *The judgement of culture: Cultural assumptions in American law*. London: Routledge.

Schechner, R. (2006). *Performance studies: An introduction* (2nd edition). New York/London: Routledge.

Snoek, J. (2006). Defining rituals. In J. Kreinath, J. Snoek, & M. Stausberg (Eds.), *Theorizing rituals: Issues, topics, approaches, concepts* (Volume 1, pp. 3–14). Leiden: Brill.

Tulloch, J. (2006). *One day in July: Experiencing 7/7*. London: Little Brown.

Van Dijk, J. (2009). Free the victim: A critique of the Western conception of victimhood. *International Review of Victimology*, 16(1), 1–33.

Wacquant, L. (2009). *Punishing the poor: The neoliberal government of social insecurity*. Durham/London: Duke University Press.

Walklate, S. (2012). Who is the victim of crime? Paying homage to the work of Richard Quinney. *Crime, Media, Culture*, 8(2), 173–184.

Part I

Ritual practices

Chapter 1

Srebrenica

Conflict and ritual complexities

Martin Hoondert

Introduction

The massacre of more than 8000 Bosnian Muslim men and boys by Serb forces led by Ratko Mladić in Srebrenica in 1995, is the worst act of genocide in Europe since the Second World War. For the Netherlands, the fall of Srebrenica has become a national trauma. This is because a battalion of Dutch UN peace-keepers in Srebrenica and the neighbouring village Potočari failed to protect the UN safe area and the people in their care. For many years, Srebrenica haunted Dutch politicians, struggling with the issue of responsibility, and Srebrenica survivors used lawsuits in their fight for recognition and justice (Attila Hoare, 2010; Spijkers, 2016).

In 2003, a memorial centre was opened in Potočari. This Potočari Memorial Centre (PMC) is located at the Dutchbat compound, a former battery factory. On the other side of the road, the victims of the Srebrenica genocide are buried (Pollack, 2003a). Every year, on the 11th of July, various commemoration practices take place here, attracting both Bosniaks – as the Bosnian Muslims are called – from the whole of Bosnia-Herzegovina and a large international public (sympathizers and delegates of governments, NGOs and international organizations). Although the commemoration on the 11th of July in Srebrenica gets the most attention in the international media, it is not the only ritual related to the fall of the enclave and, more broadly, the Bosnian War, which lasted from 1992 to 1995 (Burg & Shoup, 1999). In this chapter, I will explore the rituals and ritual-like practices in Srebrenica and neighbouring villages, showing how the ritual dynamics resurrect the (past) conflict, making Srebrenica a prisoner of its own history. Second, I will reflect on the necessity to design places of shared truths, which enhance the process of social reconstruction and reconciliation in post-war Bosnia-Herzegovina.

Rituals and counter-rituals

In Potočari

In 2015, I visited Srebrenica and attended the 20th anniversary of the Srebrenica genocide at the Potočari Memorial Centre (Figures 1.1 and 1.2). Srebrenica and Potočari, two small villages in the Eastern part of Bosnia Herzegovina, were crowded. The road leading to the Memorial Centre was full of cars and buses. The official commemoration on the 11th of July started at the Memorial Centre, located in the former battery factory. While most of the participants gathered on the other side of the road, at the cemetery, waiting for the burial ceremony to start, we listened to speeches by, among others, the Mayor of Srebrenica, former US President Bill Clinton and the Dutch Minister of Foreign Affairs Bert Koenders. One of the guests was the Serbian Prime Minister Aleksandar Vučić, who was welcomed by Bill Clinton and praised because of his courage and his endeavour to make a first step to reconciliation.

After the speeches by the officials, we all left the Memorial Centre and walked to the cemetery. There, 136 coffins with the remains of the victims of the Srebrenica genocide, recently identified using DNA analysis, were waiting to be buried. When Vučić entered the cemetery, a few people in the crowd started booing and whistling, while others shouted 'Genocide!'. Stones and other objects were thrown at him, and Vučić was forced to leave the site. Although the Mayor of Srebrenica and representatives of survivors' associations (the 'Mothers of Srebrenica') distanced themselves from these hostilities, the damage had already been done. Later that day, the Serbian Minister of the Interior, Nebojša Stefanović, declared on Serbian Pink television: 'This is a scandalous attack and I can say it can be seen as an assassination attempt. Bosnia has failed to create even the minimal conditions for the safety of the prime minister.'[1]

Apart from this incident, the mass burial of the 136 victims was an impressive and worthy ceremonial. Ten thousand Muslim men and women took part in the funeral prayers before the coffins were carried to the graves (Figure 1.3). In the meantime, the names of the victims were read by a woman as a litany of dead. Each coffin was accompanied by an imam, who said the required prayers at the graveside. Not being a Muslim, I felt like an intruder, watching a ritual in which I was not able to participate. While all the people surrounding me bowed and kneeled, I stood upright. While the survivors of the genocide and the next of kin were digging the grave and others were praying, weeping or taking pictures, I walked around on the cemetery and took pictures. Although the ceremony had started as a collective Muslim ritual, the ritual changed into 136 individual family rituals (see also Pollack, 2003b). While the

Figure 1.1 The cemetery in Potočari, a day before the commemoration and burial, July 10, 2015.

Source: © Martin Hoondert.

Figure 1.2 The monument with the names of the Srebrenica genocide, Potočari, July 10, 2015.

Source: © Martin Hoondert.

Figure 1.3 A coffin with the remains of one of the victims of the Srebrenica genocide is carried to its grave, Potočari, July 11, 2015.

Source: © Martin Hoondert.

families gathered around the graves, others left the cemetery to have lunch or to visit the exhibition in the Memorial Centre. The crowd slowly resolved, although it took hours before all the cars and buses had left the venue.

From Nezuk to Potočari

The day before the official commemoration I witnessed the arrival of the participants of the so-called 'Mars Mira' at Potočari and had informal conversations with some of them. Since 2005, several Bosnian survivors and families of the victims organize a Peace March beginning on the 8th of July. This Mars Mira memorizes the escape of 15,000 Bosnian men from Srebrenica-Potočari to Nezuk (near Tuzla) in July 1995. Because of illness, infirmity because of the war, and due to snipers and land mines along the route, only 3,500 survived the march.[2] In the Peace March, participants walk this 'path of death' in the reverse direction, from Nezuk to Potočari. Starting as a local event, the Mars Mira now attracts visitors from all over the world and thousands of people participate in this march every year. The marchers pass near mass grave sites, and at some locations they get 'history lessons' by survivors, forensic specialists and others. There are periodic stops for food and drink and three over-night camps are encompassed by the organizing committee. Nettelfield and Wagner, who described the 2010 Mars Mira, call the march a 'symbolic act of movement – an inverse trek to defy the attempts of General Mladić and his army to eradicate a people from a place' (Nettelfield & Wagner, 2015, p. 61). The arrival of the walkers is both an event of sorrow and joy: people along the road are applauding and a lot of international media pay attention to the walkers finishing. The march is framed as a 'campaign of solidarity',[3] and for some of the participants it might be a healing ritual, a symbolic walk from 'death' to 'life', symbolically bringing the beloved deceased home.

From Visoko to Potočari

A few days before July 11, 2015, the 136 coffins with the remains of the victims of the Srebrenica genocide were brought from Visoko, near Sarajevo, to Potočari. I did not witness the arrival of the coffins in Potočari, but was informed about the convoy and its route by employees of the Dutch peace organization, PAX. In the months before the official commemoration, the remains of the victims had been identified in Tuzla, in the ICMP (International Commission on Missing Persons)[4] Identification Coordination Facility (ICF) (Delpla, Bougarel, & Fournel, 2012) in cooperation with the Missing Persons Institute (MPI) of Bosnia-Herzegovina. In spite of efforts that were employed to hide or relocate the bodies of those killed to cover up the genocide, the ICMP was able to identify nearly 7000 victims of the genocide using DNA techniques. One thousand victims are still missing.

The convoy carrying the coffins of the newly identified victims of Srebrenica passed through Lapisnica, Sokolac, Vlasenica, Milici, Bratunac and Srebrenica.[5] In several towns, for example in Bratunac in the Republika Srpska (the Serb entity of Bosnia-Herzegovina; Srebrenica and Potočari also belong to the Republika Srpska), the convoy passed by posters displaying the Russian President, Vladimir Putin, who had, less than two weeks before the commemoration, vetoed a UN Security Council resolution that called the Srebrenica massacre a 'genocide'.[6]

These posters were more than a political statement and an expression of gratitude by the Bosnian Serbs towards Putin. From a ritual studies perspective they might be analysed as a materialization of genocide denial and as a counter-ritual against the Bosniaks' commemoration in Potočari, which almost exclusively dominates the media. Also in former years, from the first large-scale commemoration in 2000 and the opening of the Potočari Memorial Centre in 2003, local Serbs expressed discontent with

the commemorations, jeering the arriving mourners, welcoming them with
the three-finger Serb nationalist salute and holding pictures of the former
Bosnian-Serb General Mladić and President Karadžić. In July 2001, some
Serbs roasted pigs on a spit in Kravica, apparently set up for the Muslims
to see (Bougarel, Helms, & Duijzings, 2007). From a ritual studies perspective, this seemingly innocent barbecue party is a ritual to make the
place impure for Muslims.

In Belgrade

On the eve of the official commemoration and burial service in Potočari,
on the 10th of July, a group of women and other citizens gathered in
downtown Belgrade, the capital of Serbia. I gathered information about
this group, the so-called 'Women in Black', through literature and
online sources. The group Women in Black was formed in 1991, just
after the former Yugoslavia began to disintegrate and the war broke
out.[7] Since the very first years of the July 11 commemorations, the
Women in Black travelled to Potočari to attend the ceremony and to
show their support (Nettelfield & Wagner, 2015, p. 51). During the
war, the Women in Black were already standing in weekly vigils at the
Republic Square, protesting against the war, the killing of innocent
people, and against silencing of the perpetration of war crimes. In the
aftermath of the war, the group continued to remind the citizens of their
country of Serbia's atrocious past. The yearly gathering on the 10th of
July has become part of their commemoration calendar, but also part of
a 'war of memories'. While the Women in Black commemorated Srebrenica *as genocide*, others protested against the Women in Black,
celebrating the 11th of July as the 'Liberation of Srebrenica'. As Orli
Fridman wrote in her article regarding alternative calendars and
memory work in Serbia,

> the square became a contested territory of interpretations of the past.
> From 2006 on, police began escorting the Women in Black on their
> way to and from the square. After the 2008 arrest of Radovan
> Karadžić, in 2009 the square literally was divided into two by police
> forces standing as divider between those attending the Women in Black
> vigil and counter demonstrators [...].
>
> (Fridman, 2015, p. 218)

The presence of the Women in Black in Belgrade is an attempt to restruc-
ture the narrative of Srebrenica in the minds of the Serbs, and to offer a
counter-narrative against the genocide denial and the relativism of numbers
of victims. As the counter-demonstrations showed, the Women in Black
only partly succeeded in their pursuit.

In Zalužje

The day after the commemoration and burial service in Potočari, a memorial service and wreath-laying ceremony took place in the village of Zalužje (also: Zalažje), near Srebrenica. I did not visit this ritual myself, but was informed about it by one of the members of the delegation with which I visited Srebrenica. I interviewed this member, a former Dutchbat soldier, on the day of the Zalužje ritual and received the pictures he took during the ritual (for example, Figure 1.4).

Figure 1.4 The Bosnian-Serb memorial in Zalužje, July 12, 2015.
Source: © Marco Smit.

On the 12th of July, the Serbs commemorate the massacre of Serb civilians and soldiers by Bosnian Muslim forces under the command of Naser Orić on July 12, 1992. This commemoration, and there exist a lot more of them in the villages of Republika Srpska, receives hardly any attention in the international media.

The ceremony took place at the memorial in Zalužje and was led by Orthodox Serb priests. According to Serb sources, 69 Serbs were killed and 22 were taken prisoner. All prisoners were tortured and eventually murdered in Srebrenica camps.[8] The memorial consists of two mausoleums and a wall with the names and pictures of the 1992 victims. According to a speech, held by Borislav Paravac, a member of the Bosnia-Herzegovina Presidency, on July 12, 2005, one mausoleum contains 'those who were executed on the Christian feast of the Holy Trinity in 1943, and another containing those who perished on St. Peter's Day in 1993'.[9]

The combination of a Second World War monument next to a monument commemorating the Serbian victims of the Bosnian War is not unusual in Bosnia-Herzegovina. A striking and saddening example is to be found in Pilica were a Serbian Second World War monument and a memorial to some two dozen Serbian soldiers stand just before a cultural centre, where 500 Bosniak men were executed on July 16, 1995 (Nettelfield & Wagner, 2015, pp. 67–71).

Ritual criticism: a contextual approach

A lot of literature confirms the existence of narratives and counter-narratives regarding the Bosnian War and the fall of the village of Srebrenica. There is no shared truth in Bosnia-Herzegovina and up to now there is no reason to expect a shared truth to be realized. Writing about reconciliation and conflict transformation, Martina Fischer states:

> The politics of remembrance in the region of the former Yugoslavia has mainly been focused on the selective commemoration of war victims, each generally characterizing their own 'constituency' as the victims. Bosnia-Herzegovina in particular is marked by such polarisations, mixed with greatly differing interpretations of the past that constantly fuel disputes and (frozen) conflicts.
>
> (Fischer, 2011, pp. 418–419)

Each interpretation of the past evokes a counter-narrative and it seems to be impossible to weave an inclusive narrative that would do justice to both Bosniaks and Bosnian Serbs (Duijzings, 2008). The narratives, memorials and other practices of memorialization have been analysed as linked with ethnicity and religion[10] and are actually impeding the process of reconciliation

(Hromadžić, 2015; Magill & Hamber, 2011; McMahon & Western, 2009; Murphy, 2017).[11]

The five commemorative rituals described before, are only a small part of the rituals (commemorations and counter-rituals) regarding Srebrenica, initiated in Bosnia-Herzegovina, European countries and other parts of the world. To understand these five rituals, it is useful to grasp the main aims of the rituals in a few key words. According to my interpretation, the main aims of the rituals in Potočari on the 11th of July are to commemorate the 1995 genocide and to bury the identified victims. The Mars Mira's aims are to commemorate the 'walk of death' and to heal or restore the situation by walking the Mars in the reverse direction. The main aim of both the displaying of the posters with Putin and the commemoration in Zalužje is to resist the Bosniaks' interpretation of the past. Finally, the aim of the vigil by the Women in Black in Belgrade is to resist the Serb interpretation of the past. In overview, the main aims are the following:

- Potočari, July 11   To commemorate and to bury
- Mars Mira   To commemorate and to heal
- Displaying posters with Putin   To resist the Bosniaks' inter-
                              pretation of the past
- Belgrade, vigil by the Women in Black   To resist the Serb interpreta-
                              tion of the past
- Zalužje, July 12   To resist the Bosniaks' inter-
                              pretation of the past

From an outsider's perspective it is easy to criticize these rituals, because they do not support social reconstruction beyond ethnicity, truth finding and reconciliation, neither at the national level nor at the local level. What they do is construct victimhood. Both the Bosniaks and the Bosnian Serbs reinforce their status as victims by using rituals as cultural representations of their sufferings (Kleinman, Das, & Lock, 1997). Using John Austin's approach of performatives (Austin, 1975), we might say that victimhood is performed more successfully by the Bosniaks than by the Bosnian Serbs, for it is the Bosniaks who get full international support and media attention. Didier Fassin and Richard Rechtman speak in their book, *The Empire of Trauma* (2009) of 'the political uses of trauma'. We have to be aware of the politics of victimhood and trauma, the possibilities of agency that are linked to these politics, and the possible benefits of victimhood, before we continue criticizing the rituals from an outsider's perspective. This outsider's perspective is informed by the ideologically not neutral and perhaps too optimistic agenda of transitional justice (Simić, 2017). Inspired by this agenda, my aim is to find ways to commemorate the 1995 genocide, which both recognizes victimhood and leads to social reconstruction. In other words, I look for practices of memorialization that actually change public awareness from one-sided, ethnically framed perceptions of the past to a more dialogic sense regarding the violent and atrocious past. By analysing the five rituals described in the previous section, I hope to understand why these rituals 'go wrong', quoting the title of Ute Hüsken's book regarding ritual failure (Hüsken, 2007).

The outsider's perspective or approach I use in analysing and criticizing the five rituals is 'ritual criticism'. This approach, which is both practical and academic, is useful to analyse rituals *in their context*. This emphasis will turn out to be of major concern. Before I go into the rituals themselves, I will start with a discussion of ritual criticism as an approach to analyse rituals.

Ritual criticism

The term 'ritual criticism' was coined by ritual studies scholar Ronald Grimes in his book *Ritual Criticism: Case Studies in its Practice, Essays on its Theory*, published in 1990. He defined it as the continual and structural perspective of the critical examination and evaluation of ritual acts. In a chapter entitled 'Infelicitous performances and ritual criticism', Grimes offers a typology of ritual failures (Grimes, 1990, pp. 191–209). These failures are not mutually exclusive, meaning that a ritual can be successful from one perspective for some and a failure from another perspective for others. Here, once again, the outsider's perspective comes up. A ritual can fail for outsiders, for example, because it is unintelligible, exclusive, insulting or a violation of certain values or norms, which may not be the case for those actually engaged in the ritual. A ritual can fail and be successful simultaneously, depending on the perspective of the evaluator and the criteria that are applied.

My colleague Paul Post more precisely distinguished between critical reflection on the ritual act itself on the one hand, and criticism that emerges from the context. In the first case, the focus is on the ritual itself, including the attitudes, actors, effects, and so on. In the second case, the criticism emerges from a normative framework within a group or culture, such as group identity, political or economic interest, or ideological criteria (Post, 2015). Both approaches can be applied by both insiders and outsiders.

Both approaches of ritual criticism can be applied to the five rituals regarding Srebrenica. However, to understand the Srebrenica case in its full complexity, a contextual approach seems to be the most fruitful. For example, we might say that the official commemoration ritual on the 11th of July in Potočari as an Islamic burial ritual functions well for the participants, but performed in the context of Srebrenica, located in the Republika Srpska, something goes wrong. Srebrenica is, since the Dayton Agreement of December 1995 which put an end to the Bosnian War, part of the Republika Srpska, the Serbian entity in Bosnia-Herzegovina. The yearly return of thousands of Bosniaks to Potočari-Srebrenica and the burial of the identified victims of the genocide are not only a ritual act, but also a political statement of undoing the ethnic cleansing and reconquering the place that was once inhabited by a mixed population of Bosniaks, Serbs and Croats. We cannot describe and analyse the Potočari ceremony as just an Islamic burial ritual, because it is performed in this environment, dominated by the Serbs. The ritual itself is suitable, but something goes wrong because it is performed in this specific context.

The five rituals described in the previous section do have a function in their own right (to bury, to mourn, to commemorate, to protest or to resist) and can be analysed from the perspective of how they are efficacious to the participants (or not), but the ritual criticism approach also challenges us to analyse them using the more broad context in which they are performed and to use this context as a normative framework. Part of this contextual analysis and criticism is perspectivity and attention to social agents in the ritual context. Ritual failure or success depends on the perspective we take, which is related to intentionality and the expected, hoped for and actual efficacy of the ritual. To go into this issue more profoundly, I will analyse once again the Potočari ritual, performed yearly on the 11th of July, using the contextual multi-perspectivity approach.

Once again: Potočari

In the commemoration ritual in Potočari, we can discern three groups of participants. First, the ritual aims at the survivors and the next-of-kin, especially those of the recently identified victims of the genocide. Second, many participants belong to the Bosniak community, which is spread out all over Bosnia-Herzegovina and lives in diaspora communities outside the region. Third, the commemoration is attended by representatives of the international community, which is in itself heterogeneous. The international guests are representatives of those countries that were responsible for the safety of the inhabitants of the enclave Srebrenica during the Bosnian War (and failed in keeping the area safe!), representatives of NGOs, sympathizers, and, in the 2015 case, one representative from the perpetrators (the (Bosnian) Serbs): Aleksandar Vučić.

From the perspective of the survivors and the next-of-kin, the first aim is to bury the recently identified victims and to pay respect to the dead. The ritual is first and foremost a burial ritual, performed by the Grand Mufti, the Muslims who take part in the prayers and the numerous imams who assist the families at the gravesides. The collective and family rituals help to overcome the losses and traumas of war.

Besides the aims of the burial as a mourning ritual and a ritual of paying respect, the commemoration and burial on the 11th of July also serve political purposes. These concern both the survivors and the next-of-kin, and other Bosniaks participating in the yearly commemoration. Most of the survivors no longer live in the (ethnically cleansed) area of the Republika Srpska and they have to travel to Srebrenica to attend the commemoration and to visit the cemetery. Regular visits to the cemetery to mourn and to maintain the graves are hardly possible because of the distance. Yet, the survivors and the organizations representing them wanted to have this collective place and the once-a-year ritual and there are several reasons to do it this way. First, to save up the remnants of the identified dead to bury them collectively once per year shows the extent of the 1995 genocide in a convincing way. The imaginative power of this 'guilty landscape' (Van Alphen, 1997, p. 128; Reijnders, 2011)[12] is used to convince, in particular, the international community of the atrocities committed by the Bosnian Serbs. Second, the burial ritual and commemoration are also a 'ritual of confrontation' (Brosius, 2007, p. 297): the international community is confronted with its failure and even guilt. Third, the burial ritual and commemoration confronts the Bosnian Serbs with their past. The permanent presence of the cemetery with its Muslim grave pillars on the hill just at the border of Potočari confronts the Bosnian Serbs with the crimes they have committed. The massive turnout at the 11th of July, the impact of the burial ritual with the coffins carried through the crowd and the, perhaps annoying, view of the cemetery resist in a very strong way the denial of the 1995 genocide, which is visible at websites and audible in statements by Serbian politicians (Nettelfield & Wagner, 2015, pp. 251–284).[13] Fourth, the cemetery and the presence of so many dead bodies of killed Bosniaks is a way of reclaiming the land and in doing so claiming the right to exist in this part of Bosnia-Herzegovina. There is both a religious and a political element in this reclaiming of the land (Cornelisse, 2006, pp. 146–150). From a religious perspective, the reburial at the site where the deceased used to live reaffirms the relations between the living and the dead.

> [T]hese relations include not just mourning loved ones but also fearing them, as sources of possible harm; one must therefore closely observe the myriad rules and requirements of proper burial, for they affect the relations of both living and dead to the world that all inhabit.
>
> (Verdery, 1999, p. 107)

From a political perspective, the reclaiming of the land by burying the dead in this area, which is dominated by the Bosnian Serbs, is a way of linking land and identity. By bringing the dead bodies 'home' the Mothers of Srebrenica indirectly say: 'We belong here, this is our land' (Verdery, 1999, pp. 47, 103–110). The cemetery, the yearly commemoration and the monument referring to the 8372 victims not only refer to the past, but also claim a place in the present. Paraphrasing Katherine Verdery, reburying the victims of the 1995 genocide is uttering a territorial claim and sacralizing space as 'ours' (Verdery, 1999, p. 110). Paul Connerton refers to these kinds of practices of memorialization, which not only refer to the past but also act upon the present through ritual performance as 'performative memories' (Connerton, 1989). Christiane Brosius speaks, albeit in a totally different context, of a 'territorial ritual' (Brosius, 2007, p. 294) which aims at liberating a 'dominated site' and converting it into a 'dominant site'. It is true that the Potočari Memorial Centre and Cemetery have become a dominant site, both in the media and in the general opinion about the 'truth' of Srebrenica. But in spite of the mediagenic ritual staging, the final aim of reconquering the land fails. For after the commemoration of the 11th of July, the Bosniaks depart in their cars and buses, leaving Srebrenica-Potočari to the Bosnian Serbs.

Summarizing, we might say that, for the Bosniaks, both the survivors and next-of-kin and other Bosniak communities, the commemorative ritual is both successful and unsuccessful. It is successful as a ritual of burial and mourning, but it fails as a territorial ritual. Related to the participating representatives of the international community the commemorative rituals function as a ritual of confrontation. Instead of creating a sense of 'communitas' (Turner, 1969), the ritual confronts the international community with the consequences of the failure to keep Srebrenica a safe area. This confrontation is both successful and unsuccessful. On the one hand, it has led to much (financial) support by the US, European Countries and Saudi Arabia. The European Union, for example, provided some ten million euro to Srebrenica and the surrounding municipalities,[14] Saudi Arabia financed the memorial library at the Potočari Memorial Centre and invested a million euro to fund the return of displaced people to Srebrenica.[15] On the other hand, the Dutch government, one of the central figures in the Srebrenica case, still refuses to offer apologies and to recognize guilt. In 2002, the then Prime Minister of the Netherlands, Wim Kok, put the blame on the international community, but refused to explicitly state the role of the Dutch government in Srebrenica. Several times, representatives of the Dutch government attended the July 11 commemoration at Potočari, but refused to express apologies.[16]

One participant at the 2015 commemoration in Potočari has not been mentioned: Aleksandar Vučić, during that time he was Prime Minister (2014–2017), and since 2017 President, of Serbia. His relation to Srebrenica is complex. Just a few days after the genocide, he firmly declared: 'For every Serb killed, we will kill 100 Muslims.' Twenty years later, in 2015, he downgraded his statement by saying that he would never say such a thing again.[17] While he entered the cemetery to attend the 2015 commemoration in Potočari, he was attacked by some people in the crowd and forced to flee. Because I do not have enough empirical material, I have to be modest regarding my claims in this case. In my opinion however, there are both political and religious dynamics in the Vučić case. Before the commemoration, Vučić wrote an open letter in which he stated that 'Serbia clearly and unambiguously condemns this horrible crime and is disgusted with all those who took part in it and will continue to bring them to justice'.[18] Although his words are reconciling, he avoided denoting the Srebrenica massacre as *genocide*, for which he was blamed by representatives of the Bosniak community. On the one hand, the political dynamics of the Vučić incident were evoked by the tension in his previous and recent statements. On the other hand, as I see it, he went beyond sacred boundaries by entering the cemetery. When Vučić entered the graveyard, some people in the crowd started shouting 'Allahu Akbar', emphasizing the religious character of the ceremony. Here, the politics of territory get mixed with religious-ritual practices and ethnicity. Katharine Verdery explains that

> post-Yugoslav reburials create new, narrower, national communities, as the group of participants has come to be monoethnic. Whereas Bosnia's Muslims used to go to the burials of their Serb or Croat covillagers and vice versa, for instance, that is no longer possible. Burials bring people together, reminding them of the reason for their collective presence – relatedness – but that relatedness has now become ethnically exclusive.
>
> (Verdery, 1999, p. 108)

In Durkheimian terms, we can say that Vučić through his presence polluted the cemetery as a sacred place; sacred in many ways: as burial site, as site of commemoration and as reclaimed Bosniak territory.

Towards places of shared truths

In the previous section I have analysed the yearly commemoration in Potočari, using a contextual ritual criticism approach. As said, the context of ritual practices is of major concern in applying ritual criticism. In this section, I will use the context of post-war Bosnia-Herzegovina to reflect on the desirability and possibility of inclusive ritual practices. On the one hand, I hesitate to start this reflection because of the very strongly profiled rituals, which I have described and analysed so far. Is there anything that can go beyond ethnicity and religion in the complex situation of Bosnia-Herzegovina? On the other hand, I am urged to reflect on this issue because of the responsibility I feel as a scholar to contribute to society at large. In the field of transitional justice and post-conflict management 'scholarly diplomacy' might help (Alisic et al., 2016). At least I can do my bit to contribute to a more peaceful future for the people of Bosnia-Herzegovina.

A bottom-up approach

The context in which the described rituals and counter-rituals are performed can be summarized as: post-war Bosnia-Herzegovina. In ritual criticism this context functions as a normative perspective or authority in relation to the ritual. Although a ritual is presented as a liminal or virtual reality, it is never detached from the 'real reality' in which the ritual takes place. This reality is not just background, but functions as the ultimate authority on the ritual. The ritual is questioned: how does it act upon reality, what are its functions? The usefulness of these functions is decided upon and weighted by reality (Van Beek, 2015, pp. 10–11). If we agree on the description of the context of the rituals and counter-rituals in Srebrenica and the surrounding villages as 'post-war Bosnia-Herzegovina', then we might say that the normative element in this characterization is given by the words 'post-war'. Rebuilding the country and transforming it into a post-war society requires reflection on the normative parameters which makes the claim of being 'post-war' credible. So, a good question might be: what do the people of Bosnia-Herzegovina need to build up their society after the Bosnian War and do the rituals and counter-rituals described in the first section of this chapter attribute to their needs?

The answer to this last question is clear: no! The rituals and counter-rituals re-enact the Bosnian War and reinforce the ethnic and religious boundaries between the communities involved. The official commemoration in Potočari on the 11th of July is first and foremost an Islamic burial ritual mixed with a commemoration that is dominated by the international community, expressing their regrets and failure regarding the Srebrenica genocide, and the Bosniak community, reclaiming the territory. The commemoration in Zalužje on the 12th of July is first and foremost an Orthodox Serb ritual, exclusively attended by Bosnian Serbs. The Mars Mira has developed too much into a political protest march to be an inclusive ritual in which both Muslim and Serb victims are commemorated.

To understand what is needed in post-war Bosnia-Herzegovina, we have to listen carefully to the people living there. One of the problems in post-conflict management is that it is often outsiders who put emphasis on reconciliation as a peace-building strategy. My ethnographic approach, however, forces me to look at the situation 'from below'. Moreover, I have learned to take this approach by studying the activities of the Dutch peace organization, PAX, which has worked in Srebrenica since 1995. One of the employees, Dion van den Berg, told me in a personal conversation, during a visit to Srebrenica (February 2017): 'True reconciliation can only come from the individuals involved, not from outsiders. Only when returnees and other citizens in Srebrenica, request support, does PAX facilitate processes of co-existence and inter-ethnic cooperation.'[19] During the commemoration in Srebrenica-Potočari, I mainly heard officials talking and I had informal conversations with Bosniaks attending the commemoration – however, not enough to present the voices of the people living in Bosnia-Herzegovina.

At the 2015 Potočari ceremony, one of the speakers was Camil Durako-vic, at that time the Bosniak Mayor of Srebrenica. He voiced, at least partly, what is needed in Bosnia-Herzegovina to grow into a real post-war situation. In his speech he referred to the still 1000 missing victims of the Srebrenica genocide and asked the Bosnian-Serbian authorities to reveal the locations of the mass graves which still, after more than 20 years, have not been found. We might interpret his request as an attempt to make the Bosnian Serbs face the past. Also, the presence of the Serbian Prime Minister Vučić might be seen as an attempt to find a way to deal with the past from a shared perspective, a shared narrative, or at least the acknowledgement of the mutual and at some points conflicting interpreta-tions of the past. The fact that the Mothers of Srebrenica condemned the violence against Vučić, which made him flee from the ceremony, might be seen as an acknowledgement of his attempt to search for a shared nar-rative. The commemoration of the Serb victims in Zalužje and the Putin posters along the road to the cemetery in Potočari show that this shared narrative also has to involve the Serbs who were killed during the Bosnian War.

This shared narrative or shared truth(s) is not only a way of dealing with the past, but has also practical consequences. Before the Bosnian War, Srebrenica used to be a lively city with mine industries and a big spa that attracted a lot of tourists. In an interview with Mitra Nazar, the already mentioned Mayor of Srebrenica, Durakovic, said: 'What we need are jobs.'[20] To achieve this, mutual respect and the possibility to communicate beyond ethnic boundaries are needed. A precondition is a metaphorical place where truths can be shared, acknowledging victimhood and perpe-tratorship on both sides. Ger Duijzings stressed the importance of col-lective memory after violence as a precondition to build up the country.

> [If] Muslims, Serbs, and Croats in Bosnia cannot reach agreement on how to remember events such as the Srebrenica massacre and fail to develop mechanisms to establish a shared narrative about the war, it is difficult to see how the country can continue to exist.
>
> (Duijzings, 2007, p. 143)

As my colleague Odile Heynders expounded, this shared narrative is not an objectification of truth, but is determined by the ability to place oneself in a narrative of others (Heynders, 2014, p. 4). We can metaphorically describe this shared narrative as a book with several chapters. Each chapter tells its own story about Srebrenica; truth is not what actually happened – who knows what actually happened? – but what people witnessed. It would be a mistake to impose this book, filled with controversies, in a top-down way, as is actually done now by the international community, imposing its one-and-only truth of what Srebrenica represents. It has to be written by the people of Bosnia-Herzegovina.

Places of shared truths

Using post-war Bosnia-Herzegovina as a normative framework, we came across a shared narrative as a precondition to rebuild the country. As we have seen, however, quite the opposite happens now in what we might call a 'commemorative arena' (Duijzings, 2007, p. 163). The Srebrenica case shows that the almost sacred dictum by the American philosopher George Santayana that those who cannot remember the past are condemned to repeat it, does not hold true: those who do remember the past are condemned to repeat it! The rituals tell their own narrative, construct and define victimhood and are actually a continuation of the conflict. The Bosnian War still goes on in the rituals. Although I do not agree with the main proposition of David Rieff in his book *In Praise of Forgetting* (2016), I do agree that in the Srebrenica case the commemorative rituals do more harm than good, because they are politically exploited (Erll & Nünning, 2010, p. 208). Of course, people in Bosnia-Herzegovina need places to mourn and places to remember. As we have seen, these places are ethnically and religiously profiled; there is no other way. But if the people of Bosnia-Herzegovina want to build up the country, they have to find places where they can meet and share their narratives and truths, with all the anger and grief which go along with these narratives. Bosnia-Herzegovina requires a new kind of *loci memoriae*, not as devices of religious and ethnic identity politics, but 'to learn how to understand, to forgive, and to forget' (De Boer, 2010, p. 24).

Notes

1 Martin Williams (2015, July 11), 'Srebrenica crowds drive Serbian prime minister from anniversary event'. *Guardian*. Retrieved from www.theguardian.com/world/2015/jul/11/srebrenica-crowds-drive-serbian-prime-minister-from-anniversary-event (accessed May 2016).
2 See www.balkaninsight.com/en/blog/an-american-student-s-experience-marching-in-mars-mira (accessed May 2016).
3 See www.marsmira.org/en/faq.php (accessed May 2016).
4 See www.icmp.int.
5 See www.bosniatoday.ba/convoy-with-coffins-of-victims-of-genocide-arrives-in-potocari/ (accessed May 2016).
6 See www.trtworld.com/europe/serbs-srebrenica-hang-posters-putin-3865 (accessed May 2016).
7 See www.womeninblack.org/old/en/history (accessed May 2016).
8 See http://inserbia.info/today/2014/07/bih-22-years-since-massacre-of-serbs-in-srebrenica/ (accessed May 2016).

9 See www.spc.rs/old/Vesti-2005/07/13–7-05-e.html (accessed May 2016). The
   year of 1993 should be 1992. On Serbian victims see also: https://serbian
   journal.wordpress.com/2013/01/20/srebrenica-face-off-genocide-the-west-doesnt-
   want-you-to-know-about-warning-very-graphic-material/.
10 Although there is a link between ethnicity and religion in Bosnia-Herzegovina,
   the two categories are not interchangeable.
11 See also: Daria Sito-Sucic (2017, August 11), 'Faith, history and community in
   Bosnia', *Reuters: The Wider Image*. Retrieved from https://widerimage.reuters.
   com/story/faith-history-and-community-in-bosnia (accessed August 2017).
12 'Guilty landscape' is a notion borrowed from the Dutch painter, sculptor, writer
   and musician, Armando. Living in Amersfoort (the Netherlands) before, during,
   and after the Second World War, close to a concentration camp situated in the
   woods, he was very aware that the innocent forest of his youth had witnessed
   the horrors of war.
13 Regarding the rejection of the atrocities at Srebrenica *as genocide* and the discussion about the number of victims, see http://thesaker.is/special-report-the-truth-
   about-srebrenica-20-years-later/ (accessed September 2017). See also David
   Rohde's article in *The Atlantic* (2015, July 17): 'Denying genocide in the face of
   science'. Retrieved from www.theatlantic.com/international/archive/2015/07/
   srebrenica-massacre-bosnia-anniversary-denial/398846/ (accessed September 2017).
14 See http://europa.ba/?p=37797 (accessed September 2017).
15 See www.eurasiareview.com/31102016-bosnian-serbs-greenlight-saudi-grant-for-
   srebrenica/ (accessed September 2017).
16 Theo Koelé (July 12, 2010), 'Nederland blijft zwijgen over drama Srebrenica',
   de Volkskrant. See www.volkskrant.nl/buitenland/-nederland-blijft-zwijgen-over-
   drama-srebrenica~a1010992/ (accessed September 2017).
17 www.b92.net/eng/news/region.php?yyyy=2015&mm=11&dd=05&nav_id=95946
   (accessed September 2017).
18 www.theguardian.com/world/2015/jul/11/serbia-pm-flees-srebrenica-tribute
   (accessed September 2017).
19 See also the unpublished article by Dion van den Berg: 'Rekindling the national
   debate: How public and private recognition can shift the Dutch discourse on
   Srebrenica' (2010, June-July).
20 See www.oneworld.nl/vrede-veiligheid/burgemeester-srebrenica-wil-meer-dan-
   herdenken-wat-wij-nodig-hebben-banen (accessed May 2016).

References

Alisic, E., Letschert, R., Van den Brink, M. C. L., et al. (2016). *Fresh eyes on the
   refugee crisis: An interdisciplinary approach*. Amsterdam: Global Young
   Academy/Young Academy Netherlands.
Attila Hoare, M. (2010). Bosnia-Hercegovina and international justice. *East Euro-
   pean Politics and Societies*, 24(2), 191–205.
Austin, J. L. (1975). *How to do things with words* (2nd edition, edited by J. O.
   Urmson & M. Sbisà). Oxford: Oxford University Press.
Bougarel, X., Helms, E., & Duijzings, G. (Eds.). (2007). *The new Bosnian mosaic:
   Identities, memories and moral claims in a post-war society*. Aldershot, UK:
   Ashgate.
Brosius, C. (2007). The unwanted offering: Ubiquity and success of failure in a
   ritual of the Hindu right. In U. Husken (Ed.), *When rituals go wrong: Mistakes,
   failure, and the dynamics of ritual* (pp. 296–324). Leiden/Boston: Brill.

Burg, S. L., & Shoup, P. S. (1999). *The war in Bosnia-Herzegovina: Ethnic conflict and international intervention.* Armonk, NY: Sharpe.

Connerton, P. (1989). *How societies remember.* Cambridge, UK: Cambridge University Press.

Cornelisse, E. (2006). *Verdeeld verleden: De constructie van sociale herinneringen van Bosnische Moslims en Bosnische Serviers in naoorlogs Srebrernica* (MA Thesis). Universiteit van Amsterdam, Amsterdam.

De Boer, P. (2010). Loci memoriae – Lieux de memoire. In A. Erll & A. Nunning (Eds.), *A companion to cultural memory studies* (pp. 19–25). Berlin/New York: De Gruyter.

Delpla, I., Bougarel, X., & Fournel, J.-L. (Eds.). (2012). *Investigating Srebrenica: Institutions, facts, responsibilities.* New York: Berghahn Books.

Duijzings, G. (2007). Commemorating Srebrenica: Histories of violence and the politics of memory in Eastern Bosnia. In X. Bougarel, E. Helms, & G. Duijzings (Eds.), *The new Bosnian mosaic: Identities, memories and moral claims in a post-war society* (pp. 141–166). Surrey: Ashgate.

Duijzings, G. (2008). Commemorating Srebrenica. In O. B. E. Caucaso (Ed.), *Bad memories: Sites, symbols and narrations of the wars in the Balkans* (pp. 45–52). Rovereto: Osservatorio Balcani e Caucaso/Provincia Autonoma di Trento.

Erll, A., & Nünning, A. (2010). *A companion to cultural memory studies.* Berlin/New York: De Gruyter.

Fassin, D., & Rechtman, R. (2009). *The empire of trauma: An inquiry into the condition of victimhood.* Princeton: Princeton University Press.

Fischer, M. (2011). Transitional justice and reconiliation: Theory and practice. In B. Austin, M. Visher, & H. J. Giessman (Eds.), *Advancing conflict transformation: The Berghof handbook II* (pp. 405–430). Berlin: Barbara Budrich Publishers.

Fridman, O. (2015). Alternative calendars and memory work in Serbia: Anti-war activism after Milošević. *Memory Studies, 8*(2), 212–226.

Grimes, R. L. (1990). *Ritual criticism: Case studies in its practice, essays on its theory.* Columbia, SC: University of South Carolina Press.

Heynders, O. (2014). Speaking the self, narratives on Srebrenica. *European Journal of Life Writing, 3*, 1–22.

Hromadžić, A. (2015). *Citizens of an empty nation: Youth and state-making in postwar Bosnia-Herzegovina.* Philadelphia: University of Pennsylvania Press.

Hüsken, U. (Ed.). (2007). *When rituals go wrong: Mistakes, failure, and the dynamics of ritual.* Leiden: Brill.

Kleinman, A., Das, V., & Lock, M. M. (1997). *Social suffering.* Berkeley: University of California Press.

Magill, C., & Hamber, B. (2011). 'If they don't start listening to us, the future is going to look the same as the past': Young people and reconciliation in Northern Ireland and Bosnia and Herzegovina. *Youth & Society, 43*(2), 509–527.

McMahon, P. C., & Western, J. (2009). The death of Dayton: How to stop Bosnia from falling apart. *Foreign Affairs, 88*(5), 69–83.

Murphy, K. (2017). Education reform through a transitional justice lens: The ambivalent transitions of Bosnia and Northern Ireland. In C. Ramirez-Barat & R. Duthie (Eds.), *Transitional justice and education: Learning peace* (pp. 65–98). New York: Social Science Research Council.

38   Martin Hoondert

Nettelfield, L. J., & Wagner, S. (2015). *Srebrenica in the aftermath of genocide.* Cambridge: Cambridge University Press.
Pollack, C. E. (2003a). Burial at Srebrenica: Linking place and trauma. *Social Science & Medicine, 56*(4), 793–801.
Pollack, C. E. (2003b). Intentions of burial: Mourning, politics, and memorials following the massacre at Srebrenica. *Death Studies, 27*(2), 125–142.
Post, P. (2015). Ritual studies. *Oxford research encyclopedia of religion.* Retrieved from https://pure.uvt.nl/portal/en/publications/ritual-studies(53922eba-41ab-4c03-adad-535d1a6a4fc5).html.
Reijnders, S. (2011). *Places of the imagination: Media, tourism, culture.* Farnham, UK: Ashgate.
Rieff, D. (2016). *In praise of forgetting: Historical memory and its ironies.* New Haven: Yale University Press.
Simić, O. (Ed.). (2017). *An introduction to transitional justice.* Abingdon, Oxon: Routledge.
Spijkers, O. (2016). Questions of legal responsibility for Srebrenica before the Dutch courts. *Journal of International Criminal Justice, 14*(4), 819–843.
Turner, V. W. (1969). *The ritual process: Structure and anti-structure.* London: Routledge & Kegan.
Van Alphen, E. (1997). *Caught by history: Holocaust effects in contemporary art, literature, and theory.* Stanford, CA: Stanford University Press.
Van Beek, W. E. A. (2015). *Zwarte Piet in Afrika: Rite en ruzie.* Tilburg: Tilburg University.
Verdery, K. (1999). *The political lives of dead bodies: Reburial and postsocialist change.* New York: Columbia University Press.

Chapter 2

A monument for boat refugees

Ritual and the art of liminality

William Arfman

Introduction

The European migration crisis has been dominating news headlines, as well as national and international politics, since 2015.[1] Since then, the focus of the debate has gradually shifted from malfunctioning migration policies to issues of identity politics. This is to say that much of our current public debate has come to be centred on borders in more than just the geographical or political sense (Börzel & Risse, 2017). In fact, what is actually at stake within this public debate is otherness. In that sense, our current debates on migration sometimes mimic those of the fifteenth century, when a profound fear of so-called Islamic hordes trying to overtake Christian lands laid the foundation of the present-day conceptualization of Europe (Burke, 1980, pp. 23–24). Today, however, living in late modern societies characterized by forces of pluralization and globalization, the other can no longer be simply equated to the outsider on such a one-to-one basis. Today, the stranger refers to more than just religious foreigners or newcomers to our Western nations. Not only is the migrant a stranger to us, with increasing ideological polarization our neighbours are increasingly becoming like strangers to us as well (Rumford, 2016). The borders that have become the focal point of our public migration discourse are not just seen to divide countries or civilizations as Huntington (1993) would have it, but increasingly also concern intra-societal divisions revolving around values and our individual roles in a globalized world (Kaufman, 2016).

One of the major points of contention within the above-mentioned public debate on migration is the question of how migrants should be perceived (Van Klingeren, Boomgaarden, & De Vreese, 2017). The issue of victimhood is central to that question, tying in directly to underlying discussions about motives. Those on the progressive end of the political divide tend to emphasize a Western duty towards all those who are forced to flee due to reasons of war, oppression, and/or poverty. Those on the conservative end, in contrast, argue for a distinction between political and economic migration. From the former perspective, almost all migrants are victims of outside forces to some extent, whereas from the latter many are merely people trying to seize an opportunity.[2] This chapter asks how these different attitudes towards migration, which in their core revolve around questions of victimhood, are given shape in a world that is increasingly becoming characterized by experiences of societal estrangement. It seeks to answer this question by studying a travelling art project. The project in question concerns an interactive art installation called *Monument for Boat Refugees*, which was designed by the Dutch-Iranian artist Nosrat Mansouri Gilani. Given Gilani's own migrant background, as well as the fact that he chose to use words such as 'monument' and 'refugee' to name his artwork, it might seem almost self-evident that the artist is making a statement here about the victimhood of migrants. What will be shown here, however, is that Gilani actually presents us with something much more complex and playful than that, a cultural practice that does not set out to convince people to choose sides in these debates about the victimhood of migrants, but lures them into a liminal, in-between, zone instead.

In the following sections, the art project will first be introduced further, detailing both its conceptualization and its ultimate realization as a travelling art installation. The data presented here come from semi-structured interviews with the artist in 2015 and 2016. Next, as a first step towards analysis of our data, a ritual studies approach will be taken. This approach allows for a type of analysis that focuses on the art piece's symbolism, its interactive characteristics and, most importantly, its liminal dimensions, meaning the ways in which it deals with borders. The question here is what kind of borders are created and/or crossed in this particular art installation. After the analysis of the art installation as a ritualized practice, some possible attitudes towards victims will be presented, in order to ask which of these play a role in how the liminal situation designed by the artist portrays migrants. Finally, in the concluding remarks, the answers to these two sub-questions are drawn together to both answer how attitudes towards migration are given shape in this particular art project and how this can help us understand how issues of victimhood are resolved in today's world in general.

Monument for Boat Refugees

If we are to make sense of the social and cultural impact of the European migration crisis in general, and the way migrants are perceived in particular, focusing just on meta-level discourse does not suffice. Of course, studies of general media terminology are crucial, as the UNHCR-funded research project on press coverage of the migration crisis has shown (Berry, Garcia-Blanco, & Moore, 2015). However, another, complementary perspective is needed if we are to understand the ways in which particular attitudes towards migrants actually emerge. As this volume's introduction has already indicated, we need to study actual cultural practices in order to be able to take that perspective. Heynders does this in Chapter 7 when discussing literary strategies that aim to give a voice to migrants. Kroon, in Chapter 10, similarly looks at the specific media practices around the Cologne sexual assault case to talk about victimhood and perpetratorship. Here we focus on Nosrat Mansouri Gilani's interactive art installation called *Monument for Boat Refugees*.

Gilani was born in Teheran in 1969 and came to Amsterdam in 1992 in what he characterizes as a time of individual migration, in contrast to today's mass migration. In 1999 he graduated from the Gerrit Rietveld Academie, a fine arts and design academy in Amsterdam. When asked, he describes his art as primarily conceptual rather than being focused on materiality. Despite stemming from a very politically-minded family, Gilani argues that his art is not intended to be of an activist nature. That being said, much of his work does deal with issues such as migration or tackles political issues through a personal lens, dealing for example with the way his sister was treated under the Iranian regime (Gilani, 2016). In recent years, Gilani served as co-founder of two artist collectives that also deal with migration. The first of these is called 'Joy' or, in Dutch, *De Vrolijkheid*, and it creates opportunities for young migrants living in asylum centres to express themselves through creative workshops led by artists, most of whom have a refugee background themselves. The second, called 'Reality' or, in Dutch, *De Werkelijkheid*, aims to help asylum seekers with artistic interests to establish themselves as professional artists in the Netherlands through collaborative art projects.

The first version of Gilani's *Monument for Boat Refugees* was nothing more than a scale model made of steel and tin, of which he put an image on his personal website in 2015. The actual project only got going later that year, however, after the Dutch Foundation for Refugee Students (UAF) saw the image and contacted Gilani, asking if the installation was available for exhibition.[3] After Gilani explained that the image only showed a scale model of an installation that did not yet exist, he was hired by the UAF to redesign his original idea into an actual piece that could be exhibited at the Amsterdam University of Applied Sciences (AUAS). When interviewed, Gilani explained that tin plays an important role in his repertoire, introducing a playful element to his work by linking it to African tin toys and thus a sense of innocence. In addition, the African origin of such toys for him also means a link to issues of migration, as this is the part of the world where most migrants come from in his experience. Working with tin is not very fast, however, and given the fact that forced migration had suddenly become a hot topic, the UAF wanted to exhibit something at the AUAS sooner rather than later. As a result, the decision was made to work with wood and paper instead. One benefit of working with wood, Gilani explained, was that it allowed him to shape the entire installation as a giant bar chart (see Figure 2.1), just like the ones through which migrants are normally presented to us, as numbers entering our countries or numbers dying along the way. In its entirety, the installation is 3.20 metres wide and 2.30 metres high, consisting of 150 separate empty squares (LKCA, 2016). The next challenge, Gilani explained, was to imbue the paper that was to be used with some sort of meaning. Here, a familiar theme returned, namely that of playful innocence. The paper to be used was to come from comic books, Dutch ones in particular. For Gilani, the latter would not only point to the fact that the migration crisis had now made it to the Dutch dinner tables, but also that, according to him, all of us are involved in the wars that lie at the foundation of that crisis, even if only because of how our pension funds decide to invest our money.

For Gilani, the final challenge lay in making the art installation inter-active. For this, he indicated having been inspired by the altars he remem-bered from his childhood in Iran. When interviewed, Gilani describes this as an advantage of being a refugee: having the traditions of your country of origin to draw inspiration from while being able to explore those of your host country as well. On his website he describes Iran's street corner altars as places of final hope when all else fails, miraculous places which act as monuments that save people from being forgotten (Gilani, 2016). Gilani sees his *Monument for Boat Refugees* as an altar as well, even

Figure 2.1 Students folding paper boats for Nosrat Mansouri Gilani's *Monument for Boat Refugees* at the Amsterdam University of Applied Sciences.

Source: © Nosrat Mansouri Gilani.

calling it an altar of innocence. Taking a head start at the ritual theory to be introduced in the next section, we could add here that when art becomes an altar, some kind of performative action is implied as well. In this case, that action is the folding of paper boats by passers-by that can then be placed inside the wooden 'bar chart' frame of the installation. Again, Gilani means such an act to imply our own involvement in the migration crisis, but this is not its main function. What Gilani intends to do instead, is to offer those passing by a moment of reflection. Students and faculty members walking the halls of the AUAS would encounter the installation during their daily routine, a small sign would explain that it concerned a monument for boat refugees and before they knew it, they would be busy folding a small paper boat. Once engaged with this activity, with the general theme of the installation still in their minds, their daily routine suddenly included a moment spent on thinking about the migration crisis. When asked whether the folding of these boats was also mentioned as a gesture towards migrants, Gilani answered that he would prefer to leave that open to the actual people participating. For him it was enough that people were actually taking a moment to think about the migration crisis, *what* they were actually thinking was up to them. The UAF had originally asked Gilani the same question and he is aware that as an organization for refugee students it has goals of its own as well, but for him putting his art out there and engaging people so they spend a moment to reflect on things was sufficient for him as an artist.

Overall, the reception of the art installation at the AUAS was very positive, resulting in other venues asking for an opportunity to exhibit the interactive piece as well. After having been exhibited in two different buildings of the AUAS, it was then exhibited at VU University Amsterdam, several buildings of the University of Amsterdam and Humanity House in The Hague during the final months of 2015, as well as the National Museum of Ethnology in Leiden, and the *Karavaan* theatre festival in Alkmaar in 2016. Along the way, the original comic book pages were replaced by pages from satirical newspapers from the Middle East (LKCA, 2016). Gilani also made several media appearances because of the project, including national television.

The one criticism that Gilani did indicate he got from some people who participated was that they considered his work too light-hearted or playful for such a heavy theme. The joint magazine of the University of Amsterdam and the AUAS, *Folia*, likewise wondered why Gilani had preferred paper boats over photographs of actual refugees if his goal was to make refugees more than a number, immediately adding that the artist would luckily be at hand to tell his own story as a refugee during one of the exhibition days (Van Ewijk, 2015). As will be clear from the above, the more playful elements in Gilani's work are intentional. Gilani happily mentions that the conversations he has had with people at the exhibitions are not just about violence and fleeing, they are also about hope, about studying, future careers, and even the nostalgia associated with a practice as simple as folding paper boats. When asked whether he feels that his own background as a refugee adds anything to his work, Gilani suggests it is precisely that background that makes it possible for him to take this more light-hearted approach. For him, being a refugee is not just about suffering, it is about opportunities as well, about being able to draw inspiration from two different worlds. An outsider would likely feel a duty to approach a topic like this in a strictly serious manner, whereas he is able to mix the serious with the playful and vice versa.

Liminality in a ritual-like practice

In the introduction to this chapter, it was explained that in order to understand how attitudes towards migration are given shape in Gilani's *Monument for Boat Refugees*, a ritual studies approach would be taken. In particular, such an approach would allow us to analyse how borders are created and/or crossed in this particular art installation, using the concept of liminality. Before we can do so, however, we have to establish whether it even makes sense to apply ritual theory to an art project like this. Here, we make use of the concept of ritualization, as put forward by ritual studies scholar Ronald Grimes. For Grimes, ritualization points to those practices that are not generally culturally framed as ritual, but which show ritual characteristics nonetheless (Grimes, 2014, p. 193). Religious studies scholar Catherine Bell speaks of ritual-like activities in these instances and lists six of their characteristics (Bell, 1997, p. 138). With the first four characteristics overlapping considerably, this list of six characteristics can be summarized as three main ones: repetition, performativity and symbolism.

Repetition points to a ritual's connection to earlier, concurrent, or future rites and deals with issues of formalism, traditionalism, invariance and rule governance (Bell, 1997, pp. 139–154). Of course, the folding of paper boats is not part of any established ritual tradition, religious or otherwise. Placing these boats in a wooden framework, however, does present us with a certain link to traditional practices of placing offering on altars. Here, the connection to Gilani's own terminology is, at the very least, worthy of notice as well. Speaking more generally, the installation as a whole likewise calls for formalized, rule-governed behaviour, with only a very limited variance between the different exhibitions. Performativity, as a second characteristic, has to do with ritual as cultural practice. As something that is not just acted out, but that is acted out in a reflexive manner, conscious both of one's own acting and of the presence of others, an audience (Bell, 1997, p. 160). It is through a rite's performativity that a microcosm is created, setting itself apart from everyday routine, framing itself as special and thus significant (Bell, 1997, p. 160). This too, we recognize in Gilani's *Monument for Boat Refugees*. Designed to lure passers-by away from their everyday routine, the art installation gives people a moment in which the folding and placing of a paper boat comes to be a moment to reflect on the European migration crisis. An act that seems somewhat childish at first comes to be set apart and special through its framing. With these last points, our third ritual characteristic becomes evident as well. The wooden installation symbolizes the bar graphs we see in the news media, the paper symbolizes innocence, the fragile boat symbolizes the journey made to get here and folding it symbolizes our own Western involvement. In addition to these 'canonical' messages, those quietly reflecting on these ritual-like acts, are given space to find their own 'self-referential' symbolic messages as well (Rappaport, 1999, p. 52).

It does not take much of a stretch, then, to consider Gilani's art installation as a ritual-like practice or a ritualization. The art piece might not be culturally framed as ritual, but in offering people a moment to reflect, it clearly does rely on elements of repetition, performativity and symbolism enough to make ritual theory of relevance. Liminality in particular, a key concept in ritual studies, promises to be a useful angle here. Stemming from the Latin word *limen* or threshold, the concept has a long tradition in the study of ritual. It was first introduced in Arnold van Gennep's work on rites of passage in order to mark the three types of rites that together make it possible to transition from one social status to another: preliminal rites, liminal rites, and postliminal rites (Van Gennep, 1960 [1909]). Several decades later, anthropologist Victor Turner picked up on Van Gennep's work for his research into the Ndembu in Zambia (Turner, 1967). Seeing Van Gennep's different types of rites as stages of a larger encompassing ritual instead, Turner focused on the middle of these stages, the liminal one in particular. For Turner, the liminal stage could be found in all ritual, marking a period where participants were 'betwixt and between', being taken out of their everyday social or cultural position before being returned, somehow transformed (Turner, 1969, p. 95). It was in this middle phase of being on the threshold that a sense of *communitas* could then emerge, a state in which participants share a sort of unstructured and transformative communion (Turner, 1969, p. 96). Due to Turner's claim that liminality and *communitas* were of importance for understanding modern cultural practices as well, writing not just about Western ritual but also about theatre, the arts and various forms of leisure, his work has had a clear impact on each of these fields (Bell, 1997, pp. 254–255, 263; Thomassen, 2009, pp. 14–15).

More recently, an interest in liminality has started to emerge in a range of other fields as well, likely part of an increased interest in boundaries, and their transition, in social sciences as a whole (Lamont & Molnár, 2002). Analytically, the most important work on translating the concept of liminality to our late modern times has been done by anthropologist Bjørn Thomassen (2009, 2016). Taking seriously Turner's position that liminality refers to any in-between situation or object, Thomassen has built on the work of Van Gennep and Turner to speak about liminality in regard to a range of subjects, from individuals to whole societies, and in both spatial and temporal terms (Thomassen, 2009, p. 16). The spatial and temporal dimensions also have ranges to them, from specific spaces and objects to entire global regions and from small moments to entire epochs (Thomassen, 2009, p. 16).

If we look at our case study with these different scales in mind, a logical first conclusion would be that Gilani's *Monument for Boat Refugees* acts on the more limited end of these spectrums. The location is small and clearly demarcated by the art installation, the subjects involved are largely individuals or very small social groups and for these participants the whole thing takes just a moment. However, if we take the actual theme of the art installation into consideration as well, then things start to shift. The European migration crisis does involve whole societies, it does span a considerable period of time and it does include entire regions of the globe. Importantly, it is also on this scale that things start to get dangerous according to Thomassen. For the original ritual moments discussed by Van Gennep and Turner it was clear when a liminal stage was entered, how it was left again and who was in charge of this entire ordeal. As a result, these ritual practices could become exercises of spiritual experience. None of these things hold for liminality on the larger scale (Thomassen, 2009, pp. 21–22). Not knowing when the crisis will end, who exactly are in charge or how close things might get, creates a sort of dangerous 'permanentisation of liminality' (Thomassen, 2009, p. 22). Recent work on liminality within migration studies clearly illustrates this idea of permanentization. Research on protracted exile, for example shows that such exile fosters an ongoing sense of liminality through an idealized notion of home that transcends time and space (Den Boer, 2015; Hughes, 2016). Refugee camps or centres, similarly, can be considered spaces of 'enduring liminality' (Ramadan, 2012) or thresholds between an inside and an outside, neither here nor there, that are often regarded as a threat to the social order (Chatty, 2016). This, of course, is in addition to the persistent cultural boundaries migrants experience between themselves and local residents, and vice versa (Donati, 2016). A more permanent state of liminality will not be considered dangerous or problematic by everybody, of course. Turner discussed a whole range of more or less professionally liminal individuals, from jesters to hippies and from prophets to artists (Turner, 1969, pp. 109–113, 128). That last category also shines a different light on what Gilani called an advantage of being a refugee, namely that his 'art comes into being in the context of two environments. The one from before fleeing and that newer one' (Gilani, 2016). Being both an artist and a refugee,

Gilani is no stranger to the permanentization of liminality. Almost para-doxically, the more playful elements of his work stand testimony to that. Play, after all, is a fundamental characteristic of the liminal as well (Thomassen, 2016, pp. 141–166).

As said, however, Gilani's art installation primarily involves liminality on a small scale and, as such, the borders that are created and crossed are the typical ones for a ritualized practice. In particular, this is the border between being apart from the art piece and being part of it, between passing-by and letting yourself be engaged. This is what Gilani himself called offering someone a moment to reflect. Folding paper boats in the hallways of your university is not part of everyday routine and letting yourself be convinced to do so anyway allows you to temporarily enter a symbolic microcosm designed by the artist – temporarily, because the act of placing your boat within the wooden bar graph framework also represents you taking the step back into your ordinary world. Some elements of the liminal experience in between these two points in time have been explicitly designed by the artist, others were deliberately left open for you to fill in for yourself. And while the paper boat has been left behind, you take these experiences with you. With this *Monument for Boat Refugees*, however, borders are not just created and crossed on this small local scale, the liminal experience being offered also has clear global ties. When, as a participant, you decide to enter the limited liminal arena of the art installation, you enter the much larger liminal arena of the European migration crisis as well. Through symbolic performativity, this crisis is brought to bear upon the, in principle rather innocent, practice of folding a paper boat. Importantly, however, and in sharp contrast to most other moments in which we are confronted with this global crisis, here too the leaving behind of the boat establishes at least some degree of closure, of return to normality.

Returning to Turner's work on liminality and *communitas*, one final border needs to be addressed, namely the one between participants who would normally find themselves on different ends of the political spectrum when it comes to the European migration crisis. Of course, it seems unlikely that those who are vehemently against migration would parti-cipate in an art project like this and it is difficult to establish whether any sense of *communitas* actually emerges in a short-lived practice such as this. Nonetheless, this still leaves a wide range of people who might participate, stepping across the border into liminality together, sharing an experience despite any possible differences of opinion. Here too the difference with other cultural practices, especially those involving our (social) media, is evident. Rather than favouring polarization (Van Klingeren, Boomgaarden, & De Vreese 2017), participants are instead taken into the in-between.

Having looked at Gilani's *Monument for Boat Refugees* through a ritual studies lens, we can conclude that as a specialist in the field of liminality, the artist has designed a ritual-like experience in which several types of borders have been playfully conflated. These concern the borders between the everyday and the ritual-like, the borders between us and migrants, and eventually even the borders between us and those who might think differently about that crisis than we do. It is through the crossing of these conflated borders that the art installation has an effect on participants, offering them a moment in which the European migrant crisis is brought to bear on their everyday lives and then returning them again, slightly transformed as Turner would call it.

Attitudes towards migration

In the first part of this chapter it was argued that Gilani's *Monument for Boat Refugees* concerns the crossing of various types of borders. The question that remains, however, is how attitudes towards migration are given shape within the liminal space that lies behind these borders. Does this artwork have a particular message to share regarding how migrants should be perceived? In her book *Victims and Victimhood*, philosopher Trudy Govier (2015) distinguishes between four attitudes that people commonly display towards victims: silence, blame, deference, and agency. Of course, within current public debates on migration, the issue of whether or not migrants should even be perceived as victims remains fundamentally unresolved. As we will see, however, Govier's four attitudes towards victims have a clear bearing on how questions of victimhood are being dealt with within the migration debate as well.

With the first of the four attitudes, Govier explains, a burden is placed upon victims to remain silent and keep their suffering to themselves so as not to disrupt a societal image of safety, stability and normalcy (Govier, 2015, pp. 2–3). Where this first attitude fails, the next one emerges. Sometimes victims refuse to remain silent, or evidence of suffering can't be ignored. If denial of suffering has become impossible as a strategy to convince ourselves that we are safe, we can always convince ourselves instead that at least bad things can be protected against. Then, if bad things happen to people, this is just a matter of them not having taken the right precautions or not having responded to a dangerous situation in the right way. The blame, in other words, is at least partially on them (pp. 5–6). Both of these attitudes have come to be considered problematic. There are situations in which victims might benefit from silence (pp. 4–5) and sometimes actions leading up to victimization do require consideration (pp. 8–9), but by and large these attitudes place the burden on the wrong shoulders. This realization leads to the third attitude: that of deference. Rather than ignoring or blaming victims, they should be respected and listened to. From this perspective, victims are innocent people to whom bad things have been done and as such they deserve our support in all things (pp. 9–10). The final attitude towards victimhood is one that focuses on a victim's agency. Originally stemming from the restorative justice movement and its criticism of the control which states have over the resolution of conflicts, victims are not seen as passive victims, but as co-owners of these conflicts and active stakeholders in their resolution (pp. 12–13).

Using these four attitudes towards victims as a starting point for our second analysis, the question is, which of these play a role in Gilani's *Monument for Boat Refugees*? Which of these can tell us something about how Gilani is portraying migrants and migration? The logical starting point here is to look at Gilani's design goals, which he summarized as wanting to offer passers-by a moment to reflect. With that design goal, attitudes of silence are seemingly off the table. In fact, the art piece seems to have been designed precisely to confront us with our default attitude of reducing migrants to anonymizing bar charts. Then again, as the journalist for the *Folia* magazine pointed out, Gilani also did not set out to tell us the stories of migrants instead, or even show us their faces. Gilani's art installation seems to be pointing out our silence to us, but it does not fill it. Since Gilani's work is not actually telling us stories about migrants, an attitude of blame is not to be found either. As indicated in the introduction, the name of the installation is particularly telling in that regard, referring to those involved as refugees, rather than migrants. We talk of illegal migrants, but never of illegal refugees, there is neither blame nor a crime in being a refugee, refugees are clearly victims. This, then, seems to point us into the direction of migrants being presented in this art installation as victims to be deferred to instead. The fact that Gilani himself describes his work as an altar of innocence, certainly seems to underline that viewpoint. Interestingly, the element of innocence is crucial in Govier's analysis of how we think about victims and victimhood. Using illegal migration as an example herself, Govier points out that it is easy to consider young children of migrating parents as fully innocent victims, after all, they had no part in the choices made by their parents. When we consider the parents, however, matters become more difficult, leading to the public debates we have grown so accustomed to. At stake here is the issue of agency: do we see these migrants as passive victims of outside forces or as people in charge of their own decisions? (Govier, 2015, pp. 21–26).

How does Gilani's *Monument for Boat Refugees* relate to Govier's points on innocence? Is the only agency involved in this art piece that of the participants who have come to make their offerings to this altar for passively innocent refugees? That interpretation seems a bit too simple. After all, Gilani is not bombarding us with sad pictures or stories of suffering at all. Instead, the innocence that Gilani speaks of has more to do with the acts participants perform than with the migrants themselves. And as we have seen, this innocence acts like a double-edged sword. On the one hand, we are folding fragile paper boats made of comic book paper, but, on the other, this is meant to symbolize our own involvement in this migration crisis as well. More importantly, Gilani does not even want to predetermine what the participants should be reflecting about. This is an attempt to move them away from an attitude of silence, but whether that attitude turns into one of deference is up to them. One important caveat has to be placed here, however, and it concerns how the art installation is actually presented to passers-by. After all, the installation is accompanied by an explanatory text, printed both on a sign and on flyers. The text has not been written by Gilani but is provided by the UAF instead, asking passers-by to help the artist to complete the art installation he has built on their request. This text, too, clearly moves away from an attitude of silence by telling the participant that placing your boat in the monument will save refugees from being forgotten. At first glance, phrasing this gesture as an act of salvation also seems to construct an image of migrants as essentially passive victims. The rest of the text, however, actually goes directly against that point of view. There, agency is emphasized, telling you to envision for yourself the arduous journeys these migrants had to undertake to a safe existence. In fact, migrants are not even really depicted as victims here, but rather as survivors, some of whom will even come to share these university halls with the participants, building on their future. What we see here is that the UAF, as an organization meant to support refugee students, has a clearer message for participants than the artist has, although it too is not completely unambiguous. Govier explains that the tendency to prefer to be labelled a survivor rather than a victim is a common one, as it implies a great deal of agency and concerns a forward-looking attitude, rather than a backward-looking one. Not all victims become survivors, though (Govier, 2015, pp. 29–30). It might come as no surprise, then, that Gilani himself clearly indicates that his monument was meant for both those who did not survive and those who did. Finally, when it comes to matters of agency, the move from comic book pages to pages from satirical newspapers is also noteworthy, with the latter clearly signalling a degree of resistance against the causes behind migration, albeit it still a playful one.

Returning to our second sub-question, it is clear that Gilani's art installation, and the way the UAF has chosen to present it, actively goes against an attitude towards migrants that is dominated by silence. Attitudes of deference and agency are both present, but a choice is never fully made between them, thereby leaving a door open for an attitude of blame. After all, those who are seen as having agency are always open to blame as well. Of course, participant reception research would be needed to establish to what extent such attitudes also actually occur in practice. From the interviews with Gilani it is clear that for him the ambiguity is deliberate. The art piece serves to offer a moment of interactive reflection, rather than a clear message. It is also in this context that we should understand Gilani's earlier assertions that his work does not have activist intentions. Although the accompanying text provided by the UAF asks participants to imagine the dangerous journeys undertaken by migrants, we might even argue that these migrants do not actually seem to be the most important 'strangers' involved in this artistic exercise. Gilani does not use the artwork's aura of innocence to tell us what we should think or do about the European migration crisis, but only intends to bring us together to reflect on these matters. It is not actually the migrant who is the stranger here, it is the participant who would normally isolate him- or herself from this topic. The strangers we are meeting in this liminal arena are not migrants either, they are our fellow students and co-workers. Unlike public debate, where the emphasis is on opposing viewpoints, the cultural practice presented here is about sharing experiences despite opposing viewpoints. Ambiguity and liminality are crucial ingredients for achieving that.

Concluding remarks

This chapter set out to study attitudes towards migration as they are given shape in a late modern world where our neighbours have become like strangers. More precisely, it focused on questions of victimhood in the European migrant crisis, using an interactive art installation called *Monument for Boat Refugees* as its central case study. In regard to this art installation, two observations have been made. First of all, this art piece can be seen as a ritual-like cultural practice, meaning it exhibits characteristics such as repetition, performativity and symbolism. Calling this art installation ritual-like also points to its liminal aspects, meaning the ways in which it deals with the creation and crossing of borders so as to establish a certain experience of being in-between. In this particular case, that liminality is not just restricted to the ritual-like framing of this cultural practice, but actually brings the larger scale liminality of the European migrant crisis as a whole to bear on this limited liminal moment as well. In doing so it even has the potential to bring together different viewpoints within this one liminal experience.

The second observation that has been made about Gilani's interactive artwork concerns the way it excludes one attitude towards migrants through its design and presentation, while leaving room for the participants to reflect upon the remaining attitudes for themselves. Matters of innocence and victimhood are at the core of the artwork but these are deliberately never fully resolved. In particular, the artwork precludes a silencing attitude towards the topic of migration and not much of a blaming attitude could be identified in the project's design and presentation either. An attitude of deference to migrants as innocent victims is available for participants to reflect upon when engaging with the art work, as is an attitude that regards them essentially as agents. As already said, however, the crucial observation here is that a lot is deliberately kept open for interpretation and personal experience. Even an attitude of blame could, in principle, find itself back to this artwork in this way. Gilani's *Monument for Boat Refugees*, then, is at once a closed endeavour, that takes participants both in and out of liminal spaces of overlapping scale, as well as an open-ended one, leaving much room for ambiguity. Combined, this allows for a kind of shared experience that is actually rather rare when it comes to how we generally deal with the European migrant crisis.

Having focused on a small-scale case study, no general answers can of course be given here about how attitudes towards the victimhood of migrants are given shape in Europe today. It is possible, however, to reflect a bit further upon the relationship between questions of victimhood and the element of societal strangeness that was deemed so fundamental in the introduction. In his book *The Globalization of Strangeness*, political scientist Chris Rumford presented his ideas on strangeness to counteract earlier existing ideas about the role of the stranger, bound up as these were with the idea of an outsider entering one's clearly bounded society or social group (Rumford, 2016, p. 1). Globalization has severely undermined any such clear demarcations, leaving many with a sense of disorientation instead (Rumford, 2016, pp. 7–14). Interestingly, Horvath, Thomassen and Wydra (2018, p. 1) point to this downside to globalization as well, describing it as the cause of much uncertainty, as well as new divisions and antagonisms. To them, this emerging new reality asks for a new mode of theorizing, one in which aspects of liminality should be placed at the forefront (Horvath, Thomassen, & Wydra, 2018, p. 2).

Trying to understand issues of victimhood from a liminal perspective, as was attempted here, teaches us three things. First of all, public debates on whether migrants coming into Europe should be considered victims or not are, at their core, attempts to make sense of a world in which borders are constantly shifting. Second, this first observation in turn argues for the importance of cultural practices such as the one discussed here; cultural practices that actively make use of our liminal preoccupations to guide us into, and out of, the in-between. With late modernity supposedly having melted most of the stable traditions of early modernity without replacing them with new ones (Bauman, 2000, pp. 5–8), these late modern cultural practices no longer tell us directly what to think or feel about topics as divisive as migration or victimhood. Instead, these liminal cultural practices allow for such constructions of meaning to emerge from the interplay between creative cultural design and personal participation, from what one might call the art of liminality. Third, and finally, that art of liminality cannot be understood without taking the artist into account. Gilani's own attitude towards the victimhood of migrants, himself included, can be described as ambiguously balancing somewhere between seriousness and playfulness, between blame and innocence, and between suffering and new opportunities. Acknowledging the fundamental importance of that ambiguity will be essential for making sense of the cultural complexity of victimhood in the years to come.

Notes

1 For this chapter, the term migration has been adopted when discussing the European crisis at hand rather than the more specific term migrant (or refugee). As will be shown, this crisis is not just about how to deal with a significant amount of individuals moving to Europe, it is just as much about European inability to discuss, think about, or deal with migration in general.
2 For more on this debate, see Chapter 10, where Kroon analyses the Cologne sexual assault case.
3 The Foundation for Refugee Students UAF is a Dutch refugee organization that was established in 1948 to support Czech students who had fled to the Netherlands after the Soviet invasion. Today, the organization gives guidance and supplies grants and loans to refugees seeking to enrol in Dutch higher education (UAF, 2016).

References

Bauman, Z. (2000). *Liquid modernity*. Malden, MA: Blackwell Publishing.

Bell, C. M. (1997). *Ritual: Perspectives and dimensions*. New York: Oxford University Press.

Berry, M., Garcia-Blanco, I., & Moore, K. (2015, December). *Press coverage of the refugee and migrant crisis in the EU: A content analysis of five European countries*. Report prepared for the United Nations High Commission for Refugees. Retrieved from www.unhcr.org/56bb369c9.html.

Börzel, T. A., & Risse, T. (2017). From the euro to the Schengen crises: European integration theories, politicization, and identity politics. *Journal of European Public Policy*, 25(1), 83–108.

Burke, P. (1980). Did Europe exist before 1700? *History of European Ideas*, 1(1), 21–29.

Chatty, D. (2016). Refugee voices: Exploring the border zones between states and state bureaucracies. *Refuge*, 32(1), 3–6.

Den Boer, R. (2015). Liminal space in protracted exile: The meaning of place in Congolese refugees' narratives of home and belonging in Kampala. *Journal of Refugee Studies*, 28(4), 486–504.

Donati, P. (2016). The cultural borders of citizenship in a multicultural society. *Journal of Mediterranean Knowledge*, 1(1), 11–26.

Gilani, N. M. (2016, November). *Nosrat Mansouri Gilani: Beeldend kunstenaar*. Retrieved from www.nosrat.nl/#home.

Govier, T. (2015). *Victims and victimhood*. Peterborough: Broadview Press.

Grimes, R. L. (2014). *The craft of ritual studies*. New York: Oxford University Press.

Horvath, A., Thomassen, B., & Wydra, H. (2018). *Breaking boundaries: Varieties of liminality*. New York: Berghahn Books.

Hughes, V. (2016). Narrating 'home': Experiences of German expellees after the Second World War. *Refuge*, 32(1), 28–37.

Huntington, S. P. (1993). The clash of civilizations? *Foreign Affairs*, 72(3), 22.

Kaufmann, E. (2016, November 11). *It's NOT the economy, stupid: Brexit as a story of personal values* [Web log post]. Retrieved from http://blogs.lse.ac.uk/politicsandpolicy/personal-values-brexit-vote.

Lamont, M., & Molnár, V. (2002). The study of boundaries in the social sciences. *Annual Review of Sociology, 28*, 167–195.

LKCA (2016). *Altaar voor bootvluchtelingen.* Retrieved from www.lkca.nl/vrije-tijd/vluchtelingen/inspirerende-voorbeelden/altaar-voor-bootvluchtelingen.

Ramadan, A. (2012). Spatialising the refugee camp. *Transactions of the Institute of British Geographers, 38*(1), 65–77.

Rappaport, R. A. (1999). *Ritual and religion in the making of humanity.* Cambridge, UK: Cambridge University Press.

Rumford, C. (2016). *Globalization of strangeness.* London: Palgrave Macmillan.

Thomassen, B. (2009). The uses and meanings of liminality. *International Political Anthropology, 2*(1), 5–27.

Thomassen, B. (2016). *Liminality and the modern: Living through the in-between.* London: Routledge, Taylor & Francis Group.

Turner, V. W. (1967). *The forest of symbols: Aspects of Ndembu ritual.* Ithaca: Cornell University Press.

Turner, V. W. (1969). *The ritual process: Structure and anti-structure.* Ithaca: Cornell University Press.

UAF (2016). *About the Foundation for Refugee Students UAF.* Retrieved from www.uaf.nl/home/english/the_foundation_for_refugee_students_uaf.

Van Ewijk, W. (2015, October 16). 'Papieren bootjes moeten vluchtelingen een gezicht geven'. *Folia.* Retrieved from www.folia.nl/actueel/96528/papieren-bootjes-moeten-vluchtelingen-een-gezicht-geven.

Van Gennep, A. (1960 [1909]). *The rites of passage.* Chicago: Chicago University Press.

Van Klingeren, M., Boomgaarden, H. G., & De Vreese, C. H. (2017). Will conflict tear us apart? The effects of conflict and valenced media messages on polarizing attitudes toward EU immigration and border control. *Public Opinion Quarterly, 81*(2), 543–563.

Chapter 3

Refugee rituals

Exploring ritual repertoire of victimhood

Paul Post

Introduction

This contribution is part of a project on rituals connected with disasters, accidents, atrocities, and crises. A fair amount of work has gone into this project already. One of the foci of this project was the stream of refugees attempting to reach 'Fortress Europe' via the Mediterranean. In a previous article, published in 2015, I explored rituals having to do with border deaths on the important hub of the migration flow: the Italian island of Lampedusa (Post, 2015). In a follow-up, I want to look at refugee ritual focusing on the ritual practices that emerge from the refugee's journey, usually from Africa to Europe. I will look at which rituals, both individual and collective, emerge and which do not, which one would expect but stay absent. It is thus primarily an explorative and descriptive project, I map the field. However, in mapping the field I will introduce an analytical dimension by using three lenses or analytical themes to look at the practices: ritual processes and politics, the concept of borderland and material culture. With these lenses I try to approach the ritual refugee cycle as an exponent of repertoire of victimhood (Post, 2017; Post & Hoondert, 2019).

Structure

Before making some introductory comments, I will first present a division of the material into clusters of the sub-repertoires I deal with under the label of refugee ritual repertoire. I arrived at the following cycle of six phases that, as stated above, are linked to the course of the refugee's journey.

1 First of all, there is the departure, the beginning of the journey. This departure from hearth and home entails farewell rituals, in many cases the refugees take specific objects with them.
2 Then there is the journey itself, the journey over land and sea. The often unpredictable route is full of dangers, drama and encounters. It

includes a complex and largely unseen travel repertoire with some-times a gruesome sacrifice ritual at sea.

3   Third is the phase of grounding. Given that the worst happens – a shipwreck, a drowning, or a missing person – there are the funeral rites or the lack thereof, the reactions, the memorial rites, both large and small, collective and individual.

4   Directly related to that, seen from a distance of the fate of the refugee but certainly still related to that, I look at all kinds of often substitu-tionary memorial ritual: plans for memorial monuments, literary pro-jects, photo, video, and film productions, theatre as 'monument', cultural practices with an unmistakable ritual dimension. Important in this context are various documentation projects and databases that are intended at least to name and count the refugees who have died or are missing.

5   In a fifth cluster, I focus on the refugees who have survived the journey at sea, the life and rites in the reception and detention camps, travel-ling further, going to Europe, passing through cities and or staying in them temporarily.

6   And then we indicate a final, sixth, phase very briefly: the rituals after the refugee arrives, after the journey, which nonetheless have every-thing to do with the journey, especially the traumas.

These phases or clusters structure my exploration. Phases 3 and 4 will receive the most attention because they concern various visible collective rituals in the public domain. Before we start the exploration of the refugee ritual repertoire, I will give some background regarding the refugee crisis in the Mediterranean Sea, and about the concepts used and the research method. As said, I will present some analytical perspectives as lenses to look at this repertoire of victimhood.

Refugee crisis in the Mediterranean Sea

The general context of refugees, for the most part boat refugees, is well known and, unfortunately, still current. In my earlier article on this theme, I used 'Lampedusa' as a metaphorical indication of this ongoing refugee crisis or disaster in the Mediterranean Sea area (Post, 2015). I will briefly update the general image (situation in the spring of 2017). Referring to the most recent detailed annual report of the UNHCR, *Global Trends Forced Displacement*, which is always published in December and reports on the year before (thus, the most recent concerns 2015), the chapter 'Europe Refugee Crisis' draws a picture supported by figures.[1] In 2015, there were more than one million so-called arrivals at the southern border of Europe, thus the Mediterranean Sea area. There are three main routes to that area: by sea to Greece and Italy, and to Spain via sea and land. Of the total of

1,015,078 arrivals, 3771 died or are missing. That latter figure in particular is an estimate. In 2015, the route via Greece from Turkey to the so-called eastern and western Balkan route (856,700 refugees) was more popular. Since 2016, the focal point shifted again to the Italian route via primarily Lampedusa and Sicily from the Libyan coast. The Spanish route from Morocco and the Spanish enclaves in North Africa are often forgotten but are always used. At the time of writing (May/June 2017), the season for crossing is in full swing, and primarily via the 'old' traditional route to Italy to Sicily and Lampedusa. In May 2017, 55,000 refugees reached Italy (that is 40 per cent more than in 2016), and there have already been more than 1364 drownings and missing people (an estimate).[2]

The routes to the border regions of Fortress Europe fluctuate and are combined with the extremely dynamic and complex planning of human trafficking. For years, my colleague Mirjam van Reisen, with a team of on-the-ground assistants, has been mapping the routes from Eritrea, with all the ins and outs of the human trafficking business on that route (Post, 2015, note 2; Van Reisen & Mawere, 2017).

Communications and media studies investigate the role of reporting on this refugee crisis. As an example, I mention the work of the Finnish culture and media scholar Karina Horsti.[3] What is striking here is the role of certain key events. I will mention three for the Mediterranean crossings.

The disaster of an overloaded boat that caught fire on October 3, 2013, off the coast of Lampedusa and sank, with 366 dead and 155 survivors, was one of those key moments that immediately focused all attention on the catastrophe playing out on the Mediterranean Sea (Post, 2015, pp. 27–30).

A second boat disaster that made a deep impression was when a fishing boat loaded to capacity capsized off the coast of Libya on April 18, 2015. Only 28 of those aboard could be saved, and it is thought that more 700 victims were locked in the cargo hold. The Italian navy here did something that it never does with any other wreck: they salvaged the ship 14 months later and towed it to port in Augusta. There were 675 bodies discovered on board.[4]

A third 'iconic' moment was the publication of a photo of a young boy who washed up on the beach of the Turkish resort city of Bodrum (September 2, 2015). This image of the three-year-old Aylan Kurdi from Kobani in Syrian Kurdistan, who did not survive the voyage to the Greek island of Kos, drove the disaster home to the world. It had an enormous impact.

Because of this stream of refugees over several years, the Mediterranean Sea has become a so-called 'borderland' or liminal zone, with all the political, economic, humanitarian, juridical, cultural, ritual, and religious processes and practices that are part of such a threshold zone. One can think here of the phenomenon of border and border security, of building fences and walls, of the complex interplay of local, regional, national, and European interests and endeavours. As we will indicate in a short section below, the concept of borderland is relevant in studying refugee ritual, in particular because of its heuristic and comparative potential.

Some remarks on concepts and terminology

With respect to classifying refugees, I do not use strict, carefully defined descriptions but usually employ the terms refugees and migrants. I am well aware that there are many formal aspects tied to the various names given to this group. In addition to refugees and migrants, current terms also include boat refugees, forced migration, forced displacement, border deaths. I will forgo nuanced descriptions such as economic or undocumented migrants, asylum seekers, internally displaced persons (IDPs), stateless people, etc. I use refugees or migrants in a general way to describe displaced people in the Mediterranean border area.[5]

I will use an open (working) definition of ritual. For me, ritual is

> a more or less repeatable sequence of action units that take on a symbolic dimension through formalization, stylization and their situation in place and time. On the one hand, individuals and groups express their ideas and ideals, their mentalities and identities through these rituals; on the other hand, the ritual actions shape, foster, and transform these ideas, mentalities and identities.
>
> (Post, 2010, pp. 24–25; 2011, pp. 18–19; 2015, p. 6)

By ritual repertoire, I mean 'rituals that are connected to one another through form/performance, function, situation, time, place, actors, or occasions, etc.' (Post, 2010, p. 23). In this case, the refugee, and more specifically the refugee in the Mediterranean border area, gives the repertoire, i.e. refugee ritual, identity and profile. In the person or group of the refugee(s) many of the mentioned elements come together: time and place, situation and occasion. It is important to note that the refugee can be both subject and actor, and object of the ritual practices. A lot of refugee ritual is performed in the absence of the refugee as individual or group (cf. ritual at home by family and friends, commemoration ritual after a shipwreck, solidarity ritual by migrant communities in European cities).

For me, there is also another 'repertoire perspective', that of the broader category of repertoire of victimhood. Here, the identity and profile of the ritual repertoire are based on the victim's perspective. Like there is a narrative repertoire of victimhood (Kempny, 2011), there is a ritual repertoire of victimhood with ritual practices that has to do with central victimhood themes such as mourning, burying, healing, coping with trauma, commemoration, doing justice, restoration, reconciliation, protest, starting a new life etc. On the one hand, describing and analysing refugee rituals offer an important contribution to the study of the ritual repertoire of victimhood, and on the other hand taking victimhood repertoire into account in studying refugee rituals can have relevant heuristic value.

As we will see, a ritual or ritual repertoire can also refer to a ritual dimension or ritualization of cultural practices. This brings into view the 'modes' of rituality that are central to Ronald Grimes' theory of rites. For Grimes, ritualizing is a dynamic concept that is connected with a more or less presupposed direction towards ritual, 'ritual in the making' (Grimes, 2014, pp. 192–193). This has to do with ritualizations that are still not complete rituals; they are rituals that are still wet behind the ears and still not (widely) recognized and accepted culturally (Grimes speaks here of 'culturally framed'). But they do have 'ritual potential': 'ritualization refers [...] to activity that is not culturally framed as ritual and that someone, often an observer, interprets as if it were potential ritual' (Grimes, 2014, p. 193). With certain repertoires that I will characterize as ritualizations, such as all kinds of commemoration replacement practices such as art and documentation projects, the dynamic of 'ritual in the making' does not apply, so I do introduce another emphasis compared with Grimes: these ritualizations are cultural practices with a ritual dimension, such as marking, paying attention, or a memorial (Post, 2015, pp. 40–41).

Analytical perspectives

Although my aim is, as said, primarily explorative and descriptive – I try to map the field of refugee repertoire – I will use three lenses to look at aspects of the ritual practices.

First of all, it is an important Ritual Studies perspective to approach the ritual repertoires of refugees from the perspective of ritual processes. There are various possible accesses that link up with current research. I will refer to the concept of absent ritual (Post, 2017). In addition to ritual transfer, ritual denial, postponed ritual, grassroots ritual (Faro, 2015; Margry & Sánchez-Carretero, 2011) there is also absent ritual that can arise for all kinds of reasons. The refugee's journey includes a great deal of absent ritual: there are the unseen voodoo sacrifice ritual, the absent funeral and the absent grave, and the discouraged monuments.

Another ritual process perspective can be seen in a combination of the phases of the journey described above, now divided into an individual, private track and a collective public tract, with the taxonomy of the 'economy' or 'politics' of ritual memorial practices found in the work of the cultural geographer Ken Foote (Foote, 2003, 2010). For Foote, there is a scale or taxonomy in ritual attention. At one end, there is sanctification of the event (disaster, tragedy, crisis, atrocity) and the place and time, and, at the other end obliteration, silence, banning.

A second analytical perspective is working with the concept of border-land. The refugees' ritual repertoires play out in the liminal space of the trip. The concept of borderland has been developed in various disciplines and has comparative potential. I refer in particular to the work of the Canadian anthropologist Valentina Napolitano (Toronto) who focuses primarily on the study of migration and religion.[6] In a themed issue on 'Borderlands and Religion' from *Religion and Society*, she elaborates on that topic together with Nimrod Luz and Nurti Stadler (Napolitano, Luz, & Stadler, 2015). The following is proposed as a working definition: 'A borderland is a vague and undetermined place created by the emotional residue of an unnatural boundary. It is a constant state of transition. The prohibited and forbidden are its inhabitants' (Napolitano, Luz, & Stadler, 2015, p. 94). Borderlands usually imply control points, fences, and walls, and the politics of caring and uncaring. Ritual and religion play an important role here, as borderland studies in Latin America and Israel/Palestine show (Anzaldúa, 2012; Donnan & Wilson, 2010; Napolitano, Luz, & Stadler, 2015; Wilson & Donnan, 2012).

One final perspective I see is the important role of material culture and the major role that material remains play in rituals. In the work of Napolitano that we mentioned above, elements of material culture play a major role (Napolitano, 2016a, 2016b).

Research design and sources

This exploration fits into a Ritual Studies research design and certainly in the first phase of such research when the field is explored and mapped (Post & Faro, 2017). This exploratory mapping of the field then forms the basis for the other phases of case studies, analysis and interpretation. This is qualitative ethnographic research – in this case, a combination of working online and offline, which we might specify as net(h)nography (Post & Van der Beek, 2016, pp. 71–86).

Exploration of refugee ritual sub-repertoires

Departure and farewell

It is only by degrees that we get a picture of this first sub-repertoire in descriptions and analyses. It is sometimes described when one is looking back, in a later reconstruction of a successful or failed journey from home, somewhere in the Middle East or Africa. Once in a while, we also see it in visual reports that young refugees often make as a group with their cell phones (Post, 2015, pp. 31–33, note 38). In literary versions of travel reports or novels, the farewell is often dramatized (examples in Post, 2015, pp. 31–32). Young men often say farewell to their close family, to their community. Care is taken with respect to what they will take with them, especially money for the journey, for hiring services for transport and boat passage, and the indispensable cell phone. Some food is packed, as well as small, more symbolic and ritual objects: family photographs, a Bible or Qur'an, a prayer book, a love letter (these objects return in commemoration projects; see below under the section 'Relics and ruins' and the book project 'Bibbia e Corano a Lampedusa' cited in Post, 2015, p. 31). There are all kinds of mascots and amulets, pendants and bracelets. The actual farewell ritual is universal, with embracing and blessings by a father or grandfather, and then a final unexpected gift, extra money, or a memento. A prayer is said for a successful journey. But there is also absent ritual, i.e. no single form of farewell. The journey is often kept secret, even from close family members. Only later, when the refugee has already left, are those who have been left behind informed or come to understand what has happened.

After the start of the journey there is the establishment of a specific 'refugee ritual' in absence of the refugee. Family and friends try to get information, they pray, perform rites for a successful arrival, cherish a photograph in the house, etc.

Journey rituals

There are larger and smaller rituals during the journey: group rituals such as singing and praying, or personal rituals such as taking out and looking at a photograph or a book. Many acts have an apotropaic and prophylactic dimension; they are acts directed at safety and protection or at warding off danger, sickness, and death. Here as well, we see what we could call absent ritual – but now in the sense of silenced or denied ritual. Everywhere where boat refugees travel we find, for example, traces of gruesome sacrificial rites. They have been documented for decades already in the flow of migrants from Haiti to the US and in Asian waters, and now in the Mediterranean Sea as well (Post, 2015, p. 43, note 64). We witness here the practice of black magic and 'voodoo' rites when refugees encounter danger at sea. If they hit rough seas, if the engine quits, if those aboard the fully-laden boat become rebellious or restive, the leaders or the captain and his crew intervene, and sometimes a gruesome sacrificial ritual takes place. Women are especially vulnerable for victimization in these situations. There is proof that women have been selected and thrown overboard one by one as sacrifices to the spirits of the sea or the devil. Stories of these cruel rituals reach the authorities via the survivors. Crewmembers are sometimes arrested in Italy for these practices, and there is a trial.

According to the facts I have gathered, there are, however, no convictions because of the difficulty of finding proof. Witnesses are seldom present – they are either continuing their journey or they are dead, or they remain silent because of their vulnerable position. In 2013, the UNCHR published a separate report on this voodoo and witchcraft practice in the context of human trafficking in Europe (Dols García, 2013). The report also deals with the formal problem that voodoo can be seen as a recognized ritual/religious tradition, which complicates prosecution from a legal point of view. As far as I know, this kind of sacrificial practice is carried out by human traffickers from Nigeria and Ghana.

Both these cruel practices and the fact that they are hidden behind the scenes are linked with what we called in the introduction the perspective of borderland. Many refugee repertoires have a specific liminal character and are more or less 'out of place'. It is because of this dimension of 'out of the ordinary', of the borderland situation that it is very difficult to confront such practices with regular moral, social and legal norms, rules and procedures.

Shipwreck, grounding

In the next cluster of rituals, I focus on the scenario of a shipwreck and the rituals performed to remember and honour (or not) the dead and missing. These commemorative rituals, and in some cases also the absence of these kinds of rituals, are a good example of rituals of victimhood. These rituals are directly related to victims of the often very poor and hard circumstances of trafficking and forced migration. Here the repertoire of disaster rituals emerges. This repertoire has been mapped and analysed in a separate project on rituals following disasters, as in the Lampedusa project (Post, 2015; Post, Grimes, Nugteren, Pettersson, & Zondag, 2003; Post, Nugteren, & Zondag, 2002). The shipwreck off the coast of Lampedusa in 2013 has been well documented on this point and also shows where ritual is lacking or absent (Post, 2015, pp. 27–30). After the disaster, recovering the bodies was the first order of business. In this disaster in October 2013, the bodies were brought to Lampedusa and stored in a hangar, where they were later laid out in numbered coffins. The sight of the 366 coffins, which also held children and babies, made a deep impression via the media. It became a national affair in Italy, and the EU also seized on the disaster to show sympathy for the migrants who died, in the context of a passionate political debate on European border policy. Dignitaries on all levels, from local mayors to EU officials, visited Lampedusa, met survivors, and paraded past the coffins. The reality did not live up to the promises. A state funeral was announced for the victims, but that promise was quickly forgotten. From Eritrea and Ethiopia came calls for the bodies to be returned to their homelands, but that required that the bodies be identified. That was considered impossible for all kinds of reasons. In the end, the government opted for a general memorial service, not on Lampedusa but in Sicily (Agrigento) and for a quick burial of the bodies in several cemeteries. Some identified bodies were buried on Malta, some of the babies and children were buried together, and most were brought to Sicily and buried anonymously in several local cemeteries, often early in the morning. Sometimes, the local population took care of organizing an improvised ritual for the funeral.

The official memorial service in Agrigento resembled a civil ritual. There were addresses, national flags, representatives of the religious traditions involved, wreaths were laid. There was a great deal of criticism of the fact that the survivors were not invited and were left waiting on Lampedusa to learn of their fate (some of them appeared, for that matter, to have already continued their journeys).

All in all, the funeral rites after the 2013 shipwreck were a distressing example of absent ritual, the denial of victimhood and the political inconvenience of the lack of clear 'perpetratorship' and therefore responsibility for the deaths of so many refugees. There is a contradiction between the huge effort that is made in the event of other disasters to recover bodies or remains. One could think here of the crash of MH17 in the fields of East Ukraine (2014) and the Germanwings plane in the French Alps (2015).

In most cases, the sunken vessel becomes the grave for those refugees who died. From a political perspective, this is a way of neglecting or trying to forget the victimhood of the dead refugees. But bodies also wash up on the shores of the Mediterranean. The current takes many bodies of drowned migrants on the route from Libya to Italy, to the shores of southern Tunisia. Volunteers have been burying the bodies in a separate area outside the city of Zarzis for years (Lageman, 2017). It cannot be called a cemetery, for the graves are not marked. The authorities turned to this graveyard when burial in the local cemetery was no longer possible because of the numbers and the protests of the local population. There is no money for a more dignified burial with appropriate rituals, no more than there is money for taking DNA samples and starting a databank.

As distinct from the lack of attention paid to victims, there were all kinds of memorial rituals to remember and honour the victims, sometimes immediately following the disaster, but also later, as was the case in 2013. Wreaths were thrown on the spot in the sea where the disaster occurred. On Lampedusa itself, as well as elsewhere in Italy and Europe, there were silent processions with a mixture of mourning and silence for the dead, and speaking out in protest against the political-economic context that these kinds of disasters bring with them. In migrant communities in various European cities, there were gatherings in the public domain with candles and other lights (Post, 2015, pp. 29–30).

Before elaborating on specific forms of memoralizations, I want to mark how in the ritual reactions to the shipwrecks and the many victims we see various ritual processes that we briefly mentioned in the introduction. We see how ritual is absent: no funeral, no memorial services. It is right here to speak of 'politics' and we see the broad palette of reactions to tragedies presented by Foote lying between the extremes of obliteration and sanctification (Foote, 2003, 2010).

I will look at three specific forms of memorial through which the recognition of victimhood has been established. Two are directly connected to the ships or the remains of them. In the last ten years or so, a real cemetery for wreckage and the remains of boats came into being next to the harbour in Lampedusa. The majority were old discarded fishing boats, but there were also piles of the remains of rubber boats and life jackets. These remains appear to hold great authority for many, the piled-up boats, lying in the sunlight next to the harbour of Lampedusa were a symbol for many of the ongoing tragedy. This cemetery plays a central role in film and video projects (*Waste No. 2 Wreck*, by Ijäs, 2016). There are constant initiatives to turn the cemetery and the wreckage into a work of art, to make of the remains an artistic memorial. But the wreckage is constantly being removed by the government (usually unannounced), and the cemetery cleaned up.

We can see something similar after the salvaging of the boat in the already mentioned April 2015 disaster. The salvaged boat was brought to Agrigento and voices were raised immediately to preserve it as a monument. As we shall see below, that was a plan that was combined at Christmas with a memorial garden.

It has not yet come to the point of getting the formal status of monument for the boats, not on Lampedusa, nor in Sicily, and, as far as I know, nowhere else on the coasts of the Mediterranean Sea. Although there is no official information available about this, I suspect that it has to do with the more or less tacit policy of the local government. Just as it is considered undesirable to bury all the recovered bodies on Lampedusa – the island would already have turned into one large cemetery – declaring a boat cemetery a national monument is undesirable because it would be too dominatingly present. That was probably also true for the large salvaged boat in Augusta. Smaller remains do play a main role as relics of a sort in the memorial culture of migrants. In 2008, a monument for the border deaths had been erected: a gate in the tradition of triumph and memorial arches. This gate is a work by Mimmo Paladino and is called *Porta di Lampedusa – Porta d'Europa*. The remains of various possessions of migrants are fastened to the ceramic material out of which the gate is fashioned (Post, 2015, p. 30; Stockmans, 2011).

A second memorial form is connected directly with the boats: the *Lampedusa Cross* (British Museum, 2015a, 2015b). This form of memorial culture, which was originally started locally, acquired a European allure over time. It was a carpenter on Lampedusa, Francisco Tuccio, who originally came up with this cross. In 2011, he was in his parish church and saw migrants, Eritrean Christians, mourning the loss of their loved ones. That stimulated him not only to make furniture in his workshop but also to fashion small crosses from wood that washed up from boats lost at sea and to give them to refugees who were staying in his neighbourhood. He also made larger crosses from wreckage for certain occasions. A Lampedusa Cross was carried in the silent procession after the 2013 disaster, and Tuccio made all kinds of attributes from pieces of wreckage for the Mass during the Pope's visit to Lampedusa on July 8, 2013 (cross, altar, even a wooden chalice). Demand for the large crosses arose, and several parish churches in Sicily quickly put in orders for a cross. The British Museum curator, Jill Cook, heard the story of the cross on a BBC radio programme in May 2015. She wanted to give the story of the migrants a place in the museum and approached Tuccio about making a cross for the museum. He made a cross from the wreckage of the boat from 2013 and sent it to London. And thus the Lampedusa Cross (Figure 3.1) was included in the museum's collection as the last acquisition by the then museum director Neil MacGregor and has been on display since 2015.

Figure 3.1 The Lampedusa Cross in the British Museum (2015).

Especially in the UK, this cross was the occasion for memorial rituals for refugees in parishes, schools, and universities. Churches (especially Roman Catholic and Anglican parishes) ordered crosses, or crosses were moved from place to place like mobile relics, and were – together with life jackets – part of pilgrimages and refugee exhibitions. The Lampedusa Cross, which Tuccio himself called 'The Cross of Migrants', was an important element in campaigns about the refugee crisis by CAFOD, the Catholic Agency for Overseas Development, the official aid agency of the Catholic Church in England and Wales. Crosses were offered to the cathedrals in England and Wales and to pilgrimage sites. They could also be ordered, and messages of hope for the refugees could be sent either online or on paper.[7]

In these two tracks of memoralization, material culture in the form of relics and ruins plays a dominant role. Valentina Napolitano analysed the Lampedusa Cross in the British Museum (Napolitano, 2016a, 2016b) and sees those crosses as 'trace-relics of forced mobility, death, suffering and humanity'. The cross 'mobilizes a "politics of seduction" on migration, the nearness/distance of migrants' suffering, the (powerful) spirits of the sea, together with "the" trace par excellence: the *corpus verum* of Christ'. This perspective links up seamlessly not only with the growing interest in material culture in the study of culture, ritual, and religion (Meyer, 2012), but also in the interest in the phenomenon of relics, remains, waste and ruins. As abandoned places and spaces, ruins fascinate us by making the absent present; they receive a ritual and also an aesthetic dimension (Price, 2016).[8]

In addition to this perspective of relics and ruins, there is also the interaction of the cultural ritual zones of the memorial spot and the museum, between the ritual zone of marking and commemorating and remembering and the museum and exhibition. Both came together in the refugee exhibition in English churches, just as they do in the 'museum' near the haven of Lampedusa. That same interplay can be seen in the tradition right up to the present in the treasuries of the great cathedrals and in major pilgrimage sites in which the reliquaries are on display behind glass: it is both a *Sancta Sanctorum* and a museum. It is in that tradition that we have to see the Lampedusa Cross in the British Museum. We can also see it in museum projects on the spots where disasters and atrocities, such as genocide, occurred (Williams, 2007).

A third memorial form is planting trees and setting up a garden. After the 2013 disaster, there was a local initiative for a 'Giardino della Memoria' (Post, 2015, p. 30). A garden was to be set up in a nature park with 366 trees, one for each migrant who died. In November 2014, inhabitants of the island and a group of migrants planted 40 trees. I cannot discover precisely what happened after that, but an eyewitness who was on the spot in 2014 and 2015 could not see which were the separately planted trees in the garden and if any more had been planted after those initial 40. An installation was also set up in 2013 in the garden by an activist group, Askavusa, in the form of an upside-down tree. A storm destroyed this work of art in 2015 (Informant: Dr Karina Horsti, Jyväskylä, Finland (email November 20, 2016)).

The idea of a garden and planting trees in memory of the victims, returns, for that matter, after the cited, probably largest, shipwreck of April 18, 2015. In December 2016, the port city Augusta also came up with a plan to create a 'Giardino della Memoria'. On closer inspection, this plan was not so much a matter of trees and a garden as one concerning the wreck that had been brought to the city. It was intended to give the wreck a place as a memorial monument in a garden or park, as a major gesture of solidarity with the migrant flow.[9]

Cultural memorial practices with a ritual dimension

From a greater distance, we see all kinds of cultural practices with a clear ritual, memorial dimension, related to the victimhood of the refugees. This partly concerns the replacement or vicarious ritual: in their own way, people want to make up for a void, an empty space by absent ritual, and set up 'a monument' for the dead migrants. All kinds of variations on this repertoire are possible. In the Lampedusa project, I came across a triad of (a) literary projects, (b) photograph, film, and video projects, and (c) documentation projects (Post, 2015, pp. 31–37).

Migrant literature is omnipresent in all languages and genres. I will cite here only a few recent Dutch examples. During Spirituality Month ('Maand van de spiritualiteit', February 2017), the bookstore I go to regularly, set up a table with books on the topic of the refugee crisis. The immediate cause was the small book by Rosita Steenbeek *Heb uw vijanden lief* (*Love your Enemies*) that had been published that month (Steenbeek, 2017). I bought five books that were on the table, Steenbeek's book first of all. The author, who lives in Rome, explores the concept of 'compassion' and, for that purpose, travelled to Lampedusa. She spoke with the doctor there who, for over 25 years, has been looking after refugees who have washed on Lampedusa's shores and describes her conversations with the islands' inhabitants and refugees. She also took part in a rescue and salvage operation. She saw 140 people arrive who were rescued, 120 had drowned. Steenbeek also attended the memorial services in the church and on the church square. She was also struck by the role of material culture and relics in her compassion visit to Lampedusa:

> Close to the harbour a museum has been erected in which things have been collected that people who drowned had with them: clothes, bags, as well as a Copt's diary, money sewn into clothing and rolled up

pieces of text from the Bible and the Qur'an that they drew comfort and strength from, the psalms, Exodus.

(Steenbeek, 2017, p. 54)

Before that, the poet and writer Ilja Leonard Pfeijffer, who lives in Genoa, published some texts that had been published earlier in a volume called *Gelukszoekers: Over vluchtelingen, migranten, angst en hoop* (*Happiness Seekers: On Refugees, Migrants, Fear and Hope*). One of the contributions was the lyrics of the song 'Lampedusa' (Pfeijffer, 2015).

In 2013, a Dutch translation was published of the 2011 book *Mare al mattino* by Margaret Mazzantini, *Morgenzee* (*Sea at the Morning*) with two stories about refugees fleeing from and to Libya (Mazzantini, 2013).

The Dutch writer Tommy Wieringa published his novel *De dood van Murat Idrissi* (*The Death of Murat Idrissi*) in 2017. After an extended literary sketch of the Mediterranean Sea, the novel tells the dramatic story of the smuggling of a young man via Spain.

The year 2017 also saw the publication by Jan van Mersbergen of *Oase* (*Oasis*), a novel in which a not very successful eatery on the outside of the city centre is central, run by the father of the brothers Dahir and Sulayman (Van Mersbergen, 2017). This is the story of refugees who found a place to settle down, but the past constantly seems to overshadow the present and the future.

They are all literary productions that have been written out of the authors' engagement with the refugee tragedy. Fear, death, hope, and future prospects are constant themes. Compassion and the memory of the victims are also central themes. It is interesting to see how the covers reinforce the themes and mirror elements mentioned in this contribution. The cover of Steenbeek's book (Figure 3.2) is a drawing in which we see the island of Lampedusa, with Paladino's gate and grounded boats piled up: some on land, but most of them under water. Above is a burning, bright red sun. The books by Pfeijffer and Mazzantini depict the well-known theme of a drowned refugee in the water and washed up on shore (Figures 3.3 and 3.4), a topos that would definitely be established via the image of the drowned three-year-old boy Aylan Kurdi in 2015.

Of the boom in photo projects, which also often play a role in the refugee exhibitions cited, I will mention once again the impressive relic project by Marco Pavan from 2014: 'Dramatic Stories of Immigration Told through Objects Left Behind' (Post 2015, p. 32, note 37). As an example of a video/ film project on the boat wreckage on Lampedusa, I already cited *Waste No. 2 Wreck* by the Finnish artist Jan Ijäs (*Waste No. 2 Wreck*, 2016).

Documentation projects on refugees receive little attention as a practice with a ritual dimension. There are various projects that document the refugee dead and missing in the Mediterranean Sea. The methods of work and also the figures diverge, and not every project is up to date. But there

Rosita
Steenbeek Heb uw
vijanden lief

Figure 3.2 Cover, R. Steenbeek (2017).

Source: Amsterdam: Stichting Collectieve Propaganda van het Nederlandse Boek, in cooperation with Ambo/Anthos Publishers; illustration: Francesco Piobbichi.

WINNAAR CESARE PAVESE-PRIJS

Margaret Mazzantini

MORGENZEE

Voor wie alles kwijt is, rest alleen nog hoop

Figure 3.3 Cover, M. Mazzantini (2016).
Source: Amsterdam: Rainbow; cover design: b'IJ Barbara.

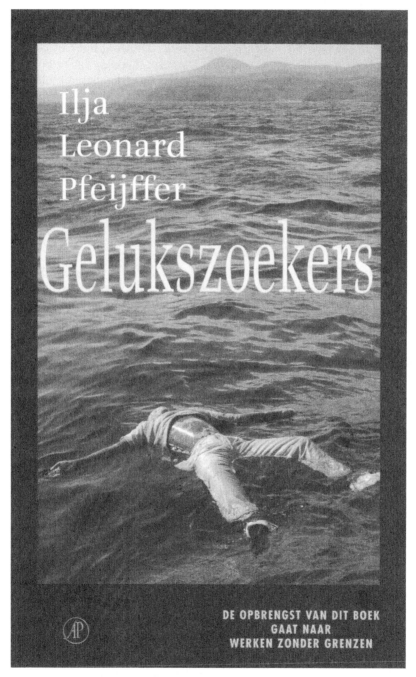

Figure 3.4 Cover, I. L. Pfeijffer (2015).
Source: Amsterdam/Antwerpen: De Arbeiderspers; illustration: Reuters/Juan Medina.

is the shared goal to not leave the migrant dead unseen, unnamed, and – at the very least – uncounted.

First of all, there is the Dutch project 'Border Deaths: Human Costs of Border Control'[10] under the direction of Professor Thomas Spijkerboer of VU University Amsterdam. Central to this project is a database of 'official, state-produced evidence on people who died while attempting to reach southern EU countries from the Balkans, the Middle East, and North and West Africa, and whose bodies were found in or brought to Europe'. The database covers the period from 1990 up to and including 2013. In addition to documentation, there is a research project on border control and the consequences for migrants.

Since the 2013 Lampedusa boat tragedy, the IOM, the International Organization for Migration, the UN migration agency, has maintained the 'Missing Migrants Project'[11] (Figures 3.5 and 3.6) that documents Mediterranean migrant deaths and the missing. The IOM published two reports on this (Brian & Laczko, 2014, 2016).

Still online is the 'List of Deaths'[12] of UNITED for Intercultural Action (Figure 3.7), a European network against nationalism, racism, fascism and in support of migrants and refugees, although the actual list stops in April 2015 (since 1993).

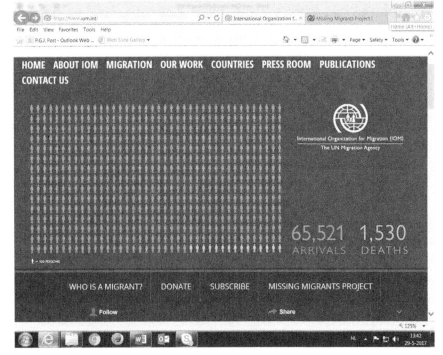

Figure 3.5 Screen shot website International Organization for Migration (IOM).

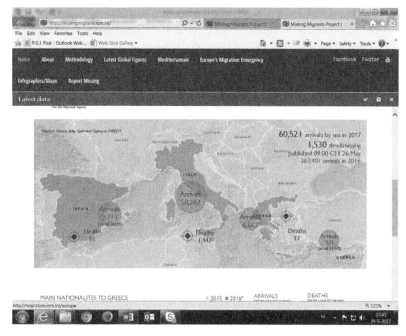

Figure 3.6 Screen shot website *Missing Migrants Project*.

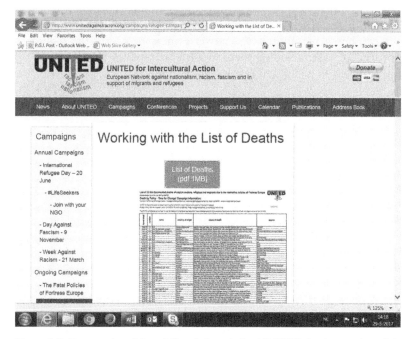

Figure 3.7 Screen shot 'List of Deaths', website UNITED for Intercultural Action.

The list in the blog by the well-known Italian journalist, Gabriele Del Grande *Fortress Europe*[13] (Figure 3.8) covers the period from 2013 to February 2016.

The database 'The Migrants' Files'[14] (Figure 3.9) by a consortium of journalists from more than 15 countries was stopped about halfway through 2016, primarily because of its overlapping with the above-mentioned database by the IOM. The database covers the period from 2000 to the middle of 2016.

These documentation projects are driven by various motivations. The general basis is formed by outrage over and engagement with the refugee crisis. The projects are intended to have a political impact, but they also have an unmistakable ritual component. Documenting and counting is not an act of dehumanization but precisely an expression of human dignity. Victims are brought into view, their fate is getting attention. In that sense, these projects are quite close to the memorial monuments where naming and/or documenting comprise a central element. One could think here of the many Holocaust memorials where documentation about the victims is central, such as the Dutch digital Holocaust monument that consists of a database of more than 104,000 Jewish Holocaust victims in the Nether-lands (Post, 2014).[15] The remarkable fact about border deaths, that several documentation projects are being done at the same time, indicates to me that there is a ritual component in play here. The importance of the act itself transcends efficiency, and repetition and doubling is not an important consideration here. There is, perhaps above all, an element of abjuration and exorcism here: one abjures the powerlessness by giving the victims a name or face. At least including them in a list with paltry facts concerning place and time fills in a gap and restores human dignity.

Refugee camps: travelling on

We now go back to a different, possibly better end to the journey, that of arrival in Europe. The first place they end up after the journey is a refugee or migrant reception camp. Not only scholars, but artists and theatre makers also emphasize the liminal character of the stay in a camp, as in the theatre project by Zlatko Ćosić: 'Liminal Rituals of Refugees'.[16] Camp life is determined by routines and rituals, small and large, individual and col-lective. It is remarkable that, for example, in the provisional migrant camp outside Calais (2015–2016), called 'the jungle', next to rickety houses built of cardboard and plastic, Eritrean Christians also built a church ('the cathedral') (Wildschut, 2016).[17]

The borderland perspective can also be seen as an analytical framework for ritual research in detention centres and hidden border camps on the edges of Europe, such as the 'The Burning' project in Morocco by the visual anthro-pologist Isabella Alexander (Emory University, US) (Alexander, 2016).

Figure 3.8 Screen shot website *Fortress Europe*.

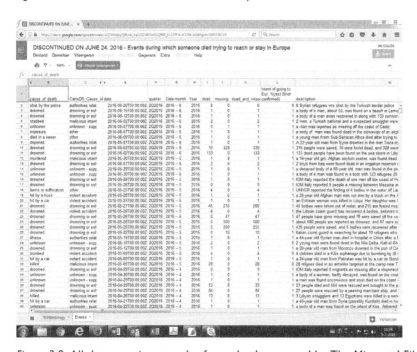

Figure 3.9 All data on migrant and refugee deaths, created by The Migrants' Files.

The stay in a camp can be long or short. The destination is often a community of fellow migrants that had formed, usually in a large European city, with family and compatriots. There are also often longer or shorter stops along the way, often also in cities. These stops have consequences for the spatial presence of (religious) rituals. Regarding these rituals, I focus now primarily on the Christian spatial presence.

In Europe there is, in addition to church closings, a major dynamic with respect to liturgical spaces that is going on. The figures regarding space for worship in the UK, which UK Church Statistics has made available, are illustrative.[18] The picture that emerges is clear: traditional churches – primarily neo-Gothic buildings – are closing, while new, growing migrant churches, primarily in the major cities, are contributing to a net increase. This picture obtains in general for all of Europe with respect to cities. Migrants are founding new communities everywhere with new churches.

In 2011, Jan Blommaert published a small local study on ritual spaces in a city district in Antwerp (Belgium) (Blommaert, 2011). In the streets of that Antwerp district there appears to be a large dynamic going on regarding churches. During his explorations, Blommaert counted 16 religious communities: two Catholic churches, three mosques (Turkish, Moroccan, one international), 11 Protestant or Evangelical churches (one local, five African, three Brazilian, two Latin American). He detected a major dynamic among the latter group: one week a church opened in a rented store, but the next week it could be in another spot, or the church had moved to a different part of the city. The internet also played a major role here: many meetings consisted of online connections with rituals and worship leaders elsewhere in the world, often in the home countries of the migrants.

Migrants also find ritual shelter in existing churches and communities. Thus, all kinds of forms of shared ritual space have emerged that have hardly been noticed and researched. In a lecture, my colleague Bert Groen from Graz invoked the interference that then takes place with respect to ritual (Groen, 2017). Everywhere in Europe there are hospitable churches: spaces are borrowed and rented, and adapted. This results in mutual tensions and influences. Armenians, Slavic Christians, Christians from Ethiopia, Eritrea, Syria and Egypt thus appropriate spaces for themselves. All kinds of ritual elements are questioned and adapted or rejected. That ritual interference concerns the language, music (traditions that did not have organ music or sing in harmony now use an organ and sing in harmony), iconography (icons, candles change the space), the role of sensory elements, the veneration of saints, the calendar, meals after the celebration, and so on.

After the journey ...

Finally, there is an arrival: the journey ends somewhere with the refugee settling down. Then too there are often rituals. It is important to tell stories about the journey, to show engagement with fellow migrants who understood the journey just as they do. Refugees are often traumatized by the gruesome experiences of the journey or the fate of those who stayed behind in a war zone. Rituals are used as coping mechanisms in therapeutic programmes. These mourning rites for refugees have been described in psychotherapeutic literature since the 1980s (Metcalf & Huntington, 1991; Van der Hart, 1984, 1992; Zwart & Nieuwenhuis, 1998).

Epilogue

We announced we would see the ritual repertoire of the refugee cycle as part of the wider repertoire of victimhood. Both of these repertoires share the perspective of the victim, in this case the refugee. But we see more elements in the refugee ritual that we know from repertoire of victimhood, for example through Holocaust studies, the study of disaster ritual (Post, Grimes, Nugteren, Pettersson, & Zondag, 2003) and practices of commemoration after atrocities, tragedies, genocides, terrorist attacks, etc.[19] We touched, in our mapping the field of refugee rituals, upon central elements, such as the dynamics of commemoration ritual, absent and present, the specific liminal setting of the rituals, the role of material culture via monuments and relics, but also – although not elaborated on here – the role of the media and the interaction of online and offline memorial practices, ritual and coping with traumas. In my view, the interference between refugee repertoire and repertoire or victimhood is fruitful. Research into refugee ritual contributes to the broader victimhood repertoire, and vice versa, and research into the repertoire of victimhood gives a focus and context to refugee ritual. And as a last remark: with both repertoires there is more work to be done.

Notes

1 See www.unhcr.org/statistics/unhcrstats/576408cd7/unhcr-global-trends-2015. html (accessed June 2017). Various organizations provide information on the refugee streams in various places. I will cite here only the UNHCR, the IOM (International Office for Migration), and the EU. Cf. http://popstats.unhcr.org/en/overview; http://ec.europa.eu/echo/refugee-crisis; www.iom.int/.
2 See http://data2.unhcr.org/en/situations/mediterranean#_ga=2.156342969.3253 43527.1495451560–543315925.1493727921 (accessed May 2017).
3 For her projects and publications, see www.jyu.fi/hytk/fi/laitokset/yfi/en/staff/horsti-karina (accessed June 2017).
4 See www.bbc.com/news/world-europe-36278529 (accessed May 2017).
5 For various definitions, see www.unitedagainstracism.org/campaigns/refugee-campaign/working-with-the-list-of-deaths/; http://popstats.unhcr.org/en/overview (both accessed May 2017).
6 See https://utoronto.academia.edu/VNapolitano/CurriculumVitae (accessed June 2017).

7 See www.stpauls.co.uk/news-press/latest-news/see-the-lampedusa-cross-at-st-pauls-on-sunday-19-june;   www.bbc.com/news/world-europe-35360682;   http://cafod.org.uk/News/International-news/Lampedusa-crosses-refugees; www.pem.cam.ac.uk/the-college/news/2017/03/arrival-of-the-lampedusa-cross/; www.youtube.com/watch?v=XFd0xeBcmDU (all accessed June 2017).
8 Cf. https://reconfiguringruins.blogs.sas.ac.uk/; http://thenewbridgeproject.com/news/artist-commission-opportunity-reconfiguring-ruins/ (accessed June 2017).
9 See   www.siracusanews.it/augusta-un-giardino-della-memoria-allinterno-del-presepe-vivente-monte-tauro-ricordare-le-700-vittime-del-naufragio/ (accessed June 2017).
10 See www.borderdeaths.org/ (accessed June 2017).
11 See https://missingmigrants.iom.int/ (accessed June 2017).
12 See   www.unitedagainstracism.org/wp-content/uploads/2017/06/UNITEDList OfDeathsActual.pdf (accessed June 2017).
13 See http://fortresseurope.blogspot.nl/ (accessed June 2017).
14 See www.themigrantsfiles.com/; https://docs.google.com/spreadsheets/d/1YNqI zyQfEn4i_be2GGWESnG2Q80E_fLASffsXdCOftI/edit# (accessed June 2017).
15 See www.joodsmonument.nl (accessed June 2017).
16 See https://vimeo.com/161774183 (seen June 2017).
17 See   also   www.volkskrant.nl/buitenland/fotograaf-zoekt-schoonheid-in-jungle-bij-calais~a4273807/ (accessed June 2017).
18 See www.eauk.org/church/research-and-statistics/how-many-churches-have-opened-or-closed-in-recent-years.cfm (from September 2014, accessed January 2017).
19 Cf. here the European research consortium PRACMEM: Practices of memoralization after atrocities and large-scale human rights abuses (a cooperation of the universities of Tilburg, Louvain, Bath and San Sebastián), see www.pracmem.eu.

References

Alexander, I. (2016). 'Burning' at the EU borders: Liminality, belonging, and Morocco's new migrant class (Doctoral Dissertation). Emory University, Atlanta. Retrieved from www.theburning.org/TEAM.php.

Anzaldúa, G. B. (2012). Borderlands/La frontera: The new Meztiza (4th edition). San Francisco: Aunt Lute Books.

Blommaert, J. (2011). The Vatican of the diaspora. Yearbook for Liturgical and Ritual Studies, 27, 243–259.

Brian, T., & Laczko, F. (Eds.). (2014). Fatal journeys 1: Tracking lives lost during migration (IOM report Geneva 2014). Retrieved from https://publications.iom.int/system/files/pdf/fataljourneys_countingtheuncounted.pdf.

Brian, T., & Laczko, F. (Eds.). (2016). Fatal journeys 2: Identification and tracing of dead and missing migrants (IOM report Geneva 2016). Retrieved from https://publications.iom.int/system/files/fataljourneys_vol. 2.pdf.

British Museum (2015a, December 18). Last acquisition under Neil MacGregor revealed [Press release]. Retrieved from www.britishmuseum.org/about_us/news_and_press/press_releases/2015/macgregors_last_acquisition.aspx.

British Museum (2015b). The Lampedusa cross [Collection online]. Retrieved from www.britishmuseum.org/research/collection_online/collection_object_details.aspx?objectId=3691920&partId=1&searchText=cross+lampedusa&page=1.

Dols García, A. (2013). Voodoo, witchcraft and human trafficking in Europe. UNHCR Research Paper, 263. Retrieved from www.ecoi.net/file_upload/1930_1 382531731_526664234.pdf.

Donnan, H., & Wilson, T. M. (Eds.). (2010). *Borderlands: Ethnographic approaches to security, power, and identity*. Lanham, MD: University Press of America.

Faro, L. (2015). *Postponed monuments in the Netherlands: Manifestation, context, and meaning* (Doctoral Dissertation). Tilburg University, Tilburg.

Foote, K. (2003). *Shadowed ground: America's landscapes of violence and tragedy* (revised edition). Austin: University of Texas Press.

Foote, K. (2010). Shadowed ground, sacred place: Reflections on violence, tragedy, memorials and public commemoration rituals. In P. Post, & A. L. Molendijk, *Holy ground: Re-inventing ritual space in modern Western culture* (Liturgia Condenda, 24, pp. 93–118). Leuven: Peeters.

Grimes, R. L. (2014). *The craft of ritual studies*. Oxford: Oxford University Press.

Groen, B. (2017, March 24). *Oosterse liturgie in het Westen: De uitdaging van inculturatie en herbronning* (unpublished lecture). Tilburg University, Tilburg.

Ijäs, J. (2016). *Waste No. 2 Wreck* [video file]. Retrieved from https://vimeo.com/groups/ijas/videos/159391660.

Kempny, M. (2011). Interpretative repertoire of victimhood. *Anthropological Journal of European Cultures*, 20(1), 132–151.

Lageman, T. (2017). Op de begraafplaats voor verdronken vluchtelingen. *Vakblad Uitvaart*, May, 26–27.

Margry, P. J., & Sánchez-Carretero, C. (Eds.). (2011). *Grassroots memorials: The politics of memorializing traumatic death*. New York/Oxford: Berghahn.

Mazzantini, M. (2013). *Morgenzee* (M. Bunnik & M. Schepers, Trans.). Amsterdam: Wereldbibliotheek.

Metcalf, P. & Huntington, R. (1991). *Celebrations of death: The anthropology of mortuary rituals*. Cambridge, UK: Cambridge University Press.

Meyer, B. (2012). *Mediation and the genesis of presence: Towards a material approach of religion* (Inaugural Lecture). Utrecht University, Utrecht.

Napolitano, V. (2016a, September). *The Lampedusa's cross: On relics and the 'politics of seduction'*. Paper presented at the international conference: On the Trace: Passing, Presence and the Persistence of the Past. Retrieved from http://conferences.saxo.ku.dk/onthetrace/accepted-abstracts/Accept_-_Napolitano__Valentina.pdf.

Napolitano, V. (2016b, November). *On the political aesthetics of Lampedusa cross(es)*. Paper presented at the conference: Inter-Religious Exchanges: Past and Present. Religion and the City: Inter-Religious Exchanges in Urban Environments. Retrieved from http://mongol.huji.ac.il/sites/default/files/Napolitano_2016_Abstract.pdf.

Napolitano, V., Luz, N., & Stadler, N. (2015). Introduction: Materialities, histories, and the spatialization of State sovereignty. *Religion and Society: Advances in Research*, 6, 90–97.

Pfeijffer, I. L. (2015). *Gelukszoekers*. Amsterdam: De Arbeiderspers.

Post, C. (2014). From site to site: The digital monument to the Jewish community in the Netherlands. In P. Post, P. Nel, & W. van Beek (Eds.), *Sacred spaces and contested identities: Space and ritual dynamics in Europe and Africa* (pp. 345–360). Trenton: Africa World Press.

Post, P. (2010). *Voorbij het kerkgebouw: Over een ander sacraal domein*. Heeswijk: Berne.

Post, P. (2011). Fields of the sacred: Reframing identities of sacred places. In P. Post, A. L. Molendijk, & J. E. A. Kroesen (Eds.), *Sacred places in modern Western culture* (pp. 13–60). Leuven: Peeters.

Post, P. (2015). The Lampedusa tragedy: Chronicles of absent and emerging ritual repertoires. *Yearbook for Liturgical and Ritual Studies, 31,* 19–43. Retrieved from http://rjh.ub.rug.nl/index.php/jvlo/article/view/19534/17012.

Post, P. (2017). Afwezig ritueel: Proeve van een typologie. *NTT Journal for Theology and the Study of Religion, 71,* 242–256.

Post, P., & Faro, L. (2017). Een ritual studies onderzoeksdesign: Ervaringen en perspectieven. *Yearbook for Ritual and Liturgical Studies, 33,* 20–39. Retrieved from http://ugp.rug.nl/jvlo/article/view/30957/28268.

Post, P., Grimes, R., Nugteren, A., Pettersson, P., & Zondag, H. (2003). *Disaster ritual: Explorations of an emerging ritual repertoire* (Liturgia Condenda, 15). Leuven: Peeters.

Post, P., & Hoondert, M. (Eds.). (2019, forthcoming). *Absent ritual: The ambivalence of hidden, disappearing, ignored, unknown, banned and forbidden rituals.*

Post, P., Nugteren, A., & Zondag, H. (2002). *Rituelen na rampen: Verkenning van een opkomend repertoire.* Kampen: Gooi & Sticht.

Post, P., & Van der Beek, S. (2016). *Doing ritual criticism in a network society: Online and offline explorations into pilgrimage and sacred place* (Liturgia Condenda, 29). Leuven: Peeters.

Price, Z. (2016). *(Re)configuring ruin: The sacred poetics of rubble in the photography of Scott Hocking* (MA Thesis). Radboud University, Nijmegen.

Steenbeek, R. (2017). *Heb uw vijanden lief.* Amsterdam: Stichting Collectieve Propaganda van het Nederlandse Boek.

Stockmans, P. (2011, August 8). Lampedusa: Van heuvel van de schande naar de poort van Europa. *MO Mondiaal Nieuws.* Retrieved from www.mo.be/wereldblog/pieter-stockmans-op-lampedusa/lampedusa-van-de-heuvel-van-de-schande-naar-de-poort-van-eu.

Van der Hart, O. (Ed.). (1984). *Rituelen in psychotherapie: Overgang en bestendiging.* Deventer: van Loghum Slaterus.

Van der Hart, O. (Ed.). (1992). *Afscheidsrituelen: Achterblijven en verder gaan.* Amsterdam: Swets en Zeitlinger.

Van Mersbergen, J. (2017). *Oase.* Amsterdam: Cossee.

Van Reisen, M., & Mawere, M. (Eds.). (2017). *Human trafficking and trauma in the digital era: The ongoing tragedy of the trade in refugees from Eritrea.* Oxford: Bamenda.

Wieringa, T. (2017). *De dood van Murat Idrissi.* Amsterdam: Hollands Diep.

Wildschut, H. (2016). *Ville de Calais.* Amsterdam: Henk Wildschut. Retrieved from http://villedecalais.nl/.

Williams, P. (2007). *Memorial museums: The global rush to commemorate atrocities.* Oxford: Berg.

Wilson, T., & Donnan, H. (2012). Border and border studies. In T. Wilson & H. Donnan (Eds.), *A companion to border studies* (pp. 1–25). Malden, MA: Blackwell.

Zwart, M., & Nieuwenhuis, L. (1998). Mourning rituals in non-verbal therapy with traumatised refugees. In D. Dokter (Ed.), *Arts therapists, refugees and migrants: Reading across borders* (pp. 62–78). London: Jessica Kingsley Publishers.

Part II

Artistic practices

Chapter 4

Representing the experience of victims at the Berlin Wall Memorial Museum

David Clarke

Memorial museums and transitional justice

The term 'memorial museum' is generally reserved for historical sites that have the dual function of commemorating the victims of injustice and informing the public about the historical circumstances of oppression (Williams, 2007). In recent years, scholars of transitional justice have emphasized the function of memorial museums and other forms of commemoration as symbolic reparations (De Greiff, 2007, p. 155) that have the potential to re-write a society's historical memory in favour of the victims of oppression (Naidu, 2014, pp. 33–34). The nature of this potential in terms of repairing harm to victims remains largely unexplored, however (Hamber, Ševčenko, & Naidu, 2010, pp. 398–399).

In the German context, and particularly in relation to memorial museums dedicated to the victims of the Soviet Occupation, the state socialist regime of the former German Democratic Republic (GDR) and the division of Germany during the Cold War, the demand of victims' organizations to have their experiences represented in memorial museums on their preferred terms has met with resistance from museum professionals and historians. Carola Rudnik (2011, 2013), who has produced the most wide-ranging study of these controversies, has identified the forceful anti-communism of victims' organizations as a key driver of conflict with heritage professionals, while other commentators have even accused these organizations of pressing a right-wing political agenda in their campaigns around memorial museums (Jander, 2013, p. 134; Winters, 2013, p. 41). While anti-communism is undoubtedly important to many of these organizations, and while some of these groups have struggled to come to terms with the questionable views of some of their members (Sachse, 2012, pp. 58–59), this chapter will argue that such a reading of these conflicts ignores a more fundamental dynamic between heritage professionals and victims.

Drawing on the systems theory of German sociologist Niklas Luhmann, this chapter will make the case that conflicts between these stakeholders are, in fact, determined by the functional systems within which they produce their communication. In this sense, for those looking to resolve conflicts over memorialization in other transitional contexts, it may be necessary to acknowledge that such systematic factors can make consensus difficult. An analysis of the Berlin Wall Memorial Museum (*Gedenkstätte Berliner Mauer*), as it has been known since 2008, will not only show how such projects are the result of 'long-term social, economic, cultural, and political processes' (Barsalou & Baxter, 2007, p. 3), but will also demonstrate how interactions between heritage professionals, victims' organizations and, indeed, the political system, condition outcomes in terms of the representation of victims' experience in the memorial museum context.

Heritage organizations, protest organizations and systems theory

Luhmann's theory of social systems, which can only be summarized very briefly here (for an overview see: King & Thornhill, 2003), is a form of constructivism (Moeller, 2012, pp. 78–87) that identifies key functional systems in the polycentric society of modernity. These systems are communicative, closed and self-producing (autopoietic). They fulfil their social function by producing communications in a particular symbolic medium. To communicate in these symbolic media, Luhmann argues, is to formulate communications according to specific binary codes (Luhmann, 1992, pp. 194–198) that are subject to historical change, even if the generalized medium of communication stays the same. For instance, the medium of power, which is the medium of the political system, would once have produced the binary subjugation/domination; yet today's modern democracies formulate their communications according to the binary of government/ opposition (Luhmann, 2002, p. 98). In other words, the political system formulates its communication according to whether that communication is more or less likely to contribute to access to government (i.e. electoral popularity).

Organizations play an important role in Luhmann's later theoretical work. He hypothesizes that organizations allow systems to communicate decisions to their environment (Luhmann, 2000, p. 388). Although not restricted to communication in one medium, organizations in Luhmann's account tend to be dominated by a particular system (Luhmann, 1998, p. 841). In this chapter, I will analyse the communication of heritage organizations and victims' organizations in the German context, assigning the former to the system of science (*Wissenschaft*) and the latter to the system of protest.

The term 'science' in English is not commonly one that would be applied to the museums and heritage sector. In Luhmann's analysis of the functional system of science, however, the term applies to any field of academic research, encompassing both the natural sciences and the humanities and social sciences. The historians and museum professionals who are charged with establishing, presenting and managing memorial museums in Germany frequently appeal to the principle of *Wissenschaflichkeit*, that is to say they claim for their approaches the status of science, or what in English we might call academic rigour.

Luhmann's account of the scientific system stresses that its social function is to produce new knowledge (Luhmann, 1992, p. 298). In order to do so, it produces communications in the medium of truth, using the binary code of true/untrue, which is to say that the communications it produces distinguish between what is and what is not the case (p. 285). This does not imply that other systems make no claims about the nature of reality. However, Luhmann argues that modern science's communications about the true and the untrue are produced in a fashion unique to that system, namely through the implementation of two kinds of programmes: theoretical and methodological (pp. 427–429). These programmes should be understood as a series of operative procedures that the system follows in order to produce its communications in the medium of truth (p. 418). Theories are propositions about the nature of reality that claim to be applicable across different cases. In other words, they are generalizations that produce a reduction in complexity (pp. 406–410). Theories alone, however, do not produce a viable communication that distinguishes truth from untruth. This final step requires the application of methodology (p. 415). Methodology provides a series of operative procedures that can be pursued in order to arrive at such a communication (p. 418).

The scientific system as a whole, however, cannot formulate such theories or methodologies, or implement the latter in order to produce scientific communication. This requires the creation of scientific organizations (p. 675). These can be universities, but are not restricted to this form (pp. 478–479). Organizations identify projects (presented as problems that require solutions) (p. 427), select and employ researchers according to professional criteria of qualification, expertise and reputation (p. 657), and communicate the results of research to their environment (p. 672).

In the years immediately following the Second World War, it was frequently the activism of victims themselves that led to the setting up of memorial museums (Haug, 2015, pp. 31–32). While these contained exhibitions in some cases, such as at Dachau, they were strongly focused on the suffering of victims and the barbarity of Nazi perpetrators, providing relatively little historical context (Marcuse, 2005, pp. 122, 132). In the 1970s and 1980s, a broadly left-wing culture of civil society engagement emerged in West Germany and West Berlin, leading to an increased involvement of non-victims in the creation of memorial museums (Haug, 2015, pp. 34–39). Despite the presence of non-victims as activists, exhibitions were nevertheless developed in close cooperation with victims and foregrounded their testimonies. However, in the late 1980s, many of these new memorial museum practitioners, some of whom became increasingly professionalized, began to debate existing practices in terms of the presentation of sites of persecution through exhibitions (Knigge, 2002, p. 384). Following German unification, these professionals have increasingly stressed the need for a new approach to sites of National Socialist persecution and to sites of political oppression in the GDR; an approach that moves away from an emphasis on emotional impact through a confrontation of the visitor with victim suffering and towards an emphasis on historical context. This development is understood in terms of new emphasis on research-based methodologies (*Verwissenschaftlichung*; Pampel, 2007, p. 53). As I have discussed elsewhere (Clarke, 2017a, 2017b), an important element of these arguments is the relative de-emphasizing of the right of victims to intervene in the presentation of memorial museum sites.

This push towards academically respectable methodologies and the professionalization of those involved in the presentation of memorial museum sites speaks of a gradual coupling of heritage organizations to the system of science. This is encouraged by the mechanisms of state funding, which insist that memorial museums are presented according to a 'scientifically and museologically [...] informed concept' (Deutscher Bundestag, 2008, p. 3; this and all following quotations from the German are my own, DC). The existence of this funding indicates that, like other scientific or research organizations (Luhmann, 1992, p. 637), heritage organizations in Germany depend for their existence on providing services to other functional systems and their organizations. Memorial museums, for example, provide services to the educational system via school visits, and to the political system via their claim to combat the emergence of anti-democratic views that threaten the reproduction of democracy in the Federal Republic.

Luhmann notes that, while remaining within the scientific system, research organizations produce communications in which the code true/untrue can take on a secondary significance. What is often at stake is the ability of that organization to convincingly produce scientific communication that persuades another system that it is fulfilling the terms of its commitment to supply services (Luhmann, 1992, p. 677). The scientific system cannot abandon its theories and methods in order to produce the output demanded by whoever is providing its resources (Luhmann, 1992, p. 638). However, in this particular case, there is, in theory, no reason why memorial museums must be run by academic historians and museum professionals. Indeed, memorial museums in Germany have been and continue to be run by organizations outside of the scientific system. Where those heritage organizations are part of the scientific system, however, heritage professionals' interest is in maintaining the authority of their communication and thus their authority over the sites in question. As Tiffany Jenkins has observed in another context, debates over appropriate museological methodologies are simultaneously processes of establishing professional authority (Jenkins, 2011). By drawing on a discourse that presents themselves as scientific (*wissenschaftlich*), heritage organizations in Germany seek to draw a line between those qualified to make decisions about the presentation of memorial museums and those who are not.

Luhmann regards protest movements as responses to the functional differentiation of modern society itself (Luhmann, 1996a, p. 103). They observe the outcomes of the functioning of the other systems, not that functioning on its own terms (Luhmann, 1996a, p. 209), and when they protest against those outcomes, they also reject them as symptoms of a functionally differentiated society. Building on Luhmann's analysis, Kai-Uwe Hellmann has proposed that the nature of the claims made by protest movements makes 'morality' a viable medium of communication through which to establish the autonomy of the system of protest (Hellmann, 1996, p. 236). Such moral coding can be seen in protest movements' construction of social problems, which they frame in terms of disappointed expectations. Those who have the power to make (political, economic and other) decisions are held responsible for negative outcomes, of which protestors themselves are figured as the victims (Hellmann, 1996, pp. 190, 237).

In relation to protest movements that focus on justice for victims of historical injustice, the medium of morality allows the formulation of a binary code of 'recognition'. The desire for recognition is one frequently invoked by victims of historical abuses (Jacoby, 2015, p. 528), but needs to be understood here in the sense proposed by Axel Honneth (1992). Honneth defines 'recognition' in relation to the desire of social movements not only to change aspects of society, but to produce a shift in the values of society. He argues that social conflicts emerge where groups seek to have their experiences, achievements and values recognized as those fundamental to the wider culture (Honneth, 1992, p. 205). Elazar Barkan has made a similar point about the importance of the recognition for oppressed groups in processes of coming to terms with the past (Barkan, 2002, p. 363). My argument here will be that victims' organizations, which operate within the system of protest, communicate about the communications of the other organizations in terms of whether they are afforded the recognition they desire. They tend to understand an apparent failure to offer such recognition as a moral failure on the part of the other functional systems and their organizations, and of society more widely.

Although Luhmann presents social systems as closed and autopoietic, their self-referentiality does not imply that each system's functioning is immune to stimulation from the other systems that make up its environment: systems are characterized by 'closure, not closedness!', as Luhmann insists (1992, p. 303; English in the original). Clearly, no system can continue to function in disregard of its environment. Indeed, in order to keep producing their own communications according to their own defining codes, systems are bound to

respond to that environment, which is made up of the communications produced by the other systems (Luhmann, 1987, p. 249). Luhmann describes the
relationships that develop between individual systems in terms of a 'structural
coupling'. This is not a direct causal relationship, in the sense that one system
makes the other do something, but rather a relationship of simultaneity
(Luhmann, 1992, p. 39). Such coupling occurs when one system produces
communications that can be responded to by another for its own purposes
(Luhmann, 1996b, pp. 122–125).

Ultimately, each system (and each organization within those systems)
seeks to respond to the communications produced in its environment, but
only ever its own systemic perspective. The example of the Berlin Wall
Memorial Museum in the Bernauer Straße in Berlin is an especially fruitful
case for studying the complexities of such interactions between heritage
organizations and victims' organizations, given the challenges to professional museology at this site that were mounted by victim activists. The
Memorial Museum itself emerged in three distinct phases, which will be
analysed below.

The development of the first memorial

A section of the notorious Berlin Wall was fenced off for preservation in
the spring of 1990 in Bernauer Straße by representatives of the city's
German Historical Museum and Museum for Germany History, supported
by Manfred Fischer, the pastor of the Reconciliation Parish (*Versöhnungsgemeinde*) in the district of Wedding, whose neo-Gothic parish church had
stood in the 'death strip' beyond the Wall until it was blown up by GDR
border forces in 1985 (Camphausen & Fischer, 2011, p. 349; Knischewski
& Splitter, 2006, p. 282). Of many possible sites for a memorial to the
Wall's victims, Bernauer Straße was particularly rich in associations. On
August 13, 1961, when the first incarnation of the Wall was constructed,
the border between East and West Berlin ran along the front of a row of
residential buildings on this street, and individuals had been able to make
dramatic escapes by jumping from their windows. Shortly after the Wall
was built, the Bernauer Straße was also the site of the famous escape by
East German solider Konrad Schumann, a 19-year-old who was photo-
graphed jumping over barbed wire into West Berlin in what became an
iconic image of the Cold War. In the months after the border was closed,
the basements of buildings on the street were also used by groups digging
escape tunnels to help East Berliners escape to the West.

On August 13, 1990, Fischer and representatives of the museums
announced their intention to set up a memorial to those who died at the
Wall. However, their press release also spoke of the difficulty of presenting
'just "pieces of the Wall" sprayed with graffiti [that] do not do justice to
the historical dimension' (*Versöhnungsgemeinde*, 1990), indicating a desire

to provide future visitors with some broader context for understanding the site. It took another year for Berlin's city government, the Senate, to approve the construction of a memorial on the site (Rudnick, 2011, p. 572) and until 1994 for a competition to be launched to find a design. This delay was chiefly the result of a dispute between the group initiating the memorial and the pastor of another adjoining parish, the *Sophiengemeinde*, which had lost a significant area of its graveyard to the border fortifications, which it clearly hoped to retrieve (Rudnik, 2011, p. 582). The pastor of the *Sophiengemeinde* claimed that the land his parish had lost contained mass graves of those killed in the city during the final stages of the Second World War. Once the graveyard had been returned to the property of his church in 1993 (Camphausen & Fischer, 2011, p. 363), he was only willing to let the land and its section of the preserved Wall be used as part of the memorial if these victims were also incorporated into the commemoration.

The guidelines for the design competition pointed to the 'necessarily complicated dialectic between this place as a site of the dead (including the victims of the Second World War) and as a site of commemoration for the victims of German division (and not only those who were killed)', which demanded a conceptualization capable of making these different traces legible (Deutsches Historisches Museum, 1994, p. 27). The entries to the competition, now held in the archive of the Memorial Museum's Documentation Centre, show how difficult it was to bring these elements together. The jury eventually chose a design by the architects Kohlhoff and Kohlhoff that was arguably a declaration of defeat with regard to the original design brief. As no entry had managed to find a convincing way of linking both sets of victims, the winning design was a compromise: it would only incorporate the stretch of Wall not situated on the land belonging to the *Sophiengemeinde*. This effectively meant that only the Wall victims would be commemorated.

The Kohlhoff and Kohlhoff design, which was completed in 1998, consists of two steel walls that close off the 70-metre section of double Berlin Wall, thereby boxing in a section of the former border area consisting largely of raked sand. The ultimately artistic intervention of the design suggests some of the border regime's original scale by reflecting the preserved Wall segments in its mirror-like internal surfaces (Trotnow, 2005, p. 162). The outside of the memorial has a different surface, made of COR-TEN or weathering steel, which develops a layer of rust. At one end, this surface carries an inscription describing the function of the memorial. In addition, the west-facing surface of the Wall, which had been damaged by souvenir hunters, was smoothed over and stabilized (Feversham & Schmidt, 1999, p. 164).

In the run-up to the opening of the memorial, victims' organizations began to focus their attention on the Bernauer Straße. First, the Circle of Victims and Surviving Relatives of Victims of the Berlin Wall and the Inner-German

Border objected to the proposed dedication of the memorial, which read 'To the Victims of the Second World War and the Division of Germany', arguing that this obscured the political and moral responsibility of the GDR regime for the building of the Wall and the border's casualties (Bernitt, 1998; Eich, 1998a). Second, the Circle insisted that the border fortifications should be reconstructed as far as possible in order to give visitors a fuller impression of the terror they must have inspired (Rudnick, 2011, p. 616). Although the victims were successful in having the inscription changed before the memorial officially opened to include a reference to 'the victims of communist despotism' (*kommunistischer Gewaltherrschaft*), at the expense of the reference to the Second World War, they nevertheless remained dissatisfied. In a speech at the inauguration on August 13, 1998, Circle spokesman Klaus-Peter Eich claimed that the new memorial failed to convey the full horror of the former border fortifications or to make explicit the link between that horror and communist ideology (Eich, 1998b, p. 8); the abstract memorial's failure to provide details of the suffering of individual victims of the Berlin Wall, he claimed, lessened its impact on the younger generation, who needed to be warned of the dangers of communism, violence and injustice (Eich, 1998b, pp. 8–9).

Carola Rudnick understands such criticisms in terms of an anti-communist agenda on the part of the Circle (Rudnick, 2011, p. 616). While it is undeniable that these victims did see their own suffering as a warning against the dangers of communist ideology, interpreting their activism only in these terms obscures a broader point. Leaving aside the specific ideology pursued by groups like the Circle, what is clear is that their protest communication conforms to that model already identified above. In other words, as a protest organization, the Circle communicated decisions about its approval or disapproval of the communications of other systems based on whether these provided adequate recognition to its own constituency. Such recognition was understood in terms of the victims' suffering taking on a central function for the rest of society, that is to say as a point of moral orientation that would underpin the values by which that society would live. The Circle's protest communication thereby also constructed the role of the victim as essential to the defence of the current social and political order against the threat of communist ideology. As I will show below, when controversy erupted again around the plans for expansion of the site at Bernauer Straße to create a more extensive memorial museum, this discourse among victims' organizations once more came to the fore.

The emergence of the 'Freedom Memorial' controversy

Already in the summer of 1997, Pastor Fischer had proposed that the soon to-be-completed Kohlhoff and Kohlhoff memorial should be complemented by a documentation centre and a new Chapel of Reconciliation. In the surrounding space, he proposed that the remaining material traces of the border system should be preserved. This proposal was swiftly agreed by the Berlin Senate (Camphausen & Fischer, 2011, p. 368) and a new private organization, the Berlin Wall Association (*Verein Berliner Mauer e.V.*), was created to plan the presentation of the space, including an exhibition in the proposed Documentation Centre (Camphausen, 1999b). The relative weakening of the influence of the *Sophiengemeinde*, once it was established that no war graves were in fact present on its land (Knischewski & Splitter, 2006, p. 284), and the willingness of the Reconciliation Parish to provide space for a memorial museum of greater scope meant that Gabriele Camphausen, who headed the new Association from 1998 until 2009, could assemble a team of historians and museum professionals to develop a concept for commemorating the Berlin Wall as a historical phenomenon.

Camphausen had already held positions at other memorial museums in Berlin and encouraged an approach very much in line with the mainstream of museological practice among professionals engaged in such work in Germany. She stressed the failure of the Kohlhoff and Kohlhoff memorial to satisfy the needs of the visitor for contextual information about the history of the Wall and German division (Camphausen, 1999a, p. 22), yet also implied that the expanded memorial ensemble would not follow the priorities of victims' organizations:

> Just as the spectrum of experiences and memories is broad, in both form and content, so the expectations of memory work are multiple and contradictory. There is no single formula for true and correct memory.
>
> (Camphausen, 1999a, pp. 21–22)

This insistence on the plurality of perspectives on the past is further borne out in the strategy that Camphausen and her team developed for the expanded site. Describing their guiding principles in retrospect, Camphausen and Fischer have stressed their desire to situate the victims' experiences as one element within a space characterized by 'an incredible density of authentic evidence' (*der authentischen Zeugnisse*) (Camphausen & Fischer, 2011, p. 375). Alongside a preference for the preservation of the fragmentary material traces of the site's past (Camphausen & Fischer, 2011, p. 376), they have also emphasized that they sought to avoid any emotionally overwhelming content, preferring instead to confront visitors with 'factual information', encouraging them to investigate the traces of the past and arrive at their own judgements (Camphausen & Fischer, 2011, p. 372; cf. Rudnik, 2011, p. 617). This stance was reflected, for example, in the format of the Documentation Centre, which presented visitors with a range of sources, including photographs, recordings of witness testimony and facsimiles of original documents, 'trusting the visitors to draw their own conclusions' (Knischewski & Splitter, 2006, p. 290).

Nevertheless, by the early 2000s, a change in the political situation in Berlin made it possible for victims' organizations to challenge this approach once more. The year 2001 saw a shift from a Senate dominated by the Christian Democrats (CDU), in a grand coalition with their Social Democrat (SPD) rivals, to a new coalition between the SPD and the Party of Democratic Socialism (PDS); the latter being the re-named East German communist party, which had formerly ruled the GDR. Following the establishment of the SPD-PDS coalition, and to mark the anniversary of the building of the Wall, the CDU organized its own commemorative event at the former Checkpoint Charlie (Sturm, 2001), distancing itself from the official ceremony at the Bernauer Straße memorial, where the PDS would be in attendance. A number of victims' organizations also chose to stay away from the Bernauer Straße event, but some protested at the official commemoration and even attacked a wreath laid by the PDS (Haselberger, 2001). Klaus Wowereit, the new SPD Mayor, and SPD Chancellor Gerhard Schröder were 'booed, jeered and verbally attacked' for their cooperation with the PDS as they attended the Bernauer Straße commemoration (Knischewski & Splitter, 2006, p. 292).

It is from this point on that we can date a convergence of the interests of the CDU in Berlin and victims' organizations. The lack of plans for further developments at the Bernauer Straße once the Documentation Centre and Reconciliation Chapel were in place allowed the CDU to accuse the so-called red-red coalition of indifference to this issue. In terms of visitor numbers, the Bernauer Straße memorial appeared to fare poorly in comparison with the Wall Museum – Checkpoint Charlie (*Haus am Checkpoint Charlie*), a privately run, unconventional, but highly popular museum dedicated to documenting escapes over the Wall and anti-communist resistance. This institution had been set up by anti-communist human rights campaigner Rainer Hildebrandt next to the most famous Allied checkpoint, soon after the building of the Wall. After Rainer's death in 2004, the museum was run by his wife, Alexandra Hildebrandt, who embarked on a strategy of provocation against what she regarded as the unsatisfactory state of Wall commemoration in the city. She acted independently of and in opposition to the left-wing Senate, which she claimed was unwilling to address the crimes of the East German regime on account of its own links to the GDR's former ruling party.

In October 2004, Hildebrandt's museum began the construction of a replica section of the Wall outside its premises. This was to form the backdrop for a memorial to those killed at the Berlin Wall. This 'Freedom Memorial', as Hildebrandt titled her 'temporary art installation' (Fülling, 2004), immediately became the object of controversy, attracting significant media attention and putting the Senate under pressure over its own plans for commemoration of the Wall. Victims' organizations supported Hildebrandt, and the battle lines were drawn between those advocates of an anti-communist discourse on GDR memory that placed the suffering of the victims of state socialism at the heart of commemoration (the Berlin CDU, victims' organizations, conservative historians) and the left-wing majority in the Senate, which was concerned primarily to wrest the commemorative agenda back from Hildebrandt.

Although Hildebrandt's memorial was taken apart under court order (when her lease on the land she was using had expired), it is widely acknowledged that she was responsible for a renewal of the debate around approaches to commemorating the Berlin Wall (Harrison, 2011, p. 85; Rudnik, 2011, p. 632; Schmidt, 1999, p. 183). Under the slogan 'They only wanted freedom!', her installation comprised 1065 crosses set in a chained-off field of white gravel, reminiscent of a cemetery. The cross motif invoked the context of martyrdom, but here in a secularized national context, in which the victims of traumatic suffering are presented as sacrificing themselves for the moment of national liberation. With the emergence of modern forms of national identity, such imagery tends to fuse together the figure of the martyr and the role of the hero (Soledad Catoggio, 2013, p. 697), converting the victim into a heroic embodiment of the community (Giesen, 2004, p. 23). This equation is perhaps even stronger in the German-speaking context, where the word *Opfer* denotes both a victim and a (self-)sacrifice. In this respect, the Freedom Memorial harked back to pre-unification West German traditions of commemoration for those who died at the border, which presented them as 'heroes of freedom' (Ullrich, 2006, p. 89), often employing Christian symbols such as the cross. The Freedom Memorial therefore signalled a reactivation of traditional West German narratives of victimhood in relation to the border, which had become less prominent during the period of FRG-GDR détente in the 1970s and 1980s (Ullrich, 2006, p. 162). The suffering of the victims of the border regime was thereby co-opted into a narrative in which they were presented as victims of the national struggle for freedom from communist oppression.

Taking up Hildebrandt's cause, victim activists from the umbrella organization *Union der Opferverbände Kommunisticher Gewaltherrschaft* ('Union of Organizations for the Victims of Communist Despotism', or UOKG) and the *Vereinigung der Opfer des Stalinismus* ('Association of the Victims of Stalinism', or VOS) presented the Wall dead as representatives of all of the victims of state socialism and, indeed, all of the victims of communist oppression both within and beyond Germany (Pohl, 2005). As with Hildebrandt's monument, the victims' understanding of their experience placed their suffering within a narrative that emphasized their contribution to the democratic freedom that Germans now enjoyed, while also stressing the memory of that suffering as a necessary defence against left-wing conspiracy and nostalgia for the GDR. Activists resisted the criticism that the Freedom Memorial was not viable due its implicit analogy to the nearby Holocaust Memorial (Pohl, 2005; Thonn, 2005a, 2005b) and sought to present their own suffering as part of the heritage of resistance to socialist dictatorship:

> We respect the [victims of the, DC] National Socialist Holocaust and the new memorial. But we also demand equal respect for the suffering, the martyrdom and the resistance [of the victims of state socialism, DC]. From Stalin's secret camps, via the people's uprising [of 17 June 1953, DC], the exodus from the GDR, the resistance to the SED's rule that led to the great citizens' movement [of 1989, DC], faced with which the communist functionaries finally had to surrender – these forty years of communist rule and in the Eastern Bloc are reason enough that we should denounce them publicly and give their victims, the living and the dead, final satisfaction.
>
> (Thonn, 2004)

While certainly anti-communist in nature, their communications in response to Hildebrandt's memorial and its removal were protest communications of the kind that have already been identified as typical for this kind of organization. The decision to remove the memorial, and the political establishment's apparent ambivalence towards it, were taken as evidence of the marginality of the victims' sacrifice to the national memory culture, and therefore as a sign of the victim's lack of recognition in the contemporary Federal Republic. This they condemned in moral terms, primarily as a failure of the political system.

The Senate's plan for commemorating the Berlin Wall

The response of the Berlin Senate, and of Culture Senator Thomas Flierl in particular, was to formulate a general plan for commemorating the Berlin Wall, informed by a series of public hearings. The Freedom Memorial had re-politicized the issue of Wall commemoration, creating a wave of media interest and allowing the CDU to make further political capital from the red-red coalition's alleged inaction on Wall commemoration. The Senate's plan, however, did not include the preservation of the Freedom Memorial, attempting instead to secure the place of the memorial and documentation centre in the Bernauer Straße as the central institution of Wall commemoration in the city, while further expanding it to create a more extensive memorial museum that would present a variety of different stories associated with the site:

The history of this street reflects the consequences of the building of the Wall in an exemplary way: the destruction of the urban space and peoples' ways of life, the dividing of families and friends. It documents the success and failure of attempts to escape the dictatorship or to help others to escape; it stands for the victims of the border regime and the dead of the Berlin Wall.

(Flierl, 2006, p. 18)

This signalled a move away from the single martyrological narrative implied by Hildebrandt's Freedom Memorial, stressing the plurality of different experiences that could be associated with the Wall.

While the plan responded to the Freedom Memorial by re-emphasizing victims to a certain extent, it did so in a way that individualized the fates of those who died at the Wall. Although the detailing of individual stories could be regarded as a means of creating empathy (Flierl, 2006, p. 19), in the context of debate surrounding the Freedom Memorial this move can also be read as an attempt to work against any unifying martyrological narrative implied in Hildebrandt's installation and supported by victims' organizations. Not only were the figures proposed by the Checkpoint Charlie Museum somewhat inflated, including suicides and unidentified corpses found floating in the river in the border zone for example (Haertle & Sälter, 2006, p. 673), they also did not seek to differentiate why and how individuals died.

As part of the consultation process for the expanded memorial concept, the Senate funded research into the number of deaths at the Berlin Wall. The results, which identified 136 confirmed cases between 1961 and 1989, were to form the basis of future commemoration. The biographies of the individual victims were published in a commemorative volume (Zentrum für zeithistorische Forschung Potsdam, 2009) and made available on the website *Chronik der Mauer* (www.chronik-der-mauer.de/todesopfer/). The texts dedicated to each victim not only give details of their deaths, but of their lives and their motivations for dissatisfaction with the GDR regime. It is striking, however, that biographies are also presented that do not fit into a straightforwardly oppositional frame, including victims who may not necessarily have been trying to flee when they were killed.

The area set aside for an outdoor exhibition now extended the length of Bernauer Straße, taking in the cemetery formerly claimed by the *Sophiengemeinde* and the underground station at Nordbahnhof, which had been a so-called 'ghost station' during the time of the Wall's existence. Although the competition brief for the renewal of the site stressed the centrality of victim memorialization and the need to use the new expanded site to show the brutal means that the SED used to cling on to power in the GDR (Senatsverwaltung für Stadtentwicklung, 2007a, pp. 93–94, 109), there was an equal emphasis on promoting 'active' participation on the part of visitors, who should be induced to engage 'thoughtfully' with the different 'levels of meaning' in the site and not be presented with a 'ready-made' meaning (Senatsverwaltung für Stadtenwicklung, 2007a, pp. 95–96). During the selection of the winning design, the plurality of perspectives offered by the site was even further to the fore. The criteria for the jury pointed to the many layers of meaning that needed to be addressed, including 'everyday life before the Wall' and 'the different perspectives of victims and perpetrators' (Senatsverwaltung für Stadtenwicklung, 2007b, p. 7).

The design eventually chosen created an open space in which the visitor could choose to move between the different elements and the different stories they represented as she pleased. There would be no set pathway through the various exhibits, which would include a 'Window of Memory' showing photographs of all those who were killed. Visitors would be able to choose to seek out information on specific events, such as the forced eviction of those living close to the Wall on the eastern side or the escape tunnels that were built near the Bernauer Staße; equally, they could choose to leave flowers at the existing Kohlhoff and Kohlhoff memorial or the Window of Memory. The Documentation Centre would continue to provide contextualizing information, including details about the Cold War, but (again) visitors would have to decide whether to include these elements in their visit. In contrast with victims' demands that the border fortifications should be re-created as realistically as possible, the new Memorial Museum design followed the Wall Association's already established principle of presenting the material traces without reconstruction. Where it was felt necessary to fill gaps in the Wall, for example where the *Sophiengemeinde* had removed some sections in 1997, this was achieved with vertical rods of COR-TEN steel, which visitors would be able to walk between (Klausmeier, 2011, p. 399).

The completed Memorial Museum takes an archaeological approach to the material the site contains. Physical remnants of the Wall's security apparatus (for example, wires that formed part of an alarmed fence in the border area) have been unearthed in places, but no attempt has been made to reconstruct the fence itself. The visitor sees these traces in trenches, which also contain remains of pre-Wall material, for example the foundations of an old memorial from the original *Sophiengemeinde* cemetery, or remains of streets and houses. This juxtaposition is not commented upon, but indicates to the visitor that the Wall was built by demolishing part of an existing community. This policy of showing the site's historical layers extends to post-unification developments, such as a wooden cross erected by the *Sophiengemeinde* on the old cemetery site and a stone memorial dedicated, in competition with the Kohlhoff and Kohlhoff memorial, to 'the victims of the Second World War and the division of Germany'. This approach allows the competing visions of the purpose and organization of the site prior to the redevelopment to remain visible: They are now as much part of the site's history as the Wall itself and relativize any potential claim to impose a single meaning on the Bernauer Straße.

The hearings at the Berlin Senate in early 2005 that preceded the final formulation of Flierl's plan showed a clear consensus among those giving evidence, who were for the most part historians and museum professionals, that there should be no radical departure from the existing museological approach to the site formulated by the Berlin Wall Association under Camphausen. The Chair of the Senate's Working Group on Wall Commemoration set up by Flierl has stressed that the response to Freedom Memorial controversy was not the acknowledgement of the need for a more emotive presentation of the Berlin Wall in the city, but rather a renewed call for a 'scientifically grounded' (*wissenschaftlich fundiert*) concept (Lemke, 2011, p. 379). From the October of 2005, Camphausen's team were given the task of developing new ideas for the site at the Bernauer Straße, based on their existing principles, and these fed directly into Flierl's eventual plan (Camphausen & Fischer, 2011, pp. 375–376). Clearly, then, the controversy surrounding the Freedom Memorial had failed to lead to a significant challenge to the professional authority of those charged with commemorating the Berlin Wall. They quickly achieved the backing of the key politician responsible, Thomas Flierl, and enjoyed the support of other influential historians and museum professionals in the city.

Flierl's proposal for a pluralized and historicized approach to commemoration of the Wall in the city as a whole should not be understood as apolitical, however. Within the political system, his communication was also inevitably political, in that it advocated a model of commemoration that defused some of the negative potential of the history of the Berlin Wall for his own party as a partner in the coalition government. The open-ended and de-centred structure of the re-developed Memorial Museum site at the Bernauer Straße recalls in many ways a previous memorial project, namely the *Denkzeichen* (literally 'think-mark') for murdered communist revolutionary Rosa Luxemburg, which was constructed in 2006 on Rosa Luxemburg Square in Berlin. Flierl played a key role in developing this memorial, which stresses an openness of interpretation in relation to Luxemburg, who is a hero to the German Left, but also a controversial figure in terms of her attitudes to liberal democracy. When the plan to construct a monument to Luxemburg was included in the 2002 SPD-PDS coalition agreement, the issue was mobilized by the CDU opposition as a means to attack the new city government (Könczöl, 2011, pp. 85–86). In response to this, the fragmented form of the memorial promoted by Flierl and his supporters 'deliberately eschew[ed] the task of setting in stone any definitive view of Luxemburg' (Bavaj, 2010, p. 292). Clearly, an open form of memorialization can also become a means of ensuring that one's own perspective at least gets heard alongside those views hostile to it, rather than functioning as a statement in favour of plurality per se. It also chimes in with the calls for 'critical' memory about the state socialist past that Flierl and others from the PDS promoted, a memory that recognized the suffering of victims, while resisting what they saw as the instrumentalization of victim memory 'to justify the current form of society, without furnishing critical instruments for questioning and further development' (Flierl & Müller, 2009, p. 12). Applied to the Berlin Wall Memorial Museum, such a strategy of apparent openness allows for the expression of the suffering caused by the GDR regime, but also insists that this is not the only experience. The call for the expression of a plurality of views is therefore not in any way politically neutral: it is in the interest of post-communists that discourses about the GDR and socialism more generally are not reduced to a single anti-communist narrative that stresses the heroic suffering of the victims of the SED regime.

The approach preferred by the Senate, as set out in Flierl's plan, also spoke to the discourse of the heritage professionals engaged in presenting the site at the Bernauer Straße. Although Flierl's principles can be understood as political communication, they chimed with the museological principles favoured among professionals. The support provided by Flierl as Senator for Culture for this concept effectively allowed the Berlin Wall Association to defend its approach to the presentation of the site against the challenge mounted by the victims' organizations and their supporters. Whereas the victims themselves sought to promote a presentation of their suffering as central to the commemoration of the Berlin Wall, the heritage professionals involved with the creation of the Memorial Museum preferred to see the victims' experience as one kind of experience of the border regime; an approach they justified in terms of the application of academically rigorous methodologies.

Perhaps rather surprisingly, once Flierl's concept had been approved by the Senate, the opposition of victims' organizations evaporated. The UKOG was invited to the Senate hearings in early 2005 and initially defended the Freedom Memorial, insisting that it should be integrated into the proposed network of memorial sites for the Wall and its victims, while also proposing that the Kohlhoff and Kohlhoff memorial should be removed (Strunz, 2005, pp. 2–3). Perhaps recognizing that the hostility of the victims' organizations stemmed at least in part from the lack of consultation with them over the building of the Kohlhoff and Kohlhoff memorial and the subsequent expansion of the Bernauer Straße site, Flierl and Mayor Wowereit engaged in something of a charm offensive with the various victims' groups, inviting them to consult both inside and outside the hearings (Lemke, 2011, p. 385). Such communication by the political system aimed specifically at victims' organizations clearly had the desired effect of allowing those organizations to communicate to their members that the victims' voice was being heard by those in power. Given the limited ability of the victims' organizations to change the Bernauer Straße memorial, the opportunity to achieve this kind of symbolic recognition on their members' behalf arguably made it easier to retreat from communicating outright opposition to the Flierl plan. In fact, Heinz Strunz, who represented both the *Bund der stalinistisch Verfolgten* (League of those Persecuted by Stalinism) and the UKOG (of which he was vice chair at the time) sat alongside Flierl on the podium in the Senate as the final 'Wall concept' was presented (Lemke, 2011, p. 386). In this way, the ruling parties in Berlin co-opted the victims' organizations into the proposals for Wall commemoration without making significant concessions to their views on how victimhood should be represented. This did not stop the Berlin CDU continuing to criticize the plans as evidence of the PDS's failure to come to terms with the past (Lemke, 2011, pp. 389–390).

Conclusion

German historian Martin Sabrow has described conflicts between heritage professionals and victims' organizations in terms of a *'liaison dangereuse* between structurally distinct partners' (Sabrow, 2008, p. 18). While some commentators have sought to portray such conflicts in ideological terms, the analysis in this chapter has sought to demonstrate that Sabrow's intuition is potentially a more productive starting-point for understanding what is at stake here. In Germany and elsewhere, it is increasingly the case that heritage professionals are tasked with presenting sites of suffering to the general public. Under such circumstances, where professional norms and the desire for academically legitimized methodologies underpin approaches to representing victims' experiences within a wider historical context, conflict with victims' organizations may seem inevitable. While that conflict can be seized upon by political actors for their own purposes, as we see in the case study discussed in this chapter, understanding the underlying systemic factors might also point a way forward to more successful management of such disputes. Ideally, it should be possible to allow heritage organizations to maintain their commitment to their museological methodologies while providing victims' organizations with opportunities for recognition. In the case of the Bernauer Straße site, for example, we see how overtures from politicians to the victims to include them in relevant consultations provided some recognition of the victims' voice. Victims' organizations were not uncompromising, but sought recognition where they could. That being said, it is in the nature of both heritage organizations as organizations within the scientific system and of victims' organizations as protest organizations that their priorities will never be entirely compatible. In the context of transitional justice, the political system arguably has a responsibility not to exploit such systemic differences for short-term gain.

References

Barkan, E. (2002). *Völker klagen an: Eine neue internationale Moral*. Düsseldorf: Patmos.

Barsalou, J., & Baxter, V. (2007). *The urge to remember: The role of memorials in social reconstruction and transitional justice*. Washington, DC: United States Institute for Peace.

Bavaj, R. (2010). Memorializing socialist contradictions: A 'think-mark' for Rosa Luxemburg in the new Berlin. In B. Niven & C. Paver (Eds.), *Memorialization in Germany since 1945* (pp. 287–297). Basingstoke: Palgrave Macmillan.

Bernitt, S. (1998, May 31). Protest gegen das Mauerdenkmal, *Welt am Sonntag*.

Camphausen, G. (1999a). Das Denkmal 'Gedenkstätte Berliner Mauer': Ein Entstehungsprozeß. In Verein Berliner Mauer – Gedenkstätte und Dokumentationszentrum (Ed.), *Berliner Mauer: Gedenkstätte, Dokumentationszentrum und Versöhnungskapelle in der Bernauerstraße* (pp. 18–22). Berlin: Jaron.

Camphausen, G. (1999b). Das Dokumentationszentrum Berliner Mauer. In Verein Berliner Mauer – Gedenkstätte und Dokumentationszentrum (Ed.), *Berliner Mauer: Gedenkstätte, Dokumentationszentrum und Versöhnungskapelle in der Bernauerstraße* (pp. 27–30). Berlin: Jaron.

Camphausen, G., & Fischer, M. (2011). Bürgerschaftliche Durchsetzung der Gedenkstätte an der Bernauer Straße. In K. Henke (Ed.), *Die Mauer: Errichtung, Überwindung, Erinnerung* (pp. 355–376). Munich: DTV.

Clarke, D. (2017a). Understanding controversies over memorial museums: The case of the Leistikowstraße Memorial Museum, Potsdam. *History and Memory*, 29(1), 41–71.

Clarke, D. (2017b). Erinnerungspolitik und historisches Lernen: Der fall DDR. In J. Hüttmann & A. von Arnim (Eds.), *Diktatur und Demokratie im Unterricht* (pp. 126–137). Berlin: Metropol.

De Greiff, P. (2007). Justice and reparations. In J. Miller & R. Kumar (Eds.), *Reparations: Interdisciplinary enquiries* (pp. 153–175). Oxford: Oxford University Press.

Deutscher Bundestag (2008). *Unterrichtung durch den Beauftragten der Bundesregierung für Kultur und Medien: Fortschreibung der Gedenkstättenkonzeption des Bundes; Verantwortung wahrnehmen, Aufarbeitung verstärken, Gedenken vertiefen*. Drucksache 16/9875.

Deutsches Historisches Museum (1994). *Architektonisch-künstlerischer Ideenwettbewerb Gedenkstätte Berliner Mauer in der Bernauer Straße: Ausschreibung*. Berlin: Deutsches Historisches Museum.

Eich, K. (1998a). Fauler Kompromiß. *Der Stacheldraht*, 1, 4.

Eich, K. (1998b). Kleine historische Requisite. *Der Stacheldraht*, 5, 8–9.

Feversham, P., & Schmidt L. (1999). *The Berlin Wall today: Cultural significance and conservation issues*. Berlin: Verlag Bauwesen.

Flierl, T. (2006). *Gesamtkonzept zur Erinnerung an die Berliner Mauer: Dokumentation, Information und Gedenken*. Berlin: Berliner Senat.

Flierl, T., & Müller, E. (2009). Kritische Erinnerungskultur. In T. Flierl & E. Müller (Eds.), *Vom kritischen Gebrauch der Erinnerung* (pp. 11–24). Berlin: Dietz.

Fülling, T. (2004, November 4). Mauermahnmal soll auf Dauer bleiben. *Die Welt*.

Giesen, B. (2004). *Triumph and trauma*. London: Paradigm.

Haertle, H., & Sälter, G. (2006). Die Todesopfer an Mauer und Grenze: Versuch einer Bilanz. *Deutschland Archiv, 39*(4), 667–676.

Hamber, B., Ševčenko, L., & Naidu E. (2010). Utopian dreams or practical possibilities? The challenges of evaluating the impact of memorialization in societies in transition. *International Journal of Transitional Justice, 4*(3), 397–420.

Harrison, H. (2011). The Berlin Wall and its resurrection as a site of memory. *German Politics and Society, 29*(2), 78–106.

Haselberger, S. (2001, August 14). Eklat be den Mauer-Gedenkfeiern. *Die Welt*.

Haug, V. (2015). *Am 'authentischen' Ort: Paradoxien der Gedenkstättenpädagogik*. Berlin: Metropol.

Hellmann, K. (1996). *Systemtheorie und Neue Soziale Bewegungen: Identitätsprobleme in der Risikogesellschaft*. Oplanden: Westdeutscher Verlag.

Honneth, A. (1992). *Kampf um Anerkennung: Zur moralischen Grammatik sozialer Konflikte*. Frankfurt am Main: Suhrkamp.

Jacoby, T. (2015). A theory of victimhood: Politics, conflict and the construction of victim-based identity. *Millennium, 43*(2), 511–536.

Jander, M. (2013). Kultur der Aufrechnung: Erneuerte deutsche Opfermythologie und radikaler Antikommunismus: Die Union der Opferverbände Kommunistischer Gewaltherrschaft (UOKG). In W. Benz (Ed.), *Ein Kampf um Deutungshoheit: Politik, Opferinteressen und historische Forschung. Die Auseinandersetzung um die Gedenk- und Begegnungsstätte Leistikowstraße Potsdam* (pp. 125–161). Berlin: Metropol.

Jenkins, T. (2011). *Contesting human remains in museum collections: The crisis of authority*. London: Routledge.

King, M., & Thornhill, C. (2003). *Niklas Luhmann's theory of politics and law*. Basingstoke: Palgrave Macmillan.

Klausmeier, A. (2011). Die Gedenkstätte Berliner Mauer an der Bernauer Straße. In K. Henke (Ed.), *Die Mauer: Errichtung, Überwindung, Erinnerung* (pp. 394–406). Munich: DTV.

Knigge, V. (2002). Gedenkstätten und Museen. In V. Knigge & N. Frei (Eds.), *Verbrechen erinnern: Die Auseinandersetzung mit Holocaust und Völkermord* (pp. 378–389). Munich: Beck.

Knischewski, G., & Splitter, U. (2006). Remembering the Berlin Wall: The Wall memorial ensemble Bernauer Straße. *German Life and Letters, 59*(2), 280–293.

Könczöl, B. (2011). Reinventing a socialist heroine: Commemorating Rosa Luxemburg after unification. In D. Clarke & U. Wölfel (Eds.), *Remembering the German Democratic Republic: Divided memory in a united Germany* (pp. 77–87). Basingstoke: Palgrave Macmillan.

Lemke, R. (2011). Das Gesamtkonzept Berliner Mauer. In K. Henke (Ed.), *Die Mauer: Errichtung, Überwindung, Erinnerung* (pp. 377–406). Munich: DTV.

Luhmann, N. (1987). *Soziale Systeme*. Frankfurt am Main: Suhrkamp.

Luhmann, N. (1992). *Die Wissenschaft der Gesellschaft*. Frankfurt am Main: Suhrkamp.

Luhmann, N. (1996a). *Protest: Systemtheorie und soziale Bewegungen*. Frankfurt am Main: Suhrkamp.

Luhmann, N. (1996b). *Die Realität der Massenmedien* (2nd edition). Opladen: Westdeutscher Verlag.

Luhmann, N. (1998). *Die Gesellschaft der Gesellschaft*. Frankfurt am Main: Suhrkamp.

Luhmann, N. (2000). *Organisation und Entscheidung*. Opladen/Wiesbaden: Westdeutscher Verlag.

Luhmann, N. (2002). *Die Politik der Gesellschaft*. Frankfurt am Main: Suhrkamp.

Luhmann, N. (2010). *Politische Soziologie*. Frankfurt am Main: Suhrkamp.

Marcuse, H. (2005). Reshaping Dachau for visitors: 1933–2000. In G. Ashworth & R. Hartmann (Eds.), *Horror and human tragedy revisited: The management of sites of atrocities for tourism* (pp. 118–148). New York: Cognizant Communication.

Moeller, H. (2012). *The radical Luhmann*. New York: Columbia University Press.

Naidu, E. (2014). Memorialization in post-conflict societies in Africa: Potentials and challenges. In S. Buckley-Zistel & S. Schäfer (Eds.), *Memorials in times of transition* (pp. 29–45). Cambridge: Interstitia.

Pampel, B. (2007). *'Mit eigenen Augen sehen, wozu der Mensch fähig ist': Zur Wirkung von Gedenkstätten auf die Besucher*. Frankfurt am Main: Campus.

Pohl, E. (2005). Maueropfer dürfen nicht verharmlost werden. *Die Freiheitsglocke*, *627*, 5.

Rudnik, C. (2011). *Die andere Hälfte der Erinnerung: Die DDR in der deutschen Geschichtspolitik nach 1989* [transcript]. Bielefeld: Verlag für Kommunikation, Kultur und sociale Praxis.

Rudnik, C. (2013). Wenn Häftlinge und Historiker straiten: Konfklite um sächsiche Gedenkstätten. In W. Benz (Ed.), *Ein Kampf um Deutungshoheit: Politik, Opferinteressen und historische Forschung. Die Auseinandersetzung um die Gedenk- und Begegnungsstätte Leistikowstraße Potsdam* (pp. 197–218). Berlin: Metropol.

Sabrow, M. (2008). Das Unbehagen in der Aufarbeitung: Zur Engführung von Wissenschaft, Moral und Politik in der Zeitgeschichte. In T. Schaurschmidt (Ed.), *Historisches Erinnern und Gedenken im Übergang vom 20. zum 21. Jahurhundert* (pp. 11–20). Frankfurt am Main: Peter Lang.

Sachse, C. (2012). *Festschrift: 20 Jahre Union der Opferverbände kommunistischer Gewaltherrschaft e.V. Rückblick und Ausblick*. Berlin: Union der Opferverbände kommunistischer Gewaltherrschaft.

Schmidt, L. (1999). Vom Symbol der Unterdrückung zur Ikone der Befreiuung: Auseinandersetzung, Verdrängung, Memorialisierung. In Deutsches Nationalkomitee für Denkmalschutz (Ed.), *Die Berliner Mauer: Vom Sperrwall zum Denkmal* (pp. 170–185). Berlin: Deutsches Nationalkomitee für Denkmalschutz.

Senatsverwaltung für Stadtenwicklung (Ed.). (2007a). *Erweiterung der Gedenkstätte Berliner Mauer: Offener Realisirungswettbewerb für Hochbau, Freiraum und Ausstellung*. Berlin: Senatsverwaltung für Stadtenwicklung.

Senatsverwaltung für Stadtenwicklung (Ed.). (2007b). *Erweiterung der Gedenkstätte Berliner Mauer: Offener Realisierungswettbewerb für Hochbau, Freiraum und Ausstellung. Erbegnisprotokoll*. Berlin: Senatsverwaltung für Stadtenwicklung.

Soledad Catoggio, M. (2013). The consecration of political suffering: Martyrs, heroes and victims in Argentine political culture. *Journal of Latin American Studies*, *45*, 695–719.

Strunz, H. (2005, March 18). *Überlegungen zum Gedenkkonzept der Berliner Mauer*. Retrieved from www.uokg.de/Text/akt039flirlkonzept.htm.

Sturm, D. F. (2001, August 1). Der Wettlauf um das geeignete Gedenken. *Die Welt*, 4.

Thonn, B. (2004). Wenn das Kreuz mit den Kreuzen die Meinungen und Pläne durchkreuzt. *Die Freiheitsglocke*, *625/626*, 19.

Thonn, B. (2005a). Erwartetes Urteil: Die Holzkreuze sollen verschwinden! Berufung angekündigt. *Die Freiheitsglocke*, *630*, 1.

Thonn, B. (2005b). Sag mir, wo die Mauer ist. *Die Freiheitsglocke*, *630*, 6.

Trotnow, H. (2005). Sag mir, wo die Spuren sind ... Berlin und der Umgang mit der Geschichte der Berliner Mauer. In B. Faulenbach & and F. Jelich (Eds.), *Asymmetrisch verflochtene Parallelgeschichte? Die Geschichte der Bundesrepublik und der DDR in Ausstellungen, Museen und Gedenkstätten* (pp. 157–167). Essen: Klartext.

Ullrich, M. (2006). *Geteilte Ansichten: Erinnerungslandschaft deutsch-deutsche Grenze*. Berlin: Aufbau.

Versöhnungsgemeinde (1990, August 13). [Press release].

Williams, P. (2007). *Memorial museums: The global rush to commemorate atrocity*. Oxford/New York: Berg.

Winters, P. J. (2013). Der Streit um die Leitsikowstraße in Potsdam. In W. Benz (Ed.), *Ein Kampf um Deutungshoheit: Politik, Opferinteressen und historische Forschung. Die Auseinandersetzung um die Gedenk- und Begegnungsstätte Leistikowstraße Potsdam* (pp. 37–63). Berlin: Metropol.

Zentrum für zeithistorische Forschung Potsdam (Ed.). (2009). *Die Todesopfer der Berliner Mauer 1961–1989: Ein biographisches Handbuch*. Berlin: Links.

Chapter 5

Victimhood in reverse

Art in the age of apology

Lieke Wijnia

Introduction[1]

The video artwork *Scratch an Aussie* (2008) by Aboriginal artist Richard Bell (1953) features a setting with a divan covered in Persian carpets, reminiscent of Sigmund Freud's office where he treated his patients. A blond woman in a golden bikini occupies this divan, while her psychoanalyst sits in a chair next to it. The woman is talking about how her bag was recently stolen from her house. She says: 'I am angry they think they have the right to come into my house and just take my stuff. They don't have the right you know. Why do people feel the right to take stuff from others?' In other scenes, the psychoanalyst, a role performed by Bell, is seeing a therapist. This therapist asks him, 'What is it with these white people that concerns you?' The psychoanalyst answers: 'They seem to carry the weight of the world on their shoulders.' After which the therapist observes, 'So you see them as people to exploit?' Onto which the psycho-analyst says, 'Yes, but it is so easy.'

In addition to the casting of two Aboriginal men in authoritative roles, the video explores post-colonial structures of exploitation, the workings of a collective consciousness, and the cultural construction of victimhood. By means of sarcasm and irony, Bell identifies a level of hypocrisy in the white patients' valuation of their life events in relation to larger questions concerning the country's history of colonization and its enduring effects in contemporary society.

This chapter uses the notion of victimhood to explore the work of Bell in a recent exhibition in the Netherlands. It analyses where a cultural studies approach to victimhood gets us in understanding the complexities of the topics Bell deals with, as well as the effects of his artistic strategies for his audiences. This chapter is structured along three particular topics: the historical and contemporary complexities of Aboriginal art; the exhibition Bell Invites for which Australian, American and Dutch artists created works on the themes of racism, inclusion and exclusion, and post-colonialism; and the relevance of a cultural studies approach to the notion of victimhood in grasping the relationship between artist and audience. Ultimately, it will lead to an exploration of the questions of who we are talking about when using the term of victimhood, what it means to identify a victim, and how visual art offers strategies to express and challenge the cultural boundaries of victimhood.

Complexities of Aboriginal art

Bell, a Brisbane-based artist, is known for his provocative performances, paintings, video works, and installations, which question the role of racism and social hierarchy in contemporary Australia. His vocabulary is strong and powerful, which he extends beyond the sites of specific artworks. 'His work is dedicated to the production of the rebellious image – both in paint and in real time' (Ziherl, 2016). His public persona can be regarded in terms of performance, in which he continuously scrutinizes the art world for its whiteness, emphasizes the secondary role fulfilled by Aboriginal artists in the Australian art world, and reinforces how the notion of Aboriginal art is a white invention (e.g. Melbourne Conversations, 2012). His work is a product of, and response to, the historical, political, and cultural dimensions of post-colonial Australian society.

The notion of Aboriginal art has a complex character, which can be traced in at least two dimensions. The first dimension relates to the historical implications of the term; the second to the requirement of knowledge. First, as Aboriginal culture traditionally does not know the notion of *art* as it exists in the West, the entire category of *Aboriginal art* is often regarded as a non-Aboriginal concept. Visual art – in the Western sense – only emerged after contact with Europeans interested in traditional iconography related to the spiritual concepts of the *Dreaming*, 'a uniquely Aboriginal way of placing people in time and space' (Morphy, 2003 [1998], p. 4), and *Country*, which refers to 'a particular area of land or water from which a person's primary identity and sense of spiritual association and belonging derives' (Sculthorpe, Bolton, & Coates, 2015, p. 14). Throughout the second half of the twentieth century, European settlers and missionaries 'encouraged people to reproduce traditional central Australian designs in an introduced medium' (Morphy, 2003, pp. 282–283). This transferal of both sacred and profane designs into new media, like acrylic paint on canvas, proved to be hugely important in the emergence of an internationally recognized sense of Aboriginal Art (Morphy, 2003).

Within the practice and appreciation of Aboriginal art, a general distinction is apparent. On the one hand, there are the practices rooted in traditional Aboriginal cultures, predominantly made in community centres in desert areas, such as Papunya Tula, Tjala Arts or Mangkaja Arts. On the other hand, there is the art dealing with contemporary topics such as post-colonialism and social inequality, made by younger generations of artists born and raised in the urban areas of cities such as Brisbane, Melbourne and Sydney. Even though the general distinction is of help in identifying different types of artistic practices, Anthony Gardner justly noted that such a distinction reinforces segregation between indigenous and non-indigenous artists, as well as between Aboriginals living in remote and urban areas. It suggests that descent and biography prescribe appropriate subject matter for artistic practices (Gardner, 2011, p. 241).

Cultural projections and normative expectations regarding Aboriginal art are recurring features in Bell's work. The normativity is derived from European modes of artistic appreciation, as distinguished by Philip Jones.

> On the one hand, Europeans have sought to appreciate Aboriginal art for what are perceived to be its universal qualities; on the other, Europeans have recognized that Aboriginal art possesses its own unique idiom and must first be understood – often through deep, immersive studies – before it may be translated.
>
> (Jones, 2011, p. 36)

The former mode, regarding the universal qualities attributed to Aboriginal art, relates to the appreciation of traditional motives for their abstract character. This created a position for the indigenous art parallel to European and American post-war abstraction.

The latter mode of appreciation directly relates to the second dimension of complexity in Aboriginal art, the necessity of study and knowledge. This results in a tension between an approach to the works for their artistic merit and the approach resulting from anthropological and ethnographic interest. Even though some argue that Aboriginal art has shaken off its anthropological status in the late twentieth century (McLean, 2011, p. 77), it is safe to state that artistic merit and anthropology still form two crucial features in the appreciation, framing and production of Aboriginal art. Many contemporary artists work against the grain of the tension between these two features. As Bell put it,

> Aboriginal art as we know it is a white construct. And that construct is anthropological. [...] It's almost impossible to separate the anthropologist from Aboriginal Art. It's been ethnicized to a really great extent, to such an extent there are certificates of authenticity. Now, white people don't have certificates of authenticity.
>
> (MCA Australia, 2016)

The anthropological approach to Aboriginal art is driven by the desire to fully grasp and categorize it. It predominantly emphasizes the historic roots of Aboriginal culture, over and against the contemporary complexities and challenges in Australian society. In relation to artistic practices, especially the traditionally rooted art created in the remote community centres, this approach implies a fixed framework that does not necessarily acknowledge a continuous cultural development. As Aboriginal artist Gordon Bennett (1955–2014) put it, 'Aborigines caught in this system of representation remain "frozen" as objects within the mapped territory of a European perceptual grid' (Morphy, 2013 [1998], p. 400). In his 'Home Décor' series, Bennett took the notion of the grid quite literally, communicating the oppressive character of European modernism by placing stereotypical Aboriginal imagery from cartoons and schoolbooks in geometric motifs reminiscent of Dutch painter Piet Mondriaan (1872–1944), an icon of European modern art.

In addition to the anthropological approach, the notion of knowledge has another dimension in relation to Aboriginal art. Dispossessed and disenfranchized by western settlers, artistic practices became a means to both preserve ceremonial iconography and to be present in the public sphere. Artistic practices provide, in very different ways both in the remote desert areas and in the metropolitan cities, opportunities for a public voice.

A remarkable example of this is the prominent role of paintings in court cases around land claims. During the 1960s and 1970s, 'the recognition of Indigenous people's rights in and to land emerged as the leading political issue' (Nugent, 2015, p. 191). In reclaiming land originally belonging to them, Aboriginal groups all over Australia actively pursued this effort – especially in response to the development of mining endeavours on the disputed pieces of land and deplorable labour conditions (Attwood, 2003). Protests were modelled on those of civil rights activists in the US, receiving widespread media coverage. 'Throughout this period, politics became increasingly inseparable from art and other forms of creative expression and performance' (Nugent, 2015, p. 195). In the 1970s, Aboriginals founded 'a literary and artistic record that said: "we exist"' (Johnson, 2014).

In addition to artistic acts as forms of protest, the traditionally rooted paintings served as an expression of knowledge, in turn indicating ownership, of the land. Paintings were officially recognized as translations of Aboriginal worldview into forms of evidence, suitable for the western judicial contexts in which the land claims were judged. The acceptance of these paintings 'entails more than a tokenistic acknowledgement of Indigenous modes of representation. They demand, rather, the recognition of Indigenous ways of being' (Nugent, 2015, p. 203). Numerous claims, following the introduction of official land rights legislation during the 1970s, have incorporated artistic evidence in the documentation of the cases (Hannam, 2017).

The notion of ownership is not only a prevalent topic in traditional painting, but in many other forms of Aboriginal art, and also in the work of Bell. However, he does not use his art to prove ancestral connection or ownership to particular sites. Rather, he uses his art as a platform to state that white people do not own the land in the first place. This reflects a primary aspect of reversal of the generally accepted point of departure, a strategy Bell widely employs in his art. It reflects a refusal to accept the status quo, a refusal to participate in the structures of argumentation resulting from colonial times. The challenging, rejection, and reversal of these structures are at the heart of his work.

The two approaches to Aboriginal art, summarized as the anthropological and the artistic approach, not only result in a tension for artistic production and reception, but also for museum practices. The challenges of this tension on the museum floor will be addressed next.

Aboriginal art in museums

Over the past few years, I have observed several exhibition practices of Aboriginal art in Western Europe. These observations underscore the complexities of exhibiting Aboriginal art. In 2015, the British Museum organized the exhibition 'Indigenous Australia, Enduring Civilization'. It covered the vast scope of Aboriginal culture from different parts of Australia, with a particular focus on the relations between Aboriginals and Western settlers since the first colonial contact of 1770.

Highlights from the large ethnographic collection were combined with a variety of contemporary artworks. Hanging high on the walls, above displays of smaller objects, many paintings were treated for their value of documentation. The painting *Yumari* (1981) by Papunya artist Uta Uta Tjangala (1926–1990), a Northern Territory masterpiece combining several Dreamings of his country, was positioned diagonally in a corner of the display, half-covered by a Plexiglas stand in front of it. This display hugely interfered with the painting's potential visual impact. Given the ethnographic character of the collection and institutional practices of the British Museum, it was apparent how in the exhibition space the paintings were treated as *ethnographic* objects, rather than as *art* in the Western sense.

To present a counter-voice to this type of practice, the Museum for Contemporary Aboriginal Art (AAMU) in Utrecht, the Netherlands, radically chose to ban the anthropological eye and instead to display Aboriginal artworks purely for their artistic qualities. As the only museum in Europe solely dedicated to contemporary Aboriginal art, the institution wholeheartedly embraced the complexities embodied by the art, its history, and its topicality. Repeatedly, artists were invited to take over the museum space and create new works in response to the identity of the museum, notably Brook Andrew's 'Theme Park' in 2008, and Blak Douglas and Adam Geczy's 'BOMB' in 2013–2014. Andrew did not wish to be identified as 'Aboriginal artist', rather wanting to position himself as an artist in the context of the international art world. In response, the museum invited him to create a *Gesamtkunstwerk* throughout the museum (AAMU, 2013).

He created Theme Park, in which he displayed his art next to ethno-graphic objects and non-Aboriginal artworks. Afterwards, curator Georges Petitjean observed, 'More than any other AAMU exhibition, "Theme Park" elicited reactions and sparked controversy. The reactions varied from downright disappointment and frustration at not having seen any "real Aboriginal art", to great enthusiasm and critical acclaim' (Petitjean, 2012, p. 128). The responses reflected the consequences of the anthropo-logical approach to Aboriginal art, resulting in fixed expectations and cate-gorizations. The trajectory towards Theme Park is representative of how the AAMU viewed its own position and responsibility as a cultural institu-tion. Petitjean further observed, 'While making it clear that no single defi-nition suffices to describe Indigenous Australian art, the exhibition also raised questions about the sustainability of a museum solely dedicated to Aboriginal art' (Petitjean, 2012, p. 128).

As a privately funded museum, the AAMU permanently closed its doors on June 15, 2017 due to the drying up of financial sources. Attempts to receive structural local, provincial, and national funding had failed. The extensive collection of 800 works was taken over by the National Museum for World Cultures, a constellation of three ethnographic museums in Amsterdam, Berg en Dal, and Leiden (AAMU, 2017).

An example of an exhibition in which the tensions between the anthro-pological and artistic approaches were integrated into the displays, was 'L'effect boomerang: Les arts aborigènes d'Australie' (2017–2018) in the Museé d'ethnographie de Genève (MEG). In the introductory text on its website, the museum acknowledged the change in approach by stating the new exhibition 'welcomes its visitors in a space evocative of a con-temporary art gallery' (MEG, 2017). The museum maintained a distinction between utilitarian objects and weapons such as boomerangs, shields, and spears, ritual objects used in exchange between communities, and art works illustrative of Dreamings. In the exhibition, an extra emphasis was on the provenance of the objects, to reinforce legal obtainment and authenticity.

Also here, Brook Andrew was invited to engage with the topics of Aboriginal art, culture, and museum practices, by means of a new installa-tion. By having a contemporary artist critically respond to the museum practices of selection, creating collections, and displaying, a platform was created that questioned the tension between the artistic and anthropologi-cal approaches. This is quite a paradox, because these tensions are par-tially caused by the very institutional history of the ethnographic museum itself. These museum practices are reflective of concerns in the broader aca-demic disciplines of anthropology and ethnography, emerging in the early 1980s, known as the 'Writing Culture' debate. This name refers to the influential edited volume *Writing Culture*, with which editors James Clifford and George Marcus unleashed ongoing discussions about ethnographic authority, reflexivity, and objectivity in anthropological research (Clifford & Marcus, 1986).

In the next section, I will explore a contemporary art exhibition in which the relationship between ethnography and art is incorporated in the works, but which does not necessarily concern a problematic characteristic in its display. By focusing on three particular geographic locations, the exhibition explored a broader significance of the themes at hand.

Bell Invites

Between January 30 and March 29, 2016, the Stedelijk Museum Bureau Amsterdam (SMBA) hosted the exhibition 'Bell Invites'. Closed later that year, the SMBA functioned as a satellite gallery to the contemporary art museum, Stedelijk Museum, in the heart of Amsterdam. While the museum is generally dedicated to the work of established artists, the Bureau served as a platform for experimental work of younger or less well-known artists. Australian-born, Amsterdam-based curator Vivian Ziherl invited Bell, introduced as 'one of the most renowned, fearless and generous figures within Australian art' (Ziherl, 2016), to exhibit in the SMBA. Bell passed on the invitation to one of his international colleagues from the US and a group of upcoming local Dutch artists. The resulting exhibition explored questions of racism and social exclusion in post-colonial times, through particular artistic means: T-shirts, murals, video and performance.

One room in the exhibition was dedicated to the significance of T-shirts in social protest. Farida Sedoc, owner of the Amsterdam-based fashion label 'Hosselaar', got widespread attention for a T-shirt design with 'Fuck the police' in Arabic. Bell presented a black T-shirt with the white imprinted slogan 'You can go now' against the contours of the Australian continent, reflecting his attitude towards the presence of white people in his country. Dutch activist Quinsy Gario got arrested for wearing a T-shirt with the slogan 'Black Pete is racism', during the national celebration of the arrival of Saint Nicholas and his black-faced helpers in November 2011. In a review of the exhibition, critic Kees Keijer recognized the significance of this T-shirt, which was on display as well. After Gario wore the shirt in 2011, 'the *Sinterklaas* event was never the same again. That shirt deserves a place in the collection of the Rijksmuseum' (Keijer, 2016).

Large murals decorated the walls of the exhibition space, resulting from collaborations between Emory Douglas, the former Minister of Culture of the Black Panther Party, and Dutch artist Brian Elstak. Amongst others, they made a mural depicting the word *minder* (Dutch for 'less') numerous times on the walls of one particular space. It referred to a speech of Dutch politician Geert Wilders during the election night of 2014. He asked a group of party supporters whether they wanted more or less (sic) inhabitants of Moroccan descent in the Netherlands. The crowd chanted 'less,

less, less', to which Wilders responded, 'then we'll fix that'. Over the course of the following two weeks, more than 5000 people filed a complaint with the police against the politician (NOS, 2016). In December 2016, the court found Wilders guilty of collective insult and incitation of discrimination. He was however acquitted from fines or punishment (RTL, 2016). The mural embodied the discriminatory chanting of the word *less* during that election night, giving physical and material expression to the extreme powerful potential of language.

At the heart of the exhibition stood an installation in homage to the 'Aboriginal Tent Embassy'. Ziherl described the significance of this installation as follows.

> Bell opens with the proposition that the Aboriginal Tent Embassy – launched with an act of street theatre by activists in 1972 – is in fact the greatest work of performance art within Australian history. Given the continuing significance and real presence of the Tent Embassy network over 50 years later, Bell's argument is a compelling one.
>
> (Ziherl, 2016)

In the catalogue to the 2015 British Museum exhibition, Maria Nugent endorsed this significance, writing that the Aboriginal Tent Embassy is 'probably the most powerful and persuasive political performance of the era' (Nugent, 2015, p. 195).

Set up in front of Parliament House in Canberra on Australia Day (January 27) 1972, members of the newly founded National Black Theatre protested against the Prime Minister's rejection of Aboriginal claims for land rights. With the theatrical embassy, four activist-actors claimed the lawns in front the parliament building. The signs used in their protests have become icons, with slogans like 'Why pay to use our own land?' and 'We want land rights. When? Right now' (Nugent, 2015, pp. 194–195). During the following years, the Embassy was dismantled and re-established multiple times, being granted permanent presence since 1992 (Dow, 2000, p. 1). While the Embassy has proven problematic for the government, it strengthened the public presence of the Aboriginal cause.

Bell's installation consisted of a large parasol, a cooling box, and two white deck chairs located on a patch of fake grass, on which were four signs stating 'Aboriginal Embassy'; 'Which do you choose?? Land rights or bloodshed!'; 'Why pay to use our own land'; and 'Destroy Arnhem Land, we destroy Australia'. The installation was flanked by a mural showing a black man holding a sign reading 'Pardon me for being born into a nation of racists'. The framing of the mural cut right through the word *racists*, only depicting the upper half of the word. These pieces resonated well with each other, and with recent events. In her introduction to the exhibition, Ziherl listed significant events such as the forced closure of over a hundred remote Aboriginal communities and mass de-registration of Aboriginal heritage sites in Australia, the surge of the 'Black Lives Matter' movement in the US, and the ongoing debates about the figure of Black Pete and the reception of refugees in the Netherlands (Ziherl, 2016). The installation and the mural indicated, like the *minder* mural, the discursive power of language in relation to social and cultural representation.

All the works in the exhibition have in common that they question the state of the post-colonial society in which they were made. The term *post-colonial* suggests the passing of colonialism, implying society has moved beyond this era from the past. This moving on does not occur naturally. 'There seems to be almost universal recognition that a society will not be able to successfully pass into the future until it somehow deals with the past' (Howard-Hassmann & Gibney, 2008, p. 1). Dealing with the past is often shaped in the form of official apologies. These apologies are expressed by later governments, consisting of individuals not personally responsible for any of the wrongdoings. However, they represent the institution held accountable, suggesting the legitimacy of such an apology. While these speeches usually tend to focus on acts in the past, the assembled artists in Bell Invites (being representative of a larger group of art activists) seek to demonstrate how histories of colonialism have impacted social, cultural, and political structures in a more structural, lasting manner.

In the attempt to understand the complexities of this lasting impact of colonial histories on current social structures, the approach to victimhood as a cultural construct is of relevance. In addition, it sheds light on the various ways in which artists question these complexities. The next section offers an exploration of how artistic practices have the potential to integrate not one, but multiple dimensions of victimhood.

Understanding victimhood through art

The earliest records of the use of 'victim' stem from the late fifteenth century, indicating the killing and sacrifice of a living creature in the honour of a deity or supernatural power. Only halfway through the seventeenth century, the term got attributed the meaning of someone who suffered death or ill treatment by another. The following century, ideas concerning the oppression by a power or situation and the notion of taking advantage were added (Hoad, 1996). In current dictionaries, the definition of 'victim' contains the notions of killing, suffering, and hurting as a result of someone else's actions. 'Victimization' implies deliberate unfair treatment (Collins Cobuild, 2001). The historical development is noteworthy, the transformation of meaning is from someone (human or animal) sacrificed for a greater good, to a focus on individual or collective harm as a result from others' wrongdoing.

The exploration of the history of Aboriginal art, and in particular the exhibition Bell Invites, suggests there are at least three key dimensions to victimhood. First, the identification of victims: externally by parties who project the label upon others and internally by those who it is attributed to or actively claim the label. Second, the rejection of the label by those who it is projected upon, who shape their identity by means of challenging this projection. And third, the strategy of reversal: establishing a confrontation for those who project victimhood based on preconceptions and biases. Artworks have the potential to communicate these dimensions simultaneously, which can lead to varying responses. The discursive frame of the artwork allows artists to intentionally play with and upset the boundaries of the three dimensions: reinforcing, challenging and unsettling their audiences.

Identification

The demand by a group of people for official recognition of their social position, in the form of an apology or court ruling, implies the self-identification of this group with being a victim or being victimized. As the editors to this volume have argued in their introduction, the use of the term 'victim' is multilayered and complex. In terms of post-colonial contexts, Stuart Hall adequately analysed one layer of complexity with the concept *self-othering*. It offers a further dimension to Edward Said's notion of Orientalism, which pinpointed how colonized people were perceived of as different within the framework of western knowledge (Said, 1978). Hall analysed another layer of perception, that of the colonized about themselves. He observed how the colonizer had 'the power to make us see and experience *ourselves* as "Other"' (Hall, 1996, p. 213, emphasis in original). By internalizing the negative view of the colonizer, the colonized began to see themselves as strange, inferior, and even uncivilized. This process did not only lead to attribution of victimhood by the colonizers onto the colonized, but just as much to the identification of the colonized with this concept themselves.

In his art, Bell does not allow for a direct external projection of victimhood upon Aboriginals, because it stems from a western structure he does not adhere to. At the same time, he continuously addresses the weaker social, cultural, and political position of Aboriginals in contemporary Australia. In that sense he acknowledges how Aboriginals have been victimized by colonialism, which has lasting effects on post-colonial society. While Bell rejects the external projections of victimhood, he simultaneously addresses the social realities of victimization, and the resulting processes of self-othering, within Aboriginal culture itself. These realities are not only reflected in a lack of power, status, or control. On the contrary, the analysis of Bell's art demonstrates how the claim to victimhood implies a moral dimension that exerts quite a lot of power. Addressing a sense of historical accountability in white Australians, the privilege of not being able to claim victimhood, and the question of how future generations relate to the consequences of colonial histories and perceptive processes such as self-othering, it is the power of challenging, upsetting, and creating discomfort.

Rejection

Hall not only described his observations of the tendency of self-othering, but also the need to actively reject it (Hall, 1996). Visual art offers a means to experiment with different forms of rejection. One such form is the denial of the social structures that make up post-colonial societies. For Bell, it is no longer a question of finding ways of collaboration or adjustment between Aboriginal and non-Aboriginal peoples. With the T-shirt stating 'You can go now', he addresses an audience of white people. He often states that white Australians should give back the continent to the Aboriginals. It is a rhetoric that returns to the original meaning of victimhood, demanding of white people to sacrifice for the greater good of reinstating Aboriginal authority and dignity. It is not a rhetoric grounded in realistic expectations, but its shocking character is intended to at least raise awareness and public discussion.

In addition to shock, another form of rejection is rhetoric grounded in unease. A relevant example can be found in the work of Vernon Ah Kee (b. 1967), one of Bell's colleagues in the Brisbane-based arts collective 'proppaNOW'. In one of his prints, he questioned the orientalism and exoticism incorporated in the anthropological approach to Aboriginal art. The slogan on the print from 2012, 'Let's not be polite about Aboriginal art', implies that most Aboriginal art is treated with a different normative framework than other artistic practices in the international art scene. He addressed a question of inconvenient character: whether the international success of the traditionally rooted Aboriginal art is based on its artistic quality, on a form of orientalism and exotic interest, or on pity and remorse.

Ah Kee's print suggests that when the latter two aspects are dominant, they impact the judgement of the former. When remorse is felt about the historical ill treatment of Aboriginals, contemporary artistic production is treated within a less critically normative framework than non-Aboriginal artworks would be treated. I would argue that Ah Kee touches upon a very relevant aspect of the cultural construction of victimhood here, one that requires more in-depth research. The approach could be described as an identification of the art as made by victims, providing a sub-dimension to the anthropological approach to Aboriginal art. Ah Kee demands equal treatment, through, indeed, a rejection of the identification of Aboriginals as victims. However, in characterizing the appreciation of Aboriginal art with the term 'politeness', Ah Kee pinpoints a particular unease for those who are appreciative of desert art. In doing so, he employs a strategy, also frequently used by Bell, which can be characterized in terms of a reversal of victimhood.

Reversal

In addition to identification with and rejection of victimhood, artistic practices allow for experimentation with the different layers of this cultural and social construct. Like no other, Bell understands the discursive potential of visual art and language, by means of which he particularly explores the reversal of self-othering. In his work he does not emphasize how Aboriginals feel inferior and less worthy as a result of the imposition of western values and social structures upon them. Rather, he turns this process around, by pointing out how those doing the projecting should question their own cultural, moral and normative frameworks. In *Scratch an Aussie*, Bell (2008) portrayed white Australians as victims of their own hypocrisy and historical ignorance. The neglect and indifference of many white Australians to finding a real and lasting treaty with Aboriginals is at the heart of much contemporary Aboriginal art (cf. AAMU, 2013). It questions not only the social inequality from Aboriginal perspectives, but even more so the attitude of white Australians towards this inequality.

In post-colonial Australia, the demand for the acknowledgement of past wrongdoings led to an official apology in 2008. In a landmark speech, Prime Minister Kevin Rudd acknowledged the consequences of historical actions for Aboriginals' weak social position as well as cultural pride. Rudd said, amongst other things: 'For the indignity and degradation this inflicted on a proud people and a proud culture, we say sorry' (Rudd, 2008). While the acknowledgement was widely appreciated, the lack of financial compensation thereafter angered many. For words are not deemed to be able to fix any structural social inequality (cf. Howard-Hassmann & Lombardo, 2008). It is exactly this tension, between apology and action, between rhetoric and attitude, which is exposed, challenged, and provoked through the artistic practices of Bell and other artist-activists.

For these artistic practices, two types of audiences are preconceived: those who have any kind of personal, familial or ethnic affiliation with histories of racism and slavery, and those who do not consider themselves to have such direct connection. While the former may be activated to reject and reverse, the latter group may feel attacked (cf. Wekker, 2016). By pinpointing neglect and indifference, artists incite a sense of embarrassment and discomfort within this latter segment of their audience. The reversal of victimhood exposes the discomfort that comes from the privilege of not being able to claim any kind of victimhood at all.

Concluding thoughts

Approaching victimhood as a cultural construct has proven a relevant exercise, of value in grasping the multi-layered character of the artworks in Bell Invites and that of contemporary Aboriginal artists in general. Central to these artistic practices is a variety of constructions of victimhood, which confronts viewers with the assumptions their perceptions are possibly based on. Addressing, openly demonstrating, and questioning the privilege of not being able to claim any kind of victimhood, the discussed art creates a certain discomfort. By means of these artworks, the self-evident, unquestioned character of living a comfortable life is turned into a discomfort for a part of the audience. This has been analysed in terms of the reversal of victimhood, a rhetoric strategy that communicates very directly to the personal awareness of art viewers.

The second half of the title of this chapter refers to the edited volume *The Age of Apology: Facing Up to the Past* (Gibney, Howard-Hassmann, Coicaud, & Steinder, 2008). This collection of excellent essays explores the many political, social, and judicial facets of the relationship between post-colonialism (and other post-conflict situations) and the role of political apologies in attempts at reconciliation and consolidation. With this chapter, I hope to deliver a small contribution to this field by raising attention to the relevant role of artistic practices in post-colonial and post-conflict societies, in which the many constructions of victimhood are of a complex character. Art has the potential to catapult issues regarding victimhood into the public sphere, to gain awareness, and get discussions going.

In a global public sphere dominated by visual culture, art is a relevant research topic for understanding social dynamics in the age of apology. These dynamics relate to the three distinguished types of constructions of victimhood: identification, rejection and reversal. In post-colonial public spheres all three types are apparent and rhetorically explored in visual art. In particular, reversal seems to offer a strategic effort, empowering those identified as victims, or purposely claiming the label of victimhood. The rhetoric of the artworks discussed in this chapter is strong, powerful and unforgiving. In its exploration of the themes of racism, social inequality and inclusion, this language is able to launch public debates primarily characterized by contributions based on the evocation of personal feelings. Especially because of emotional tendencies, these debates do not necessarily result in the most effective conversations, but do manage to get particular themes on the public agenda. The reversal of victimhood is more often than not cause for heightened emotional responses from those who actively project victimhood on others, while at the same time it provides a voice to those who are generally subjected to these projections.

The unforgiving character of much of the rhetoric used in both art and public debates leads to an easy deviation from an important aim of the activist agenda and acts of reconciliation such as official apologies: a more evenly spread social equality, inclusivity and mutual understanding. Despite the harsh language expressing fundamental disagreements with the way things are in contemporary Australia, Bell also cherishes a certain hope for a changed and improved future. In an interview he stated,

> I have to believe that art can make a difference, I have to believe that it can lead to political change. I have to. [...] There'll be lots of kids studying this work down here. [...] I wanted it to be seen by lots of young people and I am sure it will affect them, the way that they see Aboriginal people, I hope.
>
> (MCA Australia, 2016)

It was one of the rare occasions during which the usually unapologetic Bell publicly showed a slightly more forgiving side of himself.

Note

1 I am grateful to the Catharine van Tussenbroek Foundation/Nell Ongerboer Fund for its generous support of my research stay at Rocky Mountain College, Billings Mt., during which I wrote this chapter.

References

AAMU (2013). *BOMB: Exhibition catalogue*. Ghent/Utrecht: Snoeck Publishers/ Museum for Contemporary Aboriginal Art.

AAMU (2017, June 16). *Museumcollectie overgedragen: AAMU sluit de deuren* [Press release]. Leiden: Museum Volkenkunde.

Attwood, B. (2003). *Rights for Aborigines*. Sydney: Allen & Unwin.

Bell, R. (2008). *Scratch an Aussie* [video artwork].

Clifford, J., & Marcus, G. (Eds.). (1986). *Writing culture: The poetics and politics of ethnography*. Berkeley: University of California Press.

Collins Cobuild (2001). *English dictionary for advanced learners*. Entry: Victim, victimize, p. 1741. Glasgow: Harper Collins.

Dow, C. (2000). *Aboriginal Tent Embassy: Icon or eyesore?* (Chronology 1999–2000, 3). Canberra: Department of the Parliamentary Library: Information and research services.

Gardner, A. (2011). Post-provincial, still peripheral: Australian art on the global stage 1980–2009. In J. Anderson (Ed.), *The Cambridge companion to Australian art* (pp. 231–247). Cambridge: Cambridge University Press.

Gibney, M., Howard-Hassmann, R. E., Coicaud, J.-M., & Steiner, N. (Eds.). (2008). *The age of apology: Facing up to the past*. Philadelphia: Pennsylvania University Press.

Hall, S. (1996). Cultural identity and cinematic representation. In: H. A. Baker Jr., M. Diawara, & R. H. Lindeborg (Eds.), *Black British cultural studies: A reader* (pp. 210–222). Chicago: University of Chicago Press.

Hannam, P. (2017, November 8). 'Talking is not enough': Indigenous exhibition reveals the legal power of art. *The Sydney Morning Herald*. Retrieved from www.smh.com.au/environment/talking-is-not-enough-indigenous-exhibition-reveals-the-legal-power-of-art-20171107-gzgx1s.html.

Hoad, T. F. (1996). *The Concise Oxford dictionary of English etymology*. Entry: Victim. Oxford: Oxford University Press.

Howard-Hassmann, R. E., & Gibney, M. (2008). Introduction: Apologies and the West. In: M. Gibney, R. E. Howard-Hassmann, J.-M. Coicaud, & N. Steiner (Eds.), *The age of apology: Facing up to the past* (pp. 1–10). Philadelphia: University of Pennsylvania Press.

Howard-Hassmann, R. E., & Lombardo, A. P. (2008). Words require action: African elite opinion about apologies from the 'West'. In: M. Gibney, R. E. Howard-Hassmann, J.-M. Coicaud, & N. Steiner (Eds.), *The age of apology: Facing up to the past* (pp. 216–228). Philadelphia: University of Pennsylvania Press.

Johnson, D. (2014). *The Redfern story* [video file] (M. Langton, Comment). Samson Productions. Retrieved from www.youtube.com/watch?v=-IC81HnX7Ws.

Jones, P. (2011). The art of contact: Encountering an Aboriginal aesthetic from the eighteenth to the twentieth centuries. In J. Anderson (Ed.), *The Cambridge companion to Australian art* (pp. 22–37). Cambridge: Cambridge University Press.

Keijer, K. (2016, February 13). 'Minder, minder, minder' – honderden keren herhaald. *Het Parool*.

MCA Australia (2016, December 11 [2006]). *MCA artist's voice: Richard Bell on his MCA collection work 'Worth Exploring'* [video file]. Retrieved from www. youtube.com/watch?v=rf8WS9fshNo.

McLean, I. (Ed.). (2011). *How Aborigines invented the idea of contemporary art*. Brisbane: Institute of Modern Art & Power Publications.

MEG (2017). Website *Ville de Genève*. www.ville-ge.ch/meg/index_uk.php.

Melbourne Conversations (2012, March 26). *proppaNOW Artists: Melbourne conversations at the Melbourne Indigenous Arts Festival* [video file]. Retrieved from www.youtube.com/watch?v=wpwM71qMNT0&t=380s.

Morphy, H. (2013 [1998]). *Aboriginal art*. London: Phaidon Press.

NOS (2016, October 31). *Wilders' 'minder, minder'-uitspraak in 3 minuten uitgelegd* [video file]. Retrieved from https://nos.nl/op3/artikel/2140594-wilders-minder-minder-uitspraak-in-3-minuten-uitgelegd.html.

Nugent, M. (2015). Encounters in country. In G. Sculthorpe, J. Carty, H. Morphy, M. Nugent, I. Coates, L. Bolton, & J. Jones (Eds.), *Indigenous Australia: Enduring civilisation* (pp. 120–209). Exhibition Catalogue. London: British Museum.

Petitjean, G. (2012). Towards a museum of the 21st century: The ambiguity of an Aboriginal museum in Holland. In M. ter Horst (Ed.), *Changing perspectives: Dealing with globalisation in the presentation and collection of contemporary art* (pp. 122–129). Amsterdam: KIT Publishers.

RTL (2016, December 9). *Geert Wilders schuldig voor 'minder minder'-uitspraak, maar krijgt geen boete*. Retrieved from www.rtlnieuws.nl/nederland/politiek/geert-wilders-schuldig-voor-minder-minder-uitspraak-maar-krijgt-geen-boete.

Rudd, K. (2008). *Apology to Australia's Indigenous peoples* [video file]. Retrieved from   www.australia.gov.au/about-australia/our-country/our-people/apology-to-australias-indigenous-peoples.

Said, E. W. (1978). *Orientalism*. London: Penguin Books.

Sculthorpe, G., Bolton, L., & Coates, I. (2015). Introduction. In G. Sculthorpe, J. Carty, H. Morphy, M. Nugent, I. Coates, L. Bolton, & J. Jones (Eds.), *Indigenous Australia: Enduring civilisation* (pp. 12–19). Exhibition Catalogue. London: British Museum.

Wekker, G. (2016). *White innocence: Paradoxes of colonialism and race*. Durham: Duke University Press.

Ziherl, V. (2016). Introduction. *SMBA Newsletter*, 145.

Chapter 6

Basque Country competing memories at the local, regional and state levels

Promoting public artistic events versus public institutional policies

Gema Varona

Introduction: competing memories in the Basque Country

On the 11th of March 2017, the EU Remembrance Day for Victims of Terrorism – established because of the Al-Qaeda terrorist attacks in Madrid in 2004 – the Commissioner for the Security Union spoke about the 2017 EU Directive on combating terrorism and pointed to the power of victims' voices (Victim Support Europe, 2017). However, between vulnerability and a central role, some contradictions can be observed in the trend towards an increasing presence of victims in peace-building policies (Irazuzta, Rodríguez Maeso, & Villalón, 2017). This chapter will approach the current struggle in the practices of memorialization for victims of terrorism and abuse of power in the Basque Country from perspectives close to critical and visual victimology (Walklate, McGarry, & Mythen, 2014). Critical victimology holds a non-essentialist, non-antagonist and non-pathological vision of the processes of victimization, where social justice is also taken into account to underline the unequal distribution of the risk and the vulnerability of becoming a victim, as well as the inequality in recovering. Visual victimology studies show how social and political meanings are constructed through the culture of images. Images of suffering or victimization construct and reinforce cultural meanings, practices and values and, in a global world, the reproduction and spread of those images, some artistic, make us all witnesses to a degree.

While the Spanish and the Basque governments are developing different institutions, plans and initiatives with regard to the so-called terrorism and violence problem, some municipalities try to approach this controversial issue from another perspective. After a contextualization of this problem, a reflection on vulnerability and art through a brief comment on the theory of affects will follow. The rest of this chapter will concentrate on revising the contribution of the Adiorik gabe/Sin adiós project in Donostia/San Sebastián when it was 2016 European Capital of Culture. This project combines individual memorialization through music and/or theatre with a public commitment to non-violence. By an external evaluation of this project, we will explore its impact at both the individual and social levels and consider the relationship between justice and art as parallel to the search for objectivity by victimological researchers.

The Basque Country after ETA

Any account of the so-called Basque problem or terrorism, in terms of victimization, would require a deep analysis that is not appropriate here and that has been the object of recent historical research in its social dimensions (López Romo, 2014). Since the ceasefire in 2011 by ETA (*Euskadi ta Askatasuna*, meaning: 'Basque Country and Freedom') (Whitfield, 2014), the problem has persisted in the so-called memory struggle, based mostly in a controversy on qualification and quantification: who are the victims, of what kind of violence, and how many are there? The different answers to these questions condition the lack of political consensus in the way victims are remembered.

To give some figures of the impact of ETA, which are under debate according to the report of the Secretary for Peace of the Basque Government in Spain, which covers the period from 1960 to 2013, there have been 837 murders, more than 80 kidnappings, thousands of injured people, much damage done, and thousands of people affected by economic extortion and threats, together with violations of human rights by actors connected to the state or its police officers (Landa, 2013, pp. 1–2).

In 2017, 44 per cent of the Basque population agreed that it was necessary 'to turn the page', whereas 43 per cent was in favour of working for 'the memory of victims', a percentage that increased seven points over the previous two years; 83 per cent agreed that victims deserved public recognition; 47 per cent thought that victims must have an important role in education, whereas 38 per cent did not agree with this. For ETA prisoners, 74 per cent of the population was in favour of bringing prisoners closer to their homes; 61 per cent were in favour individual rehabilitation measures, but only 25 per cent agreed with granting them an amnesty (Euskobarómetro, 2017). If political ideology is a key factor in understanding this opinion, it must be recalled that, in 1995, 70 per cent of the Basque people were afraid of talking about politics in public. In 2017, that percentage was 15 per cent (Llera & Leonisio, 2017).

The end of ETA refers to its declaration of a ceasefire in 2011, half a century after its creation, during the final stages of Franco's dictatorship (1939–1975). This ceasefire was announced by ETA without achieving its goals of independence (from Spain and France) and socialism. It was also produced without securing the fate of its prisoners and exiles or full recognition of what ETA considers its own specific victimization (state terrorism in the 1980s, persecution and torture). Some authors argue that the Basque case is different from other terrorist groups and describe its singularity in the following terms:

> Despite the fact that the Basque Country enjoys a high standard of living and substantive autonomy, and despite the overwhelming rejection of their violent tactics by Basques, ETA managed to endure for over half a century.
>
> (Zulaika & Murua, 2017, p. 340)

And, in 2011, after a period of illegalization and judicial repression:

> We could say that the Basque electorate was faced with a self-fulfilling double bind: if we consider them terrorists and do not vote for them, then terrorism will continue; if we vote for them as a sign that their struggle is political and not terroristic, then terrorism will end. How ETA's terrorism ended can be summarised thus: it ended by its Basque political base telling ETA that they were not terrorists, while at the same time demanding from them not to practice terrorism in their name.
>
> (Zulaika & Murua, 2017, p. 350)

Although the latter explanation would not be shared by all historians (López Romo, 2014), it is true that many victims wonder why this social reaction did not come before 2011. For many, if it is only a politically strategic option in the climate of global battle against international terrorism, the problem of justification of violence remains, and remembrance takes a major role.

Practices of memorialization at different scales: public agents and narratives

Public agents

In 2018, there are two major public institutions in charge of promoting memory policies in the Basque Country: the Memorial Centre for Victims of Terrorism and the Institute of Remembrance, Coexistence and Human Rights.

The Memorial Centre for Victims of Terrorism (*Centro Memorial de las Víctimas del Terrorismo*) was created under the mandate of the 29/2011 Spanish Act on the Recognition and Integral Protection of Victims of Terrorism and is financed by the state (Ministerio del Interior, n.d.). According to its statutes, it aims at preserving and promoting the 'democratic and ethical values represented by victims of terrorism' and 'constructing the collective memory of victimization', as a public conscience in defence of human rights. Its stated aim is to consider victims as individuals, without forgetting their historical context.

The Memorial Centre is situated in the city of Vitoria/Gasteiz.[1] It has already started producing different encounters, reports and research by different scholars and academic institutions, which are available online. The Memorial Centre promotes exhibitions and education programmes and holds archives, among its other activities. Thus, it is not conceived as an old-style museum but, much in line with current trends, as 'an adequate place for information and reflection' for 'generating an emotional effect on the visitor', particularly the young ones, so illegitimate violence is not repeated in the future.

The Institute of Remembrance, Coexistence and Human Rights (*Gogora* in Basque) is run by a board presided over by the President of the Basque Country and has a broader scope in defining victimization in terms of the causes of violence and the period of victimization, going beyond terrorism over the last 50 years and considering the Civil War and the whole dictatorship. According to its website, 'Gogora is a forum where victims and society can share their remembrance of the past with a view to helping to build peaceful coexistence'. It aims at

> coordinating public policies on remembrance in our country. Its job is to preserve and pass on the memory of the traumatic, violent experiences of the past hundred years: the Civil War, the Franco dictatorship, the terrorism of ETA and unlawful counterterrorist attacks; memories of suffering unjustly caused and efforts to construct and defend democratic coexistence and a society based on the defence of human rights and peace, even in the most adverse circumstances.
>
> (Gogora, n.d.)

Moreover, the Institute

> seeks to establish inclusive remembrance, guaranteeing the engagement of the public. Only one limit is set on this dialogue between memories: remembrance must not be used to exclude events or seek equivalences between them. Nor must it be used to justify any form of terrorism, violence or violation of human rights.
>
> (Gogora, n.d.)

In the first anniversary of its creation, Gogora published a plan of action for 2017–2020 (Gogora, n.d.), insisting on the 'need to look for critical reflections about the past' and promoting 'plurality where everybody can be included'. The President of the Basque Country declared that it is necessary 'to manage the memory of different traumatic events, with diverse readings but the common link of including a dramatic balance sheet of human rights violations' (Díez, 2017, p. 22). This plan of action differentiates between transversal matters (including research and publications), historical memory and recent memory. The plan describes 27 projects gathered in nine initiatives.

Some of the projects seek to harmonize the memory actions developed by different public institutions, including the consolidation of the Remembrance Day on 10 November and the use of the archives of recorded victims' testimonies in schools. A guiding principle is 'the promotion of empathy' so that the work of dealing with the past can be done from a point of encounter of the whole Basque society, 'transcending subjective experiences' to include other realities. Empathy 'is a sine qua non condition to be opened to others' memory', even though it is assumed that 'it is not possible a complete agreement in the interpretation of the past' (Díez, 2017, p. 22). However, through public engagement, a minimum agreement is expected on the 'diagnosis of the guilt, responsibility, harm, suffering and their genesis'.

By reading the previous paragraphs, we can conclude that both public institutions, at the state and regional levels, manage a different concept of victimization and, in line with the globalization of practices of memorialization, use similar words and ends that are very open to different cultural and political interpretations. Finally, both institutions aim at public education and engagement with an ethical appeal. To date, the Memorial Centre seems more focused on general academic work, whereas Gogora uses the more technical language of peace studies to systematize the practices of memorialization.

Conflicting narratives

It is said that there is a 'memory battle' in current Basque Country, clearly represented in memorialization practices such as the above-mentioned Remembrance Day every 10th of November. The 10th of November was chosen because it was the only day of the calendar without a murder victim. No political agreement has yet been reached to celebrate it jointly by all political parties. The underlying debate evokes questions related to different understandings of Spanish identity, Basque identity or hybrid identities defined by culture (language and origins). There are also diverse cultural interpretations of victimhood (including aspects of cultural and structural violence).

This debate has been represented, in the summer of 2017, in the remembrance day of Miguel Ángel Blanco, an ETA victim who was a young local politician, kidnapped and murdered in 1997.[2] Marimar Blanco, sister of the victim, parliamentarian of the Popular Party and President of the Foundation for Victims of Terrorism, spoke of fighting for a narrative of winners and losers based on memory, dignity and justice. In her opinion, as the state has defeated ETA within the rule of law, efforts should now be undertaken to win the memory of this victimization, so it is not recalled as a conflict between two sides but as simple terrorism (Ferreras, 2017, p. 16).

We can define at least four elements of this battle in its cultural and narrative dimensions: language, script, categorization of victims and the public, and purposes of remembrance. The Basque Government seems to have more sympathy with conflict resolution language. In contrast, the Spanish Government rejects the so-called international mediation industry and considers the difference between conflict and terrorism in terms of state sovereignty (Zulaika, & Murua, 2017, p. 348). According to Van den Broek (2017), it is important to analyse the role of labelling in the discourse employed by the Left-Wing Nationalist movement in the Basque Country to legitimize the use of violence for political ends. Radical Nationalists develop counter-labels to define their opponents and re-label themselves, as fighters for freedom, to avoid being called fanatics or terrorists. They inscribe themselves in the logic of democracy and not terrorism.

As for the script:

> The dominant narrative in the Spanish media is clearly one of ETA's defeat at the hands of police repression and judicial intervention. There is much truth to this view, but it is by no means the full story. For this we must also listen to ETA's political arm's own narrative according to which the final decisive blow is the rebellion of its own social base.
> (Zulaika, & Murua, 2017, p. 340)

In relation to the categories of victims, some find it fair to talk about the equal suffering of all victims (including those of Francoism), whereas others underline that the historical contextualization should not be omitted. In general, some cases of perpetrators becoming victims can be found in ETA and extreme right or state-related terrorism.

In the academic sphere, this debate is translated into the use or non-use of the concepts of 'transitional justice' and the 'voice of victims' in relation to historical accounts. Although the fragmentation of initiatives is common to many post-conflict societies, some authors (Alvarez Berastegi, 2017) understand that conflicted democracies such as Northern Ireland and the Basque Country could benefit from the framework of transitional justice because it 'brings a comprehensive human rights approach to the past and promotes the principles of truth, justice, reparation and guarantees of non-repetition'. Bryson (2016, p. 63) highlights the concerns 'about the dominance of legalism within the field and the instrumentalization of those most directly affected by past violence'. He demands moving to a transitional justice theory and practice 'more open to interdisciplinary insights and perspectives' through oral history. Questioning objectivity and its 'human, humane and limited dimension', Bryson (2016) argues that 'the theory and practice of oral history can usefully illuminate the tensions between legal and historical approaches to engaging voice, and ultimately offer guidance to the shared challenge of victim-centered transitional justice'.

Finally, for the audience of the different narratives, the purpose of memory for some is to illustrate for future generations (Ferreras, 2017, p. 16) so that post-justification of terrorism and moral indifference are avoided (Montero, 2017). Others are sceptical about the possibilities of a memory without political ideology, particularly when some victims, selected in different educative initiatives, take a role in victimization story-telling at some schools. According to Irazuzta, Rodríguez Maeso and Villa-lón (2017), the increasing visibility of victims of terrorism has favoured an 'emergence and institutionalization of the figure of the victim in the field of education in the post-conflict context of the Basque Country'. These authors have analysed the 'Victims as Educators' Programme within the compulsory secondary education in the Basque Country. They question the 'sentimental education' in the field of human rights, the construction of 'appropriate feelings' in terms of fostering reconciliation and coexistence, and finally 'the construction of the figure of the victim as educator charac-terized by a resilient victim profile'.

Vulnerability, affection and art: victims of terrorism and abuse of power as a cultural category

In this section, we will consider what it means to define victims of ter-rorism as vulnerable and how the meaning of the theory of vulnerability can be related to artistic projects of memorialization through the theory of affects by the interrelation of the individual and social dimensions.

The theory of vulnerability

Victims of terrorism are catalogued as 'vulnerable victims' in the language of global legal culture. This is expressed in the 2012/29/EU Directive – establishing minimum standards on the rights, support and protection of victims of crime – and its transposition into the Spanish legal system by the 4/2015 Act on the Statute of the Victim of Crime. In practical terms, being labelled 'vulnerable' should mean more protection and rights but, in prac-tice, this categorization might only bring some symbolism and a hierarchy of victims.

In social science, Fineman's theory of vulnerability recognizes the uni-versality, yet unequal distribution, of vulnerability – sometimes innate but always socially defined – across time and different contexts, as a basis for state and social responsibility. From a similar standpoint, critical crimin-ology has highlighted that insecurity and its impact are not equally distrib-uted. The theory of vulnerability provides a way from fragmentation of identities to a universal conception of vulnerability. Some critiques note that this theory lacks a solid articulation and empirical test and must face the risk of promoting 'excessively paternalistic laws and policies', consolidating stereotyping and/or discrimination, not guiding how to allocate resources among vulnerable individuals (Kohn, 2014, p. 5).

The theory of vulnerability as formulated by Fineman (2008, 2015) started from the classical concern that formal equality cannot guarantee social or substantial equality:

> [V]ulnerability is inherent to the human condition [...] governments therefore have a responsibility to respond affirmatively to that vulnerability by ensuring that all people have equal access to the societal institutions that distribute resources.
>
> (Kohn, 2014, p. 3)

Moreover, formal equality can validate and facilitate existing inequalities, and at the same time this approach

> fails to achieve meaningful social justice because it treats vulnerability as limited to special populations, which both obscures the fact that not all persons within protected populations are disadvantaged and mistakenly treats as invulnerable people who are not members of groups that are recognized as deserving special protection.
>
> (Kohn, 2014, p. 6)

Although applied to social welfare policies, the theory of vulnerability can also be applied in relation to victim policies (as welfare policies) and, in particular, to memory policies, social responsibility and the role of the state (or other governmental institutions). Equal treatment cannot assure meeting individual needs when facing life adverse events, including victimization and other harms. For Fineman (2008), the different recognition of vulnerability is key in positive and negative social control or social cohesion.

The theory of vulnerability, beyond the debate on equality, autonomy and intersectionality, aims at transcending vulnerable group identity as exclusionary (Maglione, 2017) and advocates for a post-identity perspective recognizing vulnerability as universal in the human condition (Kohn, 2014, p. 4). This theory states that vulnerability is part of the human condition: we all can be vulnerable, and we will be at some point, because human life by definition is fragile and limited. This awareness must bring solidarity together with substantial equality based on the contextualized situation of every person. Formal equality is not enough to understand the protection or support needed when people go through vulnerable circumstances that required an individualized treatment not foreseen in general laws. Later we will explain how some victims of terrorism and violence in the Basque Country find themselves in a socially constructed vulnerable situation and that only individualized and public reparation can bring them some relief. According to the theory of vulnerability, individualization promoted by public institutions is needed. However, according to the theory of affect, this is not enough: feelings should be considered, with the risk of political manipulation, in order to reckon the intertwined multidimensionality of human beings.

The theory of affect

Victims must be treated considering their suffering or trauma and vulnerable circumstances. Their narratives can be observed as moving, in the context of their audience, and promoting understanding through the interrelation between affect and cognition. Any practice of memorialization is produced by and produces affect as personal feelings, in principle different from the social character of emotions. This is one of the reasons why the theory of vulnerability can be related to the theory of affects and its application in art. The theory of affects attracts attention from disciplines such as anthropology, cultural studies, geography, psychology, philosophy, queer studies and sociology, relating 'the aesthetic, the ethical, and the political as they play out across bodies' (Gregg, & Seigworth, 2010). The philosophers Aristotle, Descartes and Spinoza are often quoted in relation to the origin of this theory, and affect is usually taken as a synonym for sentiment or emotion, depending on the traditions of its theorization. The theory of affect studies how do (and how should) artworks produce and transmit affect (Shepard, n.d.). Affect can be produced through mimesis, and here music is quoted, not without some opposition, as inspiring virtue in Plato's words. For other authors such as Felix Guattari and Gilles Deleuze, art is 'a bloc of sensations, that is to say, a compound of percepts and affects' (Deleuze, & Guattari, 1994, p. 163) where 'affect is both embodied and bound up with consciousness' (Shepard, n.d.). Art and affect are also related in terms of temporality because the temporal experience of the viewer is mapped onto the time of the piece of art itself with its inherent manipulation risks.

Leys (2011) wonders why so many scholars today in the humanities and social sciences, including cultural studies, are fascinated by the idea of affect. Leys (2011) quotes cultural critic Eric Shouse (2005):

> the importance of affect rests upon the fact that in many cases the message consciously received may be of less import to the receiver of that message than his or her nonconscious affective resonances with the source of the message.

The power of some forms of media might lie 'in their ability to create affective resonances independent of content or meaning'.

The standpoint of current theory of affects, political argument and rationality are overvalued, and:

> [A]ffects must be viewed as independent of, and in an important sense prior to, ideology – that is, prior to intentions, meanings, reasons, and beliefs – because they are nonsignifying, autonomic processes that take place below the threshold of conscious awareness and meaning.
>
> (Leys, 2011)

Leys (2011) criticizes this interpretation of the affects as nonintentional or mere bodily reactions, in 'contrast to Freud and appraisal theorists for whom emotions are embodied, intentional states governed by our beliefs, cognitions, and desires'. Finally:

> [I]n embracing biology, many of today's affect theorists hope to avoid the charge of falling into a crude reductionism by positioning themselves at a distance from the geneticism and determinism that were a target of the previous phase of cultural theory. Instead, they seek to recast biology in dynamic, energistic, nondeterministic terms that emphasize its unpredictable and potentially emancipatory qualities.
>
> (Leys, 2011)

Affect theorists and neuroscientists seem to share the concept of affects as non-intentional and the belief that affect is independent of signification. For both, affects 'occur below the threshold of consciousness and cognition' and are 'rooted in the body'. As a result, behaviour is determined by affective dispositions 'independent of consciousness and the mind's control' (Leys, 2011).

There has been a recent application of the theory of affects to the Basque case by the Literature researcher Edurne Portela (2016). In this case, Portela aims at a rational study of affects, rejecting equidistant positions to broaden an imagination that is traditionally reduced and provokes antagonism. Thus, the category of what can be represented and expressed is more inclusive to understand the complexity of the problem. This might make us more vulnerable or insecure about having all the answers, particularly those related to identity (Portela, 2016, pp. 202–203).

As a way of a sociobiographic account, Portela reflects on her own experience of living in the Basque Country, in a context described without the accuracy of a historian. According to her, the literature and visual language play a key role in creating a subjectivity born out from a new sensitivity that makes possible structures of empathy and responsibility. The language of affect can contribute to an imaginative change entailing ethics. Portela has analysed some intimate narratives constructing what occurred in the Basque Country from a cultural perspective. To do this, she considers the concept of ethical imagination by Spinoza (Portela, 2016, p. 201). According to her, an ethical imagination allows a better knowledge or cognition and amplifies our affects so that the encounter with 'the other' is possible beyond identity stereotypes. It is not a question of moral denouncing, but of placing ourselves in 'affective spaces of discomfort and uncertainty' from which collective responsibility can also be recognized (Portela, 2016, p. 206).

A case study of ephemeral public artistic events (Adiorik gabe/Sin adiós project) versus public institutional policies: applying the theories of vulnerability and affects

European capitals of culture

Created in 1985 by the European Commission, the programme of European capitals of culture aims at promoting the cultural diversity and common grounds of Europeans.[3] 'Transforming Culture for a Decade of Coexistence' was the title of the programme of the candidature for the European Capital of Culture, for 2016, submitted by three Basque institutions four years before. Those institutions were the Basque Government, the Provincial Government of Gipuzkoa and the City Council of Donostia/San Sebastián. The programme 'sought to respond to the huge collective challenge that Basque society faced, and it aimed to do so through culture', 'to achieve peace and create a model of coexistence to share with other European cities, based on respect for Human Rights, a culture of peace, education in values and linguistic and cultural diversity'. Culture and education were seen as essential tools to 'prevent and combat violence, intolerance and the conflicts suffered by European society, and to make European cities spaces for coexistence'. According to its website (Donostia/San Sebastián, 2017), in turn, all this required 'active, responsible and solidary citizens', equipped with the strength of 'their capacity for transformation'. This idea justified the themes of 'Citizens' Waves of Energy' and 'Culture for Living Together' under which many cultural activities occurred.

Under the projects in relation to peace building, the project Adiorik gabe/Sin adiós ('Without saying goodbye') was prepared at the end of 2015 and developed in 2016.[4] The University of the Basque Country was asked to carry out an external evaluation, which was completed at the beginning of 2017 (Varona Martínez, 2017). This section considers the results of this evaluation.

Without saying goodbye: music and literature, in memoriam

This project is defined as art serving the memory of victims through music and literature work 'to collect and reconstruct their musical and literary memory'. The project was divided into three acts that, avoiding several election days in the Basque Country in 2016, occurred on the 2nd of July, the 30th of October and the 18th of December, in three different scenarios. Advertised in the media, people were freely invited, and the full capacity of each theatre was reached (seating approximately 450 people in every act). Each day of representations, four victims were remembered through music, words and pictures or videos. Assuring diversity and avoidance of 'partisan temptations', four local artists were in charge of one artistic piece per victim in each one of the three acts. Every act lasted approximately two hours and occurred on either Saturday or Sunday.

According to its website (Donostia/San Sebastián, 2017), the project meant:

> A few moments to share and remember sensorially the individuals that were violently taken from us. Those to whom we could not say goodbye. [...] The result of the process was an inclusive artistic offering that resulted in a collective expression of memory and recognition, including the respect of and commitment to human rights.

The external evaluation was very positive in this sense, particularly if we compare it to the lack of consensus and the risk of political manipulation of other practices of memorialization carried out by different institutions, as described above. However, a deeper analysis makes us conclude that some minor problems were detected in relation to the selection of victims and the purposes of memorialization. These are the issues that we will discuss in this section.

Trying to evaluate the process and the results of the project, from June to December, 2016, victims, artists, promoters and the support psychotherapist were interviewed, following a semi-structured protocol, before and after each act. Additionally, after each act, the audience was asked to fill in a brief written questionnaire collecting their opinion, using a Likert scale, and their socio-demographic profile. A final focus group with three participating family members of three different victimizations occurred at the end of 2016.

The direct and indirect victims

The project partially aimed for collaborative art between the four artists and the participating victims who were close family members of the 12 murdered people remembered. The idea was that the artists could talk to those family members and collect material from which to construct an ex profeso creative piece of musical and/or literary art. During the act, a written programme was delivered to the public explaining who was the victim and the kind of victimization suffered and containing the names of the artists.

The victims were protected from the media in the sense of limited media coverage during the act itself and lack of access to victims, and any politician's protagonism was avoided. This has been considered one of the fundamental elements of society's and victims' positive evaluation of the project.

The 12 remembered victims were selected on the basis of the document of the Basque Government (Secretaría de Paz y Convivencia, 2014) on violations of the right to life in different municipalities, without expressly mentioning 'terrorism' or 'counter-terrorism'. A snowball technique was followed to select the 12 victims. Only in two cases did family members decline the invitation, one because of doubts about the goals of the project and the other because the widow did not feel strong enough to face the emotions that the project entailed for her. In another case, there were clear opposing opinions of different family members on participation, and the artistic piece was done with those who wanted it.

The 12 remembered victims were killed between 1979 and 2001, and they were between 16 and 59 years old. Nine were victims of ETA, two of one extreme right-wing terrorist group (Batallón Vasco Español) and one of suspected police abuse. Two of the victims were women, ten were men. In several cases, no perpetrator could be condemned, and the cases are now under the statute of limitations. Thus, legal proceedings can no longer be brought. For some of these victims, particularly of abuse of police power, the artistic act also fulfilled a function of socially denouncing the injustice suffered and shortly acknowledged in juridical and social terms. For most victims, many years have passed since the victimization, even decades. Regarding the way they were produced, all victimizations were very hard, but most victims, in one way or another and to different degrees, could recover and go back to a life without their loved ones.

The selection of victims was not done considering a statistically representative sample. From 1968 to 2001, Donostia/San Sebastián represented the Basque city with the most casualties generated by terrorist groups: 94 persons, a figure only surpassed by Madrid (125; López Romo, 2014, p. 169). All those 94 deaths were caused by ETA, but this number does not consider a limited number of neighbours of San Sebastián killed outside the city, mainly by ETA but also by other terrorist groups. When considering those people, according to the Basque Government (Secretaría de Paz y Convivencia, 2014), 107 persons were killed by ETA, four by extreme-right terrorist groups, 11 by police abuses and nine of unclear authorship.

Some participating victims were sceptical about the local government supporting them so many years after the victimization and about considering other victims in addition to ETA's victims. Before the project, a minority of the participating victims also feared 'banalization' under the idea of an aesthetic or cultural product. However, after the event, they all declared that their expectations were positively surpassed in their personal experience. They underlined the innovative way of expressing suffering and silence with a different format and language. They valued the subjective creativity combined with individual and social intelligibility of that suffering. Participating victims were very surprised by the audience's reaction in terms of age, assistance, emotions and words of support expressed at the end of the act.

Finally, after the first act, when pictures of some murdered victims' faces were shown, many participating family members of the remaining acts asked to project pictures to put a face to their lost loved ones, something that some artists had not considered before, and it was later appreciated as one of the needs of the survivors in terms of individualization.

The artists and the support psychotherapist

Artists always confront their art with the public in a sort of dialogue. In this case, they had to work first with family members of victims, some of them of their own age, neighbourhood or acquaintance. In some cases, they gave more thought to that suffering, in part because they learned it from the family members' narratives, than they had when the victimization occurred.

Artists did not look for a representation of the violent act, not even of its explicit consequences, but, as a request from most victims, for a celebration of lost lives with the inherent ambiguities of emotions: a sad unjust event gathers the public and is in the origin of the artistic project, but it is done to remember something valuable and to celebrate the value of human life. Beyond art as therapy, the question is how to avoid a suffocating memory and help in incorporating suffering to a larger social life that, wanted or not, continues.

Artists were challenged to listen to victims, mostly quite distant from cultural issues and abstract aesthetical worries. In their creations, family members were the first targeted audience, and they felt relief knowing that the family liked the artwork.

Artists worked with a support psychotherapist who had experience in other projects with victims in the Basque Country. His role was not working with victims, but assisting the artists in their relationship with them so that they could be sensitive to their needs. He was also satisfied with the process and results of the project and insisted that the external evaluation should be respectful towards victims. This was expressed in a friendly debate about protection, vulnerability and autonomy prior to the final focus group used in the evaluation methodology.

The promoters within the municipal authority

The singular character of this project relies in its individualized and personalized character, with its implementation by a local public authority that finances a programme with an artistic base. This is striking because this sort of memorialization practice is usually done by private agents because of the number of victims involved and the controversial political meaning of their victimization.

In this case, despite public financing, the direct promoters were a small team of people engaged in grassroot peace movements. This team was well evaluated by all stakeholders. They worked hard to gain trust and understand different needs and worries. This includes the worries of politicians of different political parties who understood the non-partisan character of the project, limited to the year 2016.

The audience

The 544 people who filled in our questionnaire answered that the objective of the act had been fulfilled, mainly when remembering all victims through a personalized remembrance.

Most family members selected Spanish as the language for the songs or theatre pieces. Five questionnaires emphasized the need for more use of the Basque language in these artistic events. Considering that the family members selected the language most significant to them, this demand is related to the public audience and can be attended with new language formats to communicate the victims' memory. This should exclude the abuse of that memory to serve ideological positions about the Basque language.

Society was invited as the observer of something created between the artists and the living witnesses (family members of the murdered person). There was no problem in agreeing what was to be remembered: the basic idea that killing, in the way it was produced, is always a grave violation of human rights without justification. In this sense, memory is never a question of the past because it is prospective and aimed at the future generations, in an individual and social perspective and through an act of making visible the darkness of victimizations, particularly those victimizations more hidden.

In the legal and philosophical sphere, there is much debate on the conceptualization of remembrance or memory as duty and right, including as cultural right. Cultural rights are understood by United Nations as rights, individually and collectively, to express humanity and different views and meanings of the world through values, thoughts, languages, knowledge, arts and ways of living, among others (Shaheed, 2014). There are aspects of grave victimizations that cannot be encapsulated in philosophical, historical or victimological knowledge. There is another kind of knowledge, such as art. Even if not scientific, it might help beyond the so-called universal character of the artistic language. Amos Oz (2016, p. 18), in a text created for the programme of Donostia 2016, refers to the art as a gift and not having a function. For Oz, the art invites us to temporarily get out of our own existence and broaden our knowledge and emotional territory.

However, the question remains in artistic events: how to get a non-dichotomic understanding between memory and knowledge, emotion and reason, subjectivity and objectivity? Justice is said to be one of the basic human needs: the need of having been acknowledged as a person suffering an injustice in search of some form of reparation.

Final remarks: Adiorik gabe/Sin adiós as a form of restorative justice?

With all its many limitations, as described by Braithwaite (2017), restorative justice deals with stakeholders taking active responsibility for justice as a better future. Justice is understood first as reparation to victims instead of punishment to offenders. The external evaluation on Adiorik gabe/Sin adiós concluded that this project contained some elements of restorative justice, taking memory as a form of justice (Varona Martínez, 2017). Those elements were free participation and dialogue in creating reparation of victimization through art, where the community is involved. In this sense, some relation can be found between restorative justice, the theory of vulnerability and the theory of affects. This is so because the project aimed at the symbolic reparation of victims under the hypothesis that reparation can only be real and meaningful to victims if done in an individualized manner, in a public scenario, and bringing interpellating feelings to victims and the whole audience.

Mieke Bal (2016) has explored the different meanings of movement, in relation to the still image, which also moves, according to her. The project Adiorik gabe/Sin adiós is related to the idea of movement as argued by Bal. Following Henri Bergson (1911) and his attention to the body as material entity, from the theory of affects, Bal underlines the act of perception as 'a selection by the perceiving subject and that subject's memories' where there is a 'nature' in seeing and, as result, 'the potential to move us to action in the political domain'. Thus: 'Contemporary art that seeks to have political effect is groping for strategies that avoid the drawbacks of reductive representation, facile emotion, and instant recognition of critical issues' (Bal, 2016, pp. 29–30). Freely adapting Bal's (2016, p. 30) words, we are facing not just a mimesis (reproduction/abstraction) of the real victimization in a musical or dance event or a piece of theatre, but an encounter of the two, emancipating the victims from invisibility and vulnerability as defined in narrow legal terms, and turning the victims into a visible presence (Huyssen, 2003), much in line with current visual victimology.

> Art has great political potential if it disentangles the good from true. Then, it compels viewers who are affected by it to make judgments about such issues as, for example, justice [...] Making such judgments is an exercise of democratic agency. I understand the latter term to

require contexts where the issues that make up the political can be spoken [...] The spaces that democratic agency necessitates are contexts in which the antagonism can be enacted without resulting in the enmity that leads to war, terrorism, and other forms of lawless violence. They are places where, instead, judgments and acts of democratic dispute – even silently, in the form of thought and deliberation – are not only allowed but actively enabled and stimulated.

(Bal, 2016, pp. 37–38)

Culture, from an anthropological point of view (Eagleton, 2016), consisting of knowledge, values, practices and language as a corridor between past and present, can act as a key to change and a possible element of democratic cohesion beyond ideology, political parties, identity and closed communities. This is also related to assemblage thinking:

Assemblages, temporary and deliberate heterogeneous arrangements of material and immaterial elements, are about the relationship of in-betweenness. I further suggest that sensoriality and affectivity, memory and multi-temporality are key features of assemblage thinking, and that assemblages also imply certain political effects.

(Hamilakis, 2017, p. 169)

However, risks have to be recognized. The theory of vulnerability by Fineman (2008) expresses the failure of current legalism to attend inequalities and to conceptualize subjects in its dynamic dimensions, but there exists the temptation of patronizing victims. Moreover, art mobilizes emotions, either provoking them or starting from them. Emotional encounters with the past mediated by the media might exaggerate collective responsibility (Gallagher & Kalin, 2017) and be politically abused.

Alison Landsberg's (2004) prosthetic memory, in relation to representing and responding to events one did not experience (Lury, 1998; Schult & Popescu, 2016), is unsustainable for some authors because her concept of memory is just a combination of knowledge and empathy (Berger, 2007). Moreover, if 'remembering the past fosters a sense of the self, providing the idea about who we were in the past and who we are in the present' (Chiba, 2017), can remembering be separated from identity construction (Maglione, 2017)?

To what extent did Adiorik gabe/Sin adiós create an atmosphere, beyond the concept of place, where people could come because it was not related to partisan ideas of which most of Basque society seems tired and which young people do not understand? The limited success of the project in terms of number of participating victims and the actual possibility of narrating the memory of grave victimizations has been outweighed by the public satisfaction of the audience and other stakeholders. This has been achieved by an interdisciplinary team assuring participation (Cox, 2017) and care for victims and independence from politics, perhaps because it was just limited to 2016.

Within a variety of interpretations, the public shared the main idea that the artistic pieces were carried out as an individualized practice of memorialization for all society. Other direct and indirect victims, who were present among the audience, made the project theirs and were satisfied by the atmosphere of respect and recognition. Thus, the represented micro-narratives achieved a public echo. The project broke with the stereotyped image of victims whose entire life is dominated by their victimization and who are isolated from the rest of their life dimensions and other people. By representing small details of their lives and tastes, the humanity of the absent person was recognized in a more enhanced and real way (De Saint-Laurent, 2017).

To be fully restorative, perpetrators' participation wishing to repair might be envisaged in future projects. For the moment, current artistic projects might allow us to imagine the perpetrator outside his 'absolute otherness' (Portela, 2016, p. 126). Without legitimizing violence, some artistic atmospheres might build bridges among different stakeholders and generations. In this sense it is possible to reconceptualize the term 'drauma' by James Joyce, as dream and trauma (Harty, 2015). Dreaming prepossessing traumas can be thought of as celebrating unique lives that were broken because of violence. Like the angel of history, an open concept used by Walter Benjamin (Werckmeister, 1996) to criticize a linear conceptualization of rational progress, the past, present and future might be related as ways of reversing part of the irreversible.

Clamp (2016, p. 16) comments on three characteristics that restorative justice should meet in the context of grave violations of human rights:

1   It must include all affected persons, from a conceptualization of multi-dimensional and open identities.
2   It must be adapted and be culturally relevant in each concrete context.
3   It must look to the future in a sustainable manner to be transformative.

Drawing from literary theory and cultural psychology, Brescó (2017) applies the notion of prolepsis ('narrative manoeuver consisting of narrating or evoking a future event in advance') to collective memory to examine 'how imagined futures are brought into the present by means of particular ways of reconstructing the past, thus mobilizing collectives towards certain political goals'. He reflects on the role of politics of imagination 'in promoting different ways of relating past, present and future', depending on each context (Brescó, 2016; Brescó & Wagoner, 2016). This entails a meaning of politics in its best sense as non-partisan.

The report of the Truth and Reconciliation Commission of South Africa (1998, p. 110) dealt with four differing types of truth: factual and forensic truth; personal and narrative truth; social truth; and healing and restorative truth where acknowledgement is relevant as 'an affirmation that a person's pain is real and worthy of attention. It is thus central to the restoration of the dignity of victims' (Naqvi, 2006, p. 254). Memory as restorative memory is a concept close to the social dimension of truth as public acknowledgement, within the general obligation of the state to provide victims, their families and society with information about victimizations and their circumstances (Niebauer, 2017). Artistic knowledge on victimization and reparation is linked to that public acknowledgement. This is the small victimological discovery about a limited project, Adiorik gabe/Sin adiós, carried out in the Basque Country in 2016.

Notes

1 Another site is foreseen in Madrid with a special focus on jihadist terrorism.
2 For the first time, a Bildu parliamentarian participated in a commemoration in Ermua, the hometown where Miguel Ángel Blanco lived. Bildu is a coalition of the Abertzale Left. This term refers to the Nationalist Left, the political movement to which ETA belongs in broad political terms, banned by the Supreme Court but later legalized by the Constitutional Court and winning great support in the 2011 elections. ETA threatened to execute Blanco unless the government met its demand of transferring approximately 500 ETA inmates to the Basque country prisons in two days (Özçelik 2017, p. 1061) (today there are approximately 250 prisoners). The general reaction to Blanco's murder represented a change in an increasing social mobilization against ETA.
3 For more information on this initiative, see its website in different languages at https://ec.europa.eu/programmes/creative-europe/actions/capitals-culture_en.
4 Some brief images and sound of part of the acts can be seen at www.youtube.com/watch?v=4NhWVlxE7PA.

References

Alvarez Berastegi, A. (2017). Transitional justice in settled democracies: Northern Ireland and the Basque Country in comparative perspective. *Critical Studies on Terrorism*, *10*(3), 542–561.
Bal, M. (2016). El movimiento y la imagen fija. *Espacio Tiempo y Forma, Serie VII, Historia del Arte*, *4*, 15–41.
Berger, J. (2007). Which prosthetic? Mass media, narrative, empathy, and progressive politics. *Rethinking History*, *11*(4), 597–612.
Bergson, H. (1911). *Matter and memory* (N. M. Paul & W. S, Palmer, Trans.). New York: Macmillan.
Braithwaite, J. (2017). Hybrid politics for justice: The silk road of restorative justice II. *Restorative Justice*, *5*(1), 7–28.
Brescó, I. (2016). Conflict, memory and positioning: Studying the dialogical and multivoiced dimension of the Basque conflict. *Peace & Conflict: Journal of Peace Psychology*, *22*(1), 36–43.

Brescó, I. (2017). The end into the beginning: Prolepsis and the reconstruction of the collective past. *Culture & Psychology, 23*(2), 280–294.

Brescó, I., & Wagoner, B. (2016). Context in the cultural psychology of remembering. In C. Stone & L. Bietti (Eds.), *Contextualizing human memory* (pp. 69–85). London: Routledge.

Bryson, A. (2016). Victims, violence, and voice: Transitional justice, oral history, and dealing with the past. *Hastings International and Comparative Law Review, 39*(2), 1–56.

Chiba, N. (2017). *The erasure of collective memory about war in The Big O: A case of the fictional paradigm City*. Retrieved from http://repo.lib.hosei.ac.jp/bits tream/10114/13192/1/%E7%A4%BE%E4%BC%9A%E5%BF%97%E6%9 E%9763–4chiba.pdf.

Clamp, K. (Ed.). (2016). *Restorative justice in transitional settings*. London: Routledge.

Cox, J. L. (2017). Book review: Popular memories: Commemoration, participatory culture, and democratic citizenship by E. V. Haskins, Columbia, University of South Carolina, 2015. *Quarterly Journal of Speech, 103*(3), 1–5.

De Saint-Laurent, C. (2017). Personal trajectories, collective memories: Remembering and the life-course. *Culture & Psychology, 23*(2), 263–279.

Deleuze, G., & Guattari, F. (1994). *What is philosophy?* New York: Columbia University Press.

Díez, T. (2017, July 11). Gogora plantea conciliar una memoria plural con la reflexión crítica del pasado. *Diario de Noticias de Álava*. Retrieved from http://m.noticiasdealava.com/2017/07/11/politica/gogora-plantea-conciliar-una-memoria-plural-con-la-reflexion-critica-del-pasado.

Donostia/San Sebastián 2016, European Capital of Culture (2017). *European Capital of Culture, a legacy of coexistence*. Retrieved from http://dss2016.eu/en/.

Eagleton, T. (2016). *Culture*. London: Yale University Press.

Euskobarómetro (2017). La sociedad vasca ante la memoria del las víctimas y el final del terrorismo. *Avance de resultados, Informe del Centro Memorial de las Víctimas del Terrorismo*. Retrieved from www.ehu.eus/documents/1457190/1547454/informe±centro±memorial±y±euskobarometro.pdf.

Ferreras, B. (2017, July 14). El proyecto de ETA sigue vivo: No se ha terminado el trabajo. *El Mundo*.

Fineman, M. A. (2008). The vulnerable subject: Anchoring equality in the human condition. *Yale Journal of Law & Feminism, 20*(1), 9–15.

Fineman, M. A. (2015). Vulnerability and law. *New legal realism conversations*. Retrieved from https://newlegalrealism.wordpress.com/2015/11/30/fineman-on-vulnerability-and-law/.

Gallagher V. J., & Kalin J. (2017). Collected debris of public memory: Commemorative genres and the mediation of the past. In C. Miller & A. Kelly (Eds.), *Emerging genres in new media environments*. Basingstoke: Palgrave Macmillan.

Gogora (n.d.). *Presentación*. Retrieved from www.gogora.euskadi.eus/aa82-home/en/.

Gregg, M., & Seigworth, G. J. (Eds.). (2010). *The affect theory reader*. Durham: Duke University Press.

Hamilakis, Y. (2017). Sensorial assemblages: Affect, memory and temporality in assemblage thinking. *Cambridge Archaeological Journal, 27*(1), 169–182.

Harty III, J. (Ed.). (2015). *James Joyce's Finnegans wake: A casebook* (Volume 3). London: Routledge.

Huyssen, A. (2003). *Present pasts: Urban palimpsests and the politics of memory.* Redwood City: Stanford University Press.

Irazuzta, I., Rodríguez Maeso, S., & Villalón, A. M. (2017). 'Victims as educators': Sentimental education in a peace-building context. *Journal of Human Rights Practice, 9*(1), 50–67.

Kohn, N. A. (2014). Vulnerability theory and the role of government. *Yale Journal of Law & Feminism, 26*(1), Article 2. Retrieved from http://digitalcommons.law.yale.edu/cgi/viewcontent.cgi?article=1345&context=yjlf.

Landa, J.-M. (2013). Human rights and politically-motivated violence in the Basque Country. *Journal on Ethnopolitics and Minority Issues in Europe, 12*(2), 7–29.

Landsberg, A. (2004). *Prosthetic memory: The transformation of American remembrance in the age of mass culture.* New York: Columbia University Press.

Leys, R. (2011). The turn to affect: A critique. *Critical Inquiry, 37*(3), 434–472.

Llera, F. J., & Leonisio, R. (2017). *La estrategia del miedo: ETA y la espiral del silencio.* Vitoria/Gasteiz: Centro Memorial de las Víctimas del Terrorismo.

López Romo, R. (2014). *Informe Foronda: Los contextos históricos del terrorismo en el País Vasco y la consideración social de sus víctimas 1968–2010.* Vitoria/Gasteiz: Instituto Valentín de Foronda.

Lury, C. (1998). *Prosthetic culture: Photography, memory and identity.* London: Routledge.

Maglione, G. (2017). Communities at large: An archaeological analysis of the 'community' within restorative justice policy and laws. *Critical Criminology, 25*(3), 453–469.

Ministerio del Interior (n.d.). *Centro Memorial para las Víctimas del Terrorismo.* Retrieved from www.interior.gob.es/web/servicios-al-ciudadano/ayudas-y-subvenciones/a-victimas-de-actos-terroristas/cuadernos-del-centro-memorial-de-las-victimas-del-terrorismo.

Montero, M. (2017, July 14). Nosotros, los culpables. *El Correo.* Retrieved from www.elcorreo.com/opinion/culpables-20170714002905-nt.html.

Naqvi, Y. (2006). The right to the truth in international law: Fact or fiction? *International Review of the Red Cross, 88*(862), 245–273.

Niebauer, A. M. (2017). Historical justice and memory. *Quarterly Journal of Speech, 103*(3), 1–4.

Oz, A. (2016). Prólogo. In H. Abad & F. Aramburu Irigoyen (Eds.), *Correspondencias.* Zarautz: Erein.

Özçelik, S. (2017). The analysis of Basque conflict and ETA in the 1990s: The kidnapping of Miguel Angel Blanco. *Journal of Human Sciences, 14*(2), 1058–1069.

Portela, E. (2016). *El eco de los disparos: Cultura y memoria de la violencia.* Barcelona: Galaxia Gutenberg.

Schult, T., & Popescu, D. I. (2016). *Revisiting Holocaust representation in the post-witness era.* Basingstoke: Palgrave Macmillan.

Secretaría de Paz y Convivencia (2014). *Retratos municipales de las vulneraciones del derecho a la vida en el caso vasco. Donostia/San Sebastián, 1960–2010. Documento informativo ofrecido a los ayuntamientos para facilitar el impulso de actuaciones memoriales y de reconocimiento a las víctimas.* Vitoria/Gasteiz:

Gobierno Vasco. Retrieved from www.irekia.euskadi.eus/uploads/attach ments/5609/Retrato_Donostia-SS_cas.pdf?1418828779.

Shaheed, F. (2014, January 23). Report of the special rapporteur in the field of cultural rights: *Memorialization processes*. *U.N. Doc. A/HRC/25/49*. Retrieved from http://webcache.googleusercontent.com/search?q=cache:Op18bWDA-OAJ:www. ohchr.org/EN/HRBodies/HRC/RegularSessions/Session25/Documents/A_ HRC_25_49_ENG.DOC+&cd=1&hl=nl&ct=clnk&gl=nl&client=firefox-b-ab.

Shepard, B. (n.d.). *Theory of affect*. Retrieved from http://csmt.uchicago.edu/ glossary2004/affect.htm.

Shouse, E. (2005). Feeling, emotion, affect. *M/C Journal*, 8(6). Retrieved from: http://journal.media-culture.org.au/0512/03-shouse.php.

Truth and Reconciliation Commission of South Africa (1998). *Report* (Volume 1). Retrieved from www.justice.gov.za/trc/report/finalreport/Volume%201.pdf.

Van den Broek, H. P. (2017). Labelling and legitimization: Justifying political violence in the Basque Country. *Terrorism and Political Violence*, 29(1), 119–136.

Varona Martínez, G. (2017). *Arte, memoria y justicia en victimizaciones graves: Adiorik gabe/Sin adiós. Un proyecto artístico de memoria local e individualizada abierto a la sociedad*. Bilbao: University of the Basque Country. Retrieved from http://dss2016.eu/images/Ebaluazioa/proyectos/ADIORIK-GABE/ARTE-MEMORIA-UPV-EHU-2017.pdf.

Victim Support Europe (2017). VSE's Vice-President Helgard van Hüllen speaks at EU Remembrance Day for victims of terrorism. Retrieved from http://victim support.eu/news/vice-president-of-victim-support-europe-speaks-at-eu-remembrance-day-for-victims-of-terrorism/.

Walklate, S., McGarry, R., & Mythen, G. (2014). Trauma, visual victimology and the poetics of justice. In M. H. Jacobsen (Ed.), *The poetics of crime: Understanding and researching crime and deviance through creative sources* (pp. 263–284). Surrey: Ashgate.

Werckmeister, O. K. (1996). Walter Benjamin's angel of history, or the transfiguration of the revolutionary into the historian. *Critical Inquiry*, 22(2), 239–267.

Whitfield, T. (2014). *Endgame for ETA: Elusive peace in the Basque Country*. London: Hurst & Company.

Zulaika, J., & Murua, I. (2017), How terrorism ends – and does not end: The Basque case. *Critical Studies on Terrorism*, 10(2), 338–356.

Chapter 7

Who speaks for the victim?

Experiences of migrants and refugees in Jenny Erpenbeck's novel *Go, Went, Gone* and Mikhail Shishkin's *Maidenhair*

Odile Heynders

> Stories are just things we fabricate, nothing more.
>
> (Viet Thanh Nguyen, 2017, *The Refugees*)

Introduction

On August 30, 2011, Italian journalist Gabriele del Grande posted a short video on his blog, *Fortress Europe*. The clip, entitled *We are the gray area*, shows a part of the city of Torino in which we see a CIE: Centre for Identification and Expulsion.[1] This 'iron cage' in the words of Del Grande, is encapsulated in a neighbourhood of middle-class apartment buildings, and the journalist points at how common citizens, from their balconies, have a view of the site but prefer to look the other way. With a reference to Primo Levi's 'gray zone',[2] a zone in which good and evil become mixed up, Del Grande accuses Italy of being indifferent and irresponsible: 'The gray area is Italy, country of the disinterested. The third element between victims and executioners, which gives body to both.'[3] By underlining this third element, Del Grande takes the notion of victim out of a binary system, as in victim *versus* perpetrator, and underlines the moral responsibility of the bystander. Following Del Grande, we could convey that thinking about the circumstances in which migrants are received and perceived in Europe implies rethinking the opposition of victim versus executor, migrant versus resident, clandestine people versus legal ones, etc. The eyewitness might look away but is still involved in legal procedures and ethical consequences. Del Grande's claim is that we can ask the spectator to assume a responsibility (cf. Butler, 2004, p. 129).

Del Grande's blogpost is supported by a series of journalistic reportages in which he investigates the deaths in the Mediterranean, published as *Mamadou va a morire* (Del Grande 2008 [2007]).[4] In one of the reports in this volume, 'Li ciuri – Die Blumen', Del Grande describes how he travelled to the Tadla Azilal region in Morocco, from which 27 young people departed to first take a trip to Libya and then to Italy. Six of them died when the boat they were on – 120 persons were travelling together – capsized in night of August 18, 2006, in the Strait of Sicily. The accident happened after a collision with an Italian naval vessel that was sent to rescue them. Fifty people drowned or went missing. Del Grande describes that families could not afford to get the bodies of their loved ones back to Morocco. The cost of the transfer was about €5000, but many families still had to pay for the loaned money that was used for the journey. The conclusion of the reportage is that those young people could have easily taken a plane to Italy – just about €200 by Royal Air Maroc – if they only had had a travel visa for Europe. According to Del Grande, poor North-African people do not get such a permit.[5]

Del Grande's journalistic work is on the victims of illegal immigration, it is about people travelling on unseaworthy boats organized by smugglers as part of the illegality industry (Andersson, 2014, p. 8). Journalism is based on facts and on serious information (Viner, 2017) and as such needs to be representative and fair. In this chapter, however, I will not focus on journalism but on two literary novels portraying migrants, and I will gauge how much knowledge of the experiences of migration we can find in them. The hypothesis is that novels as artistic texts are useful in the study of contemporary society not because they are 'serious' representations of facts, but rather because they approach a new space of politics and human awareness in-between the presentation of facts and the fictional invention of facts (Boletsi, De Mul, Hoving, & Minnard, 2015; Keren, 2015). Novels can be about facts, so to say, but they also mould facts into a specific imaginary scenario (Heynders & Bax, 2016). It is not my intention to start an in-depth analysis on aesthetic theory here,[6] but my point of departure is that contemporary literature creates a *Vorstellung*, which implies a faithful reflection of reality and, therefore, the invention of characters that stand for real people or certain kinds of human experience in the world. As such, the literary text delivers social knowledge and increases 'a deeper sense of everyday experiences and the shape of social life' (Felski, 2008, p. 83). The fictional dimension of literature can be hailed as the source of its cognitive strength.

This brings me to the specific material that I would like to explore in this chapter: two novels focusing on migrant experiences and asylum-seeker procedures. *Go, Went, Gone* (2017 [2015]) is written by German author Jenny Erpenbeck (b. 1968) and describes how refugees are received in Berlin. The novel is of significance because of the realistic characters created on the basis of interviews by the author with actual migrants. Even if the novel could at times be considered somewhat rigid, it is convincing in the critical and detailed way in which it represents and questions discourses and procedures in Germany. *Maidenhair* (2013 [2005]), written by Russian author Mikhail Shishkin, is a more complicated read, as it is a fictionalized account of interviews with imagined refugees, who tell about the atrocities they have suffered, or that they have fabulated, or heard from someone else. The novel, situated in Switzerland, opens a labyrinthine space of stories in stories on violence and war, and as such it brings the reader close to experiences of displacement and deportation.

It is the stylistic and spatial difference of the two novels that draws us, so is the main claim of my contribution, to understand various perceptions of victimhood and provide knowledge on experiences of migration. To build up this claim, I first argue that the literary authors take a critical position of identification when framing migrants as victims of political circumstances and economic scarcity. They represent as well as imagine the conditions in which migrants live, and they make it possible to acknowledge various individual stories. Second, it is argued that the knowledge provided by literary texts contributes to societal discussion on migration and at the same time makes an affective appeal to human solidarity.

In what follows, I will first briefly conceptualize the notions of migrant, refugee and victim. Subsequently, I will conduct a close reading of both novels, contextualizing my analyses with criticism on the novels. Then, I will focus on the epistemological status of literary novels and discuss how literature can offer knowledge in a context of researching social issues regarding migration and victimhood. Raymond Williams' notion of 'experience present' is crucial here, as is also underlined in the concluding remarks.

Playing out concepts

Reading Del Grande's work as well as the two literary novels on migration requires us to explain and interrogate the intertwined concepts of migrant, refugee and victim(hood).[7] Khalid Koser (2007) distinguishes three categorizations of the migrant. First, there is a difference between voluntary and forced migrants. The latter have to move because of conflict, persecution or environmental reasons. Forced migrants are often described as refugees or asylum-seekers. The second distinction is between people who move for political reasons and those moving for economic ones. They are usually described as labour migrants, and divided into low- and high-skilled people. In between them are migrants who move for social reasons: often women and children joining their husbands and fathers. The third category is the distinction between legal and illegal or irregular migrants, the so-called *sans papiers*, without, or with forged, documents. All these categorizations of migrants are fluid: someone can lose a job because of race or religion, and thus for political as well as economic reasons. There also is the phenomenon of return migration, people moving back to origin countries because political circumstances have changed. During the course of 2015, over a million refugees would come to Europe, where a coherent plan on how and where to receive these people was missing (Betts & Collier, 2017).

Migrants applying for international protection are still judged by the criteria of the United Nations Convention relating to the Status of Refugees. The core principle of this Geneva convention of 1951 is non-refoulement, which asserts that a refugee should not be returned to a country where they face serious threats to their life or freedom.[8] The principle as such is as relevant today as when it was first developed, but the international context has changed significantly, and the Geneva ideal seems not compatible anymore with the reality of large numbers of refugees moving from the poorer regions of the world to the richest, often organized by human traffickers (Betts & Collier, 2017).[9] The scale of migration currents from war-torn and mal-administered countries does not match the Geneva principles anymore, and is forcing the EU to rethink the policies and procedures in the context of the commitment to its 'responsibility to protect'.[10] Furthermore, as Betts and Collier (2017, p. 3) claim, while the European situation was absorbing political and media attention, 'the parallel tragedy was the neglect of the nearly 90 per cent of the world's refugees who remained in the developing world'. There is no clear strategy for the future of a global refugee system.

Some scholars argue that humans have always migrated and that there have been refugees for as long as there have been political communities (Betts & Collier, 2017; Evans Braziel, 2008; Nederveen Pieterse, 2009; Sollund, 2012), others emphasize the current increase in numbers due to mobile phones and mobile money. In the 1960s, major refugee populations were on the move as a result of decolonization (Koser, 2007). In the 1970s many refugees had to leave nations in South-East Asia; in the 1990s refugee flows (ethnic and religious) were generated in the former Yugoslavia as well as in the Horn of Africa, Rwanda, Afghanistan and East Timor. Today there are the refugees from the civil war in Syria, economic refugees from Nigeria and other African countries, the Rohingya as religious refugees in Burma, and so on. The United Nations estimated that by the year 2006 there were 200 million international migrants.[11] Betts and Collier (2017, pp. 6–7) refer to the fact that the majority of refugees today are fleeing not because of persecution by their state, but because of disorder and breakdown of the state. They claim that refugees 'should be entitled to expect three things: rescue, autonomy, and an eventual route out of limbo'. In this context of disorder migrant-smuggling has become big business. Human trafficking is a new form of illegal migration or even modern slavery. Trafficking has become a profitable industry.[12] According to a CNN documentary[13] there are slave auctions in Libya, a chaotic transit state for tens of thousands of migrants seeking to reach Europe.

In addition to sociological and anthropological studies on migration, Thomas Nail (2015) offers a political-theory perspective, and researches the migrant as an abstract figure of movement who can be characterized as 'the floating population, the homeless, the stateless, the *lumpenproletariat*, the nomad, the immigrant, the emigrant, the refugee, the vagrant, the undocumented, and the barbarian' (Nail, 2015, p. 11). Nail claims that figures of the migrant emerge and coexist throughout history relative to specific sites of expulsion and mobility: 'just as there are different types of societies, so there are different types of migrants, different degrees of mobility, and different forces of expulsion' (Nail, 2015, p. 15). The figure of the migrant therefore is not a fixed identity or specific person but a mobile social position.

The third concept that requires clarification in the context of this chapter is victim. According to the *Oxford Dictionary*, the term implies a person harmed, injured or killed as a result of a crime, accident or action, and can also refer to someone who feels helpless and passive in the face of misfortune or ill-treatment. Victims, indeed, are the people who drowned in the boat accident in the Strait of Sicily, but not all migrants are victims, or experience being victims in the same sense.[14] Many migrants are traumatized because of the circumstances of war and disorder in their country or because of the unsafe travel experiences. Conceptualizing migrants as victims, however, may have negative consequences, as Williams conveys: 'it may be demeaning and disempowering for migrants themselves, may not reflect their actual self-perception and create an inaccurate image of migrants in a society' (Williams, 2014, p. 438). More and more researchers and support institutions transform a victim-discourse pointing at passiveness, loss and ongoing suffering into the recognition of migrant's strengths, agency and independence. But having power and being strong on the other hand does not mean that someone is not victimized in the manifestation of a specific context of reception. Staying in an asylum-centre with no work options and no official papers, makes people dependent and depressed (Al Galidi, 2016). Indeed, refugees have various identities and sometimes feel a victim while at other times they might feel a survivor.

In sum, migrant, refugee and victim are converging notions referring to various movements and experiences of individual human beings who have left their home region to find a safe haven. Migrants are mobile figures in a specific political history and situation, who in today's globalized and digitalized world are becoming more and more visible. We see migrants on our television screens, in newspapers and on the internet. But we do not often hear about their personal stories and circumstances; we mostly observe that they are part of a group, entering in boats, crossing borders as long rows of people. The individual background and narrative of the migrant is often missing, and that hinders our knowledge as well as empathy.

This is where literature comes in and is indispensable. Both Erpenbeck and Shishkin represent and create personal stories of migrants, and demonstrate how various stories differ but also refer to similar experiences. The literary authors bridge the gap between residents and newcomers by telling narratives of both sides. Most plainly, this is the case in the novel *Go, Went, Gone*, in which various refugees arriving in Berlin are portrayed from the third-person narrative perspective of Richard, an emeritus professor of classical philology. The German professor deliberately collects the various ordeals from the migrants he meets in a temporary asylum centre. He asks the travellers personal and very specific questions. In *Maidenhair*, the protagonist works as an interpreter in the Swiss migration service, where he translates hearings for political asylum seekers. Transcripts of the hearings get intertwined with other personal stories, and with the classical histories of Darius and Artaxerxes that the interpreter reads at home. Images from one story appear in another, figures seem to transcend place and time: migrants from a former Soviet republic run into an Ancient Greek army. One (unhappy) love story mixes up with the other. As such, both literary novels construct an image of migrants as victims of political systems as well as courageous individuals who take a life-changing decision to leave home. Rather than drawing a sharp distinction between the mobile migrant and permanent resident, the one a victim and the other living a comfortable life, Erpenbeck's and Shishkin's novels can be read as an exploration of various experiences of belonging, moving and transforming in a contemporary European space marked by history and global conflicts. The authors demonstrate how people negotiate between various categorizations of migrants as well as various identities, and how tensions emerge between self-perspective and external frames. In the following two sections I will elaborate on this, while engaging in a close reading of both novels.

Dialogues: refugees in *Go, Went, Gone*

The central narrative of Erpenbeck's novel is a story of borders and separation. Jenny Erpenbeck (b. 1967) was born in the former East Germany and still lives in Berlin. The narrative is closely focalized around Richard's experience, giving us a particular perspective on migration in the city of Berlin after the reunification. The reader becomes part of Richard's world, of the monotony of everyday life, and his growing interest in the newcomers from Africa. Richard – without surname, so as to partly underline his identity as Everyman – first notices the refugees when they are on television in a reportage on their hunger strike at Oranienplatz, and a few weeks later starts meeting them after they have moved to an old nursing home in his neighbourhood. The narrative is told chronologically in 55 chapters covering almost one year (from August to the next summer).

Richard's decision to speak to the migrants is driven by his own feeling of dislocation and loss of time: he has lost his wife, is retired, and also feels alienated in Berlin after the wall has been pulled down. Although he has been living in the same house for decades, in the 1990s he 'suddenly found himself a citizen of a different country, from one day to the next, though the view out the window remained the same' (Erpenbeck, 2017 [2015], p. 81). The experience of estrangement and the doubt about 'the actual nature of time' (p. 38) determines his plan to convene with the migrants, and ask them open and simple, and sometimes even silly questions. 'It is important he asks the right questions. And the right questions aren't always the ones you put into words' (p. 39), Richard realizes when drawing up a catalogue of questions. The third-person focalization or internal focalization[15] draws the reader in as if having an ongoing self-conversation:

> To investigate how one makes the transition from a full, readily comprehensible existence to the life of a refugee, which is open in all directions – drafty, as it were – he has to know what was at the beginning, what was in the middle, and what is now. At the border between a person's life and the other life lived by that same person, the transition has to be visible – a transition that, if you look closely enough, is nothing at all.
>
> (Erpenbeck, 2017 [2015], p. 39)

Richard, used to doing research as an academic, starts reading books and articles in preparation for the conversations and explores the map of Africa. Erpenbeck makes clear that this educated European philologer as a matter of fact knows little about Africa, about the different nations, capitals and the languages spoken. 'The languages in northern Nigeria include Yoruba and Hausa. Yoruba? Hausa? The Yoruba are mostly Christians. Rashid is Yoruba and Muslim' (p. 47). Erpenbeck ingeniously uses Richard's naiveté as well as his academic strategies to put assorted information on refugees in her novel. Richard is uninformed and unexperienced, even after a life as university professor, 'Richard has read Foucault and Baudrillard, and also Hegel and Nietzsche, but he doesn't know what you can eat when you have no money to buy food' (p. 64). The migrants that Richard meets and talks to did not have an extensive education, but they know how to survive on the streets after having experienced suffering and disaster. Some migrants have lost children, some saw parents being killed, some watched from boats as friends drowned. Once they entered Europe, they were safe, but not allowed to work or develop themselves. Erpenbeck underlines this absurdity by describing Richard reading the 'Dublin II regulation',[16] an EU document from 2013 requiring that someone arriving in the EU has to request asylum in the first country they reach – thus putting the burden on countries such as Italy and Greece with long sea borders that are hard to police. To educated Richard, the document is so complicated that it takes him a day to understand that it 'doesn't concern itself with the questions of whether or not these men are victims of war' (p. 66). The document, as Richard recognizes, 'allows all the European countries without a Mediterranean coastline to purchase the right not to have to listen to the stories of the arriving refugees' (p. 67). Richard ponders that the Italian laws have different borders in mind than do the German laws, and he realizes that these laws imply another type of border than the tangible one he knows from his Berlin background: fortified barriers, barbed wire, sharp control procedures. What is changed is that the 'law has made a shift from physical reality to the realm of language' (p. 68). The legal language and internal differences between European countries have nothing to do with the actual disorder and civil wars that the migrants are escaping from.

Various conversations make up the narrative of the book. I refer to some of them here. The first conversation partner is Rashid from Nigeria, a 'burly fellow' (p. 47), who wants to work but is not allowed to. The scene takes place in one of the rooms in the red-brick building that is now a refugee centre; the men sit on the bed – there aren't any chairs – and the television is on. Rashid's story comes out in fragments, and Richard – and the reader – have to fill in the missing pieces. Erpenbeck, effectively, tries to avoid melodrama, but in the fragments of speech the experiences talked about are heart-breaking. Richard asks the simple questions from his catalogue, and in their silliness they open a space for telling about lived experiences:

> Did you go to school? Rashid couldn't swim. He grabbed onto a cable, and this is how he remained above water. Zair can't swim either, but as the boat began to tip upside down, he climbed over the edge of the boat sticking up in the air to its underside, and from there he was rescued. What kind of place did you like to hide when you were a child? But 550 out of 800 drowned. The TV now shows a large number of fish on a conveyor belt, women's hands in rubber gloves pick up each fish and in just a few seconds slice it into filets with a large knife. In Hamburg they ran into each other again, Rashid and Zair, and recognized each other at once.
>
> (p. 47)

Erpenbeck uses the narrative technique of the intertwining of discourses that the Russian literary scholar M.M. Bakhtin called 'quasi-direct speech'. This implies that authorial and character intentions are combined in a single intentional hybrid. The discourse belongs in its emotional structure to a represented character, whose inner speech is transmitted and regulated by the author (Bakhtin, 2008 [1981], p. 433). Whereas Erpenbeck creates Richard and Rashid as literary characters, she refers to the actual experiences of migrants travelling from North Africa to Lampedusa, as is evidenced by many newspaper articles published in the last decade.[17]

A second migrant story comes from a young man, whom Richard gives the name Apollo, because he imagines the Greek god would look like this. Richard meets him in another room of the brick building. The story connected to this boy, however, is not heroic or godlike at all. The boy comes from the desert and was forced by the Tuareg people to work as a slave 'for as long as he could remember' (p. 52). Importantly, this is one of the few places in the book in which the third persons focalization is disrupted and transformed into free focalization, where the narrator knows more than the character. We enter the mind of Apollo, who ponders what he could tell the stranger and if he should show him the scars on his body left by beatings. Apollo reveals details about ordinary life – how they traversed the desert on camels – but he does not tell about the traumatic experiences.

Awad Issa (called Tristan by Richard) is the third conversation partner. He comes from Ghana, his mother died giving birth to him, and he was brought up by his grandmother and later by his father who worked in Tripoli as a driver for an oil company. 'My father told me who I am,' Awad says. But then the father was shot, Awad was taken by the military to a camp and was later put on a boat to Italy. He arrived in Sicily, worked for some days in a kitchen and then could afford to travel to Germany. He ended up in the campsite on the Berlin square, where other refugees gave him something to eat and a place to sleep. 'Oranienplatz provided for him, as his father had provided for him in Libya' (p. 65). Later in the book, there is again a focalization switch, and we read the perceptions from Awad's perspective. He looks at 'the older gentleman, who is very polite but perhaps also crazy' noting down in his notebook what is in Awad's bag, what the boy packed for the journey. Awad imagines then that the man is his father and tells him what to do.

Hermes, Karon, and other men – significantly, there are no women among Richard's conversation partners – share their stories as well. Slowly, Richard develops relationships that go further than the conversations. So, in the case of Osaboro, an 18-year-old boy wearing a jacket that is much too thin for a German October, he is invited to Richard's house to play the piano. Richard notes the scars on his arm. After a few hours Richard takes a map of Berlin and shows Osaboro how to walk back to the refugee home, but the boy does not understand how to read the map:

> He sees Osaboro trying to understand the map, and then he knows that Osaboro, who travelled from Niger by way of Libya to Italy, and then from Italy to Berlin, has never before seen a map of any city or country on earth.
>
> (p. 123)

When the Berlin Senate decides that the refugees have to move again, from the old nursing home to a proper asylum-seekers' facility in Spandau, the migrants protest heavily but finally accept the move. Once in Spandau, things are 'normal' due to the fact that here there are families and children. Rashid organizes jobs without pay: raking leaves in the park, mopping floors in schools, washing dishes in a community centre. In Spandau, the first official applications for a residency permit start. Up until this moment the refugees only had a *Fiktionsbescheinigung*, a document that Richard related to 'the English word *fiction*', but then came to understand that 'this *certificate of fiction* was merely a confirmation that this person existed who had not been granted the right to call himself a *refugee*' (p. 82). Erpenbeck, via Richard, demonstrates that German bureaucracy is ridiculous: the certificate itself does not entitle its holder to any rights.[18] Now the migrants have to apply to the Foreigners office, have to have an interview and prove that they are not coming from safe countries. Osaboro returns to Italy to renew his papers, and has to pay €680 for tickets, an address to stay and the fee. Only then can he get the *permesso di soggiorno* that he needs for health insurance and for the refugee application in Germany.

On Christmas Eve, Richard invites Rashid to his home and lets him choose a winter jacket from the closet. In the room decorated with a Christmas tree and Advent candles Rashid tells about his life in Tripoli, and how one day war broke out and he had to flee with his children. They were kept in barracks for a few days and then forced onto a boat that stayed at sea for almost two weeks. The boat collapsed when a rescue vessel finally brought food and water. The boat tipped over, many people drowned. Rashid lost both his children. The story is heartbreaking and unbearable. After having listened to this cruel survival narrative, Richard asks Rashid (again) a simple question, namely to draw a sketch of the gate he was working on at the day of the deportation. Rashid starts doing this:

> He draws, corrects, goes on drawing, until Richard can clearly recognize what the gate looked like that Rashid had built for his final commission in his life as a metal worker, a gate that surely still guards the entrance of some property in Libya.
>
> (p. 194)

It is a question that helps Rashid to overcome grief, and to transcend his identity as victim and guilty father.

Later, 12 migrants are removed from Spandau due to the fact that their applications for asylum are not correct. Richard is flabbergasted by the force that is used, 'forty heavily armed men are [...] necessary to remove twelve African refugees from a residential facility, not to mention the other 150 or so police officers waiting in the squad cars' (p. 209). Richard knows that the newspapers will complain about the money spent on this exercise. It again demonstrates the absurdity of the system.

Over the course of months, Richard gets more and more physically involved in the lives of the migrants. He buys a portable piano for Osaboro, he takes care of Rashid, reads Dante with Rufu and takes the man to the dentist, and he buys property in Ghana for Karon's family. Richard's ordinary life continues as well: he socializes with friends, and delivers a lecture in Frankfurt. In February, letters from the Foreign office arrive and – in accordance with the Dublin agreement – all the men who have arrived via Italy are sent back there: 'the legal responsibility for the men who landed in Italy is borne by Italy alone' (p. 265). Rufu, Apollo, Tristan, Karon and even Rashid have to go. But 'where can a person go when he doesn't know where to go?' Erpenbeck writes this question on two pages full of white (pp. 266–267), marking its importance and ulti-mate simplicity.

In the final part, the ordinary Berliner people become active. The church houses seven men in a small apartment, other migrants are taken by minis-ters and congregation members in their own homes, 12 people find a place in Richard's house, and in the end 147 out of 476 men have found a place to sleep. The book ends with a summer party in Richard's garden. It is a promising, even utopian final scene of a realist narrative. The dislocations of Richard as Berlin resident and of the refugees as people on the move have turned into a form of permanent temporariness or temporary togeth-erness. Importantly, the migrants still have dreams, and Richard finally has the courage to look back on his marriage and the memory of his late wife. Whereas in the beginning of the novel, the migrants on Oranienplatz asked for attention by writing 'We become visible' on a piece of cardboard, at the end of the book they are seen and met and addressed. They are visible to Berlin residents and the friends and acquaintances of Richard. Being visible means being present and being included in a community. Reading this, I would argue in line with Eileen Battersby (2017) in the *Guardian*,[19] will make readers more alert, more aware, and more human in regard to the migrant issue in Europe.

Two contrasting reviews in the German press qualified the novel on the one hand as *Stand der Dinge* ('State of the Art') and on the other as *Wohlstandsbürger-Klischees* ('upper-class clichés'). In a very positive piece, Elke Schmitter (2015) wrote that the book does not offer solutions but *aktiven Ratlosigkeit* ('active desperateness') about events happening in today's society. Facts in the novel and in the world are the same, but Erpenbeck succeeds in being the author and not a documentary maker. In 'high art' she establishes a balance. In the other review, Dana Buchzik (2015) praises the documentary passages in the novel as important contri-bution to the refugee debate. Negative, however, is the figure of the prot-agonist with his colonial mindset, who profits from the refugees. Taking the two reviews as exemplary for the reception of this novel, I would argue that the fact that the book invites contrasting interpretations and evaluations, is a proof that it is ambivalent and demanding – such as Joseph Conrad's *Heart of Darkness* is – and thus relevant. More important however, and as both reviews underline, is the fact that the book is written on the edge of reality and fiction, deliberately mixing facts and imagination. As such, it demands a negotiation of various framing and identification strategies. Before I elaborate on this, I will first deal with the second novel.

Heteroglossia: Q&A in *Maidenhair*

Maidenhair, written by the Russian writer Mikhail Shishkin (b. 1961), who moved to Zurich in 1995 and now lives in Berlin,[20] is the opposite of the realist documentary novel Erpenbeck wrote. Shishkin's narrative is experimental as well as fragmented and goes constantly back and forward in time. It seems as if the stories told are contingently connected and randomly put aside or taken back. Some stories are dramatic and documentary, others are historical or diary-like. A huge part of the book has the structure of 'Question and Answer', as such representing the asylum intake in Switzerland. The protagonist of the narrative works as an interpreter at a Swiss asylum centre, just as Shishkin himself has done. The official of the centre is a man called Peter Fisher, and the protagonist mediates between Fisher and the various asylum seekers. At the beginning of the book the procedure looks like a standard one:

> Question: Have you ever engaged in political or religious activity?
> Answer: No.
> Question: Have you ever been tried or investigated?
> Answer: No.
> Question: Have you ever sought asylum in other countries?
> Answer: No.
>
> (Shishkin, 2013 [2005], p. 6)

But, in due course, questions and answers get disconnected, and the stories told get more absurd, cruel and incomprehensible. Some of the asylum seekers tell accounts of persecution, corruption and humiliation somewhere in the east of Europe (Kazakhstan, Chechnya), others make deliberate intertextual connections to historical texts, so that what they are telling is in fact (part of) a story told or written by someone else. The point, I would argue, is that it is not clear whose individual story is told in a specific asylum procedure. Individuals are always related to others and the stories, reports and perspectives of others. In one of the accounts of life in a prison camp, there is no sharp distinction between being a victim or perpetrator of violence: 'In prison, they rape men convicted of gang-raping minors. It's violence, but that way justice prevails' (p. 76). In this specific case, the interrogator fills in for the interviewee. As a consequence, the whole procedure of asking questions and formulating answers gets disrupted, questions are extended and become answers and vice versa:

> Question: Let's take a break.
> Answer: What do you mean? Don't you believe brigands fell on us?
> Question: I don't know. There's no finding out who you really are anyway. You walk into this fishery office [there are photographs of sport fishing on the walls of the office, OH], you tell us what did and didn't happen, you stammer, gasp, sniffle, and weep, you show your notes from hospitals, you roll up your sweater and shirt to show your scars, as if someone could believe you were hung up on a hook, you ask for a drink of water, you wipe your tears and snot with tissues, a pack of which is always in front of you on the table, you don't know what to do with your hands, you chew your nails and dig at your hangnails, scratch the mosquito bite on your ankle, but in actual fact there is no real you.
>
> (p. 133)

This could be the sceptical voice of the official Peter, but it could also be the one of the interpreter. The questioner becomes sarcastic, uninterested and disengaged. The asylum-seeker stories need to be convincing, but how can one be sure of truthfulness when the stories are de-contextualized in the Swiss office? Importantly, refugee claims have to be justified or otherwise the *rejected* stamp will be put on the case file.

Stories and voices of asylum seekers intertwine in the course of the book with those of the interpreter himself, who reads Greek historical texts and writes emails to his son. The interpreter has experienced an unhappy love story with a woman, Isolde, the mother of his son. This story forms a second thread in the narrative. It shows how the interpreter, when he still was in the relationship, was traumatized by his work. At a party with friends he showed a video shot by the Chechens in which torture, beheading and rape of a pregnant woman are performed. The interpreter watched stoically, while the guests left. The issue of victimhood is pivotal here. Certainly, the murdered people are victims, but the interpreter seems to be a victim as well.

In opposition to the stories on cruel and violent experiences told by male asylum seekers, a third storyline, evidently the most conventionally written one, is the diary and narrative of a Russian singer and actress, Isabella Danilowna Jurjewa. The interpreter reads her diary in his free time because he aims to write her biography. Jurjewa, actually, is a historical figure, she lived from 1899–2000, and her diary reads like a sentimental female adolescent's writing. She is in love, she goes to the theatre, her loved one dies, she meets another man, and so on. It is a very stereotypical early twentieth century female story, the opposite of all the discourses on violence expressed by the male asylum seekers. Shishkin, of course, in weaving this thread through the narrative invites us to think about fact and fiction, experienced and real events, heard and made up stories, and male and female voices. All the stories are linked to each other in their combination of sadness and joy, brutality and hope, virility and vulnerability (Meek, 2012). As is stated by the interpreter in one of the Q&A sessions: 'None of this is the real thing. Your story is the groom and you're the bride. Stories choose the person and start wandering' (p. 121).

Page after page the stories with distinctive styles, memories, Greek histories and actual descriptions intertwine. Motives from one story reappear in another, images from the singer's narrative appear in the asylum hearings. Poignant portraits of Russian military misbehaviour, and of innocent fellows without any luck in their life come together. The actual process of interpretation and translation is described in detail, for instance in a scene in a Swiss prison when the interpreter has to assists a young female lawyer and they have to interrogate a typical refugee from Belarus, 'immer die gleichen Geschichte' and 'immer heissen sie Sergej Ivanov' the interpreter claims. Ivanov has received a 'negative' long ago, but is still in Switzerland and making trouble. He affronts the interpreter,

> 'Take you, interpreter, you phony, you've got yourself all set up here, but maybe I want to live like a human being too! What makes you better than me? Maybe you're even worse! Except you've got clean clothes and smell like cologne, while I have nothing to change into.'
> 'Was Sagt er?' Frau P. asked.
> 'Das gehört nicht zur Sache', the interpreter replied.
> 'Ich möchte, dass Sie alles überstezen', she said.
> 'Gut.' And the interpreter began interpreting everything the other man said for her.
>
> (p. 377)

The switch from English (originally Russian) to German underscores how in this type of interviews many languages are used, and create space between the words spoken and intended. The interpreter in the institutional space talks German to the lawyer, and in another space talks Russian to the prisoner. The third person in the interview setting is excluded from what the other two discuss.

The maidenhair of the title is a fern that grows wild among the Roman ruins the interpreter visited with his former wife. The idea is that the weed grew there before the city was built and will continue growing; spores spread and new plants appear. The fern spreads as stories spread and migrants dwell. The book ends with the story of the Russian singer who is pregnant and in Italy. It is not a closure of the narrative, but an open ending, hallucinating as well as drifting away. The typical Russian details and nostalgia on the one hand, as well as the universality of themes such as love, war and memory on the other, refer, I would argue, at one theme that is dominating: the preservation of human dignity is important, even in harsh circumstances. Ultimately, we are connected, and there is not much difference between the refugee and the interpreter.

Even though Shishkin is a renowned writer who has received prestigious prizes and is considered one of the most prominent writers in contemporary Russian literature,[21] just like Erpenbeck's *Go, Went, Gone*, Shishkin's novel received very positive as well as critical reviews. Phoebe Taplin (2013) praised the 'great novel' in which the interlocking narratives fuse and an unbearable intensity can be experienced as metaphors sprout and writhe. She states that the various stories become aspects of a shared human experience. Dutch literary critic and respected writer Cyrille Offermans (2015) characterizes Shishkin as 'a universalist' whereas 'we are the asylum seekers'. But Offermans does not appreciate the moralism '*a la russe*' and the holistic idea that everything is connected to everything else. Furthermore, he disapproves of the parts on Jurjewa as too sentimental, while he also thinks that irony and stylistic superiority are missing in the book.

Maidenhair clearly is a work of experimental fiction, and, I would argue, interrogates the status of fiction. James Meek (2012) in the *London Review of Books* claims that the book 'stretches the definition of the novel' since the 'enveloping structure of Shishkin's work is not so much a story as a prose portfolio, an exhibition you walk through in a particular order because that's the way the pages are put together, as you might walk clockwise round a gallery'. Whereas Erpenbeck in her book uses plain facts and real events in the fictional framing of the protagonist, Shishkin imagines and invents stories that also have a link to today's reality in the sense that asylum procedures are taking place in many countries. Shishkin's novel as experimental and fragmented fiction keeps further away from reality than Erpenbeck's more obvious documentary novel. Readers, however, have to negotiate between the fiction and reality parts, and have to accept and recognize or identify with the characters and their stories. Thus, both books give insight in the experiences of migrants as victims – experiences of dislocation, misunderstanding, loss and separation from everyday life.

Martha C. Nussbaum in *Poetic Justice* (1995, p. xvi) underlines how literary imagination invites an ethical stance that asks readers to concern themselves with the good of other people whose lives are distant from their own. As such, fictional literature has the potential to make a contribution to public reasoning in general. I would take this one step further, and argue that in the context of researching migrants and victimhood, we need to implement the analysis of literature because it helps to experience what people have gone through and are undergoing today. The process of experiencing by the reader of the book – the sharing of experience, so to say – acquires identification instigating critical reflection. It is in Raymond Williams' famous keywords, in his description of experience, that we find a relevant conceptualization. Williams distinguishes 'experience past' (as lessons) from 'experience present' (as full and active awareness). They are different but connected. Experience present

> involves an appeal to the whole consciousness, the whole being, as against rehance on more spezialized [sic] or more limited states or faculties. [...] The strength of this appeal to wholeness, against forms of thought which would exclude certain kinds of consciousness as merely 'personal', 'subjective' or 'emotional', is evident.
>
> (Williams, 1985, p. 127)

Literature as social knowledge

The two novels that I focus on in this chapter lead us to the heart of Europe, marked by history – the breaking up of the Soviet Union as well as the disappearance of the Iron Curtain and socialism in East Germany – and the present: the arrival of large numbers of global migrants in search of safety, autonomy and a good life. Hundreds of thousands of people-on-the-move are entering the EU, travelling on migration routes that are constantly being reshaped, and ending up at places where they often are not visible or seen by others. Researchers such as ethnographers, anthropologists and sociologists study the circumstances of actual migrants as well as the resilience of society and communities, using methods of observation, interview, survey and so on. My argument is that literary scholars should take a role in this research context as well, and bring in literary close reading analyses in order to give an insight into personal experiences and the diversity of narratives. Following Williams, the experiences we talk about are both experiences past (lessons) and experience present (awareness). The idea is that the reader of the book acknowledges the difference.

Many literary scholars emphasize ambiguity and ambivalence as characteristic of literature. Boletsi, De Mul, Hoving and Minnard (2015) refer to the 'lightness of literature' implying that fiction and imagination are not representations of 'real' problems or 'real' historical events, but are in the first place language and as such ephemeral. Fiction is 'not serious', and therefore it is relevant in the context of the public debate just because it is not a journalistic account. My position, obviously, is different. In the context of my reading of the two novels, I do take the literary texts as a hermeneutic warning system about what is currently happening in the world. The two books help us to become aware of social practices that we take for granted, the attitudes towards refugees, and to learn from the stories and memories of individual migrants. The two books open perspectives on personal narratives. Referring to Richard Rorty (1989), rhetorical questions that could be asked are: do we really know what is happening in today's society? Does it help to establish an imaginative identification with the details of others' lives? The argument I propose is, that literary data on migrant experiences can be distinguished from data found in ethnographic, anthropological or sociological (empirical) research, in that literary data can reveal what people think, imagine and (do or do not) say. In particular, the devices of focalization (through whose eyes are we seeing the events in the narrative) and chronotope (time–space density) can be explored and exploited in order to understand individual narratives, even when told by an author/narrator using imagination.

This pushes us to reflect on what we learn (experience past) and what we become aware of (experience present) when reading the two novels in the context of migrant research. I sum up my observations.

- It is difficult to share a coherent story, because of trauma or shame, or because it is impossible to describe the world left behind and the unsafe trajectory taken. Telling in fragments, in disruptive sentences, often seems the only adequate form of speech for refugees as victims.
- The categorization of migrants has not much to do with their reality; most migrant narratives are about fragility and force and not having the right papers, or not being informed about the right procedures. At which moment does victimhood start and when does it stop?
- How to ask questions? The questions in standard protocols do not always lead to clear answers or to the relevant information. Direct and simple questions, however, seem more inviting. These can open a dialogue.
- Stories about migration and victimhood lead to other stories. Most of the time there is no conclusion to a story, there is no specific beginning or closure. The story is not over once the voice stops telling.
- Not all migrants are victims or consider themselves a victim. But clearly many of them are hurt, vulnerable, sad, lost and displaced. Not doing a practical job or something useful is frustrating. Sleep is comforting.
- Most migrants are male, and their discourses and stories are also from a male perspective – that becomes clear when we see those stories confronted with the diary of a young woman. Are interviewers aware of this gender void?
- Most refugees already speak various languages, what is the point of learning a new language if one does not know if one can stay?
- Reality should be opened to imagination and the other way around. The edge between fiction, fabulation, traumatized reframing, and feigning is fluid. Asking about 'real' facts is irrelevant when an interview is about what people have experienced. Closing off literature

from the real world – encapsulating high art as autonomous artefact or as 'lightness' – is irrelevant as well.

To make this last observation more clear. The all too utopian scene with which Erpenbeck's book ends, situating migrants in Richard's home after they did not have a place to go to, relates to real practices. The final scene of the novel refers to grassroots movements that currently can be observed in many European cities. In Amsterdam there is the 'We Are Here' movement,[22] born from the 2012 protest camp in Amsterdam-Osdorp. People gathered together in tents in an empty city space, as they did not have legal papers, and thus could not identify or prove where they came from. Consequently, they could not go back, neither could they move forward in the Dutch asylum procedure. Since 2012 this group of about 200 people has moved from one temporary place to another supported by individuals, church organizations and sympathizers. They have their own website to make themselves visible, and to show that they are still on the move and change place every few months, so as to underline Erpenbeck's universal question: where can a person go when he doesn't know where to go?

Conclusion: giving voice to victims

Today, many literary writers are interested in the issue of migration, and represent and imagine in their novels the lives of people on the move. The two writers discussed in this chapter are a case in point, they explore the conditions under which refugees speak about what they have experienced in their home regions and on the route to Western Europe. They give their characters voice, they create a speaking personality, a speaking consciousness. A voice, as Bakhtin explained, always has a will or desire behind it, its own timbre and overtones (Bakhtin, 2008 [1981], p. 434). It is relevant is that both authors use facts and information from the 'real' world in their voicing; they represent the real world, but at the same time they mould the world into a fiction in order to experience (past and present, cf. Williams, 1985 [1976]) perceptions of migration. The literary novel invents a *Vorstellung*, an imaginary scenario, of what happens and could happen in society, and as such the novel invites readers to become aware of what the literary characters have gone through, and to identify with them.

The two novels that were read in this chapter demonstrate that refugees are victims of circumstances of civil war, disorder and violence. Many of them are traumatized and not capable of telling about their experiences in a plain way. And the conditions under which migrants live, once they have entered Europe, are not really comforting and peaceful as well: without papers and the right entrance administration forms, people are denied a place to stay. Refugees often get stuck in bureaucratic procedures. In sociological and political studies categorizations of migrant figures are established in order to understand the diverse motives and practices of moving and to analyse the various institutional procedures of receiving people. In the reading of the novels, the categorizations disappear and become fluid, and the personal stories emerge as far more significant than institutional reports.

In consequence, I argue that literature-research can make a relevant contribution to interdisciplinary research projects on migration and victimhood. Literary authors take a critical position of identification when framing migrants as victims of political circumstances and economic scarcity. Furthermore, they represent as well as imagine the conditions in which migrants live, and they make it possible to acknowledge and experience various individual stories. Literature offers social knowledge as ground for reasoning and identification. As Williams (1985 [1976], p. 129) wrote 'in the deepest sense of experience all kinds of evidence and its consideration should be tried'. Eileen Battersby (2017), the reviewer of Erpenbeck's novel underlined the same idea:

> Great fiction doesn't have to be real, but it does have to be true. Erpenbeck's powerful tale, delivered in a wonderfully plain, candid tone, is both real and true. It will alert readers, make us more aware and, it is to be hoped, more human.

Notes

1 See http://fortresseurope.blogspot.nl/2011/08/we-are-gray-area.html (accessed October 2017).
2 As Giorgio Agamben (2002, p. 21) described in *Remnants of Auschwitz*, the discovery made by Primo Levi is that the grey zone is a place in which the long chain of conjunction between victim and executioner becomes loose, the oppressed becomes oppressor and the executioner in turn appears victim. Good and evil, and 'all the metals of traditional ethics reach their point of fusion'. See also Primo Levi (1989), *The Drowned and the Saved*.
3 See http://fortresseurope.blogspot.nl/2011/08/we-are-gray-area.html (translation Camilla Gamba).
4 I use the German translation *Mamadou Fahrt in den Tod, Die Tragödie der irregularen Migranten in Mittelmeer* (Karlsruhe: Von Loeper Literaturverlag, 2008).
5 'Aber nicht alle bekommen eben ein Einreisvisum für Europa. Besonders nicht die Kinder der Armen' (Del Grande, 2008 [2007], p. 40).
6 See Christopher Prendergast (2000), *The Triangle of Representation*.
7 See also Heynders (2017).
8 See www.unhcr.org/1951-refugee-convention.html (accessed November 2017).
9 See www.theguardian.com/commentisfree/2016/jan/18/geneva-refugee-convention-crisis-demand-eu (accessed December 2017).
10 See www.responsibilitytoprotect.org (accessed December 2017).
11 See 'Preface' in Evans Braziel (2008).
12 See www.theguardian.com/world/2017/nov/26/emmanuel-macron-visits-africa-human-trafficking-slavery (accessed December 2017).

13 See http://edition.cnn.com/specials/africa/libya-slave-auctions (accessed December 10, 2017).
14 Experience, as Raymond Williams (1985 [1976]) explained is 'the fullest, most open, most active kind of consciousness, and it includes feeling as well as thought'.
15 I follow James Phelan (2005, p. 111) in *Living to Tell about It*: 'Internal focalization: center of consciousness narration such as we find in the fiction of Henry James, where the narrator perceives and knows only what the central consciousness perceives and knows'. Only a few times does Erpenbeck implement 'free focalization', where the narrator perceives and knows more than the main character, e.g. in Richard's first conversation with a young boy from Niger, who has never known his parents, who grew up in the desert as a slave of the Tuareg people, and who seems traumatized (Erpenbeck, 2017 [2015], pp. 52–53). Another example is when Richard is at a party and various conversations and discourses are intertwined (pp. 70–71).
16 See www.refworld.org/pdfid/4445fe344.pdf (accessed December 2017).
17 See news articles such as www.theguardian.com/world/2015/apr/14/400-drowned-libya-italy-migrant-boat-capsizes (accessed December 2017) and www.reuters.com/article/us-europe-migrants-egypt-ship-specialrep/special-report-500-migrants-drowned-at-sea-no-one-investigated-idUSKBN13V1DE (accessed December 2017).
18 This is what it entails: ein so genannte Fiktionsbescheinigung wird Personen ausgestellt, die sich in Deutschland aufhalten und die Erteilung oder Verlängerung einer Aufenthaltserlaubnis oder Niederlassungserlaubnis beantragt haben, über den die Ausländerbehörde nicht gleich entscheiden kann oder will. See www.nds-fluerat.org/?s=fiktionsbescheinigung (accessed December 2017).
19 www.theguardian.com/books/2017/sep/23/go-went-gone-review-jenny-erpenbeck (accessed December 2017).
20 See www.theguardian.com/books/2013/mar/13/light-and-dark-mikhail-shishkin-review (accessed December 2017).
21 See http://theamericanreader.com/a-conversation-with-mikhail-shishkin/ (accessed December 2017).
22 See http://wijzijnhier.org/2017/11/ (accessed December 2017).

References

Agamben, G. (2002). *Remnants of Auschwitz: The witness and the archive* (D. Heller-Roazen, Trans.). New York: Zone Books.
Al Galidi, R. (2016). *Hoe ik talent voor het leven kreeg*. Amsterdam: Jurgen Maas.
Andersson, R. (2014). *Illegality, Inc.: Clandestine migration and the business of bordering Europe*. Oakland: University of California Press.
Bakhtin, M. M. (2008 [1981]). *The dialogic imagination: Four essays* (C. Emerson & M. Holquist, Trans.). M. Holquist (Ed.). Austin: University of Texas Press.
Battersby, E. (2017, September 23). *Go, went, gone* by Jenny Erpenbeck review – humanising migration: The plight of African asylum seekers in Europe is vividly drawn in this powerful, candid novel. *Guardian*.
Betts, A., & Collier, P. (2017). *Refuge: Rethinking refugee policy in a changing world*. Oxford: Oxford University Press.
Boletsi, M., De Mul, S., Hoving, I., & Minnard, L. (2015). *De lichtheid van literatuur: Engagement in de multiculturele samenleving*. Leuven/Den Haag: Acco.

Buchzik, D. (2015, September 2). Roman von Jenny Erpenbeck: Trifft ein Berliner Professor auf Flüchtline. *Der Spiegel.* Retrieved from www.spiegel.de/kultur/ literatur/gehen-ging-gegangen-von-jenny-erpenbeck-rezension-a-1050518.html.

Butler, J. (2004). *Precarious life: The powers of mourning and violence.* London/ New York: Verso.

Del Grande, G. (2008 [2007]), *Mamadous Fahrt in den Tod: Die Tragödie der irregulären Migranten im Mittelmeer.* Karlsruhe: Von Loeper Literaturverlag.

Erpenbeck, J. (2017 [2015]). *Go, went, gone* (S. Bernofsky, Trans.). London: Portobello Books.

Evans Braziel, J. (2008). *Diaspora: An introduction.* Malden, MA: Blackwell Publishing.

Felski, R. (2008). *Uses of literature.* Malden, MA: Blackwell Publishing.

Heynders, O. (2017). The figure of the migrant: Tommy Wieringa's intellectual intervention. *Werkwinkel: Journal of Low Countries and South African Studies, 12*(2), 19–34.

Heynders, O., & Bax, S. (2016). Imaginary scenarios: Literature and democracy in Europe. *Pivot: A Journal of Interdisciplinary Studies and Thought, 5*(1), 247–276.

Keren, M. (2015). *Politics and literature: At the turn of the millennium.* Calgary: University of Calgary Press.

Koser, K. (2007). *International migration: A very short introduction.* Oxford: Oxford University Press.

Levi, P. (1989). *The drowned and the saved* (R. Rosenthal, Trans.). New York: Random House.

Meek, J. (2012). Cloud-brains. *London Review of Books, 34*(22), 31–32.

Nail, T. (2015). *The figure of the migrant.* Stanford: Stanford University Press.

Nederveen Pieterse, J. (2009). *Globalization and culture: Global mélange.* Lanham: Rowman and Littlefield Publishers Inc.

Nussbaum, M. C. (1995). *Poetic justice: The literary imagination and public life.* Boston: Beacon Press.

Offermans, C. (2015, June 10). In het teken van de duizendpoot. *De Groene Amsterdammer.*

Phelan, J. (2005). *Living to tell about it: A rhetoric and ethics of character narration.* London: Cornell University Press.

Prendergast, C. (2000). *The triangle of representation.* New York: Columbia University Press.

Rorty, R. (1989). *Contingency, irony, and solidarity.* Cambridge: Cambridge University Press.

Schmitter, E. (2015, September 5). Der Stand der Dinge: Jenny Erpenbecks Roman über das Flüchtlingselend in Deutschland. *Der Spiegel.* Retrieved from www. spiegel.de/spiegel/print/d-138493614.html.

Shishkin, M. (2013 [2005]). *Maidenhair* (M. Schwarz, Trans.). Rochester: Open Letter.

Sollund, R. A. (2012). Introduction: Manoeuvring rights: Immigrants' experiences of inclusion and exclusion In L. Leonard & R. Sollund (Eds.), *Transnational migration, gender and rights* (pp. 1–10). Bingley: Emerald Publishing Group Ltd.

Taplin, P. (2013, March 13). The light and the dark by Mikhail Shishkin. *Guardian.*

Viner, K. (2017, November 16). A mission for journalism in a time of crisis. *Guardian.*

Williams, K. K. (2014). Beyond stories of victimhood: Narrating experiences of displacement. *Life Writing, 11*(4), 437–455.

Williams, R. (1985 [1976]). *Keywords: A vocabulary of culture and society* (revised edition). New York: Oxford University Press.

Part III

Media practices

Chapter 8

#BlackLivesMatter

Understanding anti-police protest as a cultural practice

Paul Mutsaers[1]

'On va vous débarrasser de cette racaille'.
(Nicolas Sarkozy, 2005)

'Maybe he should have been roughed up'.
(Donald Trump, 2015)

Introduction: who is the victim?

A cop, a court, a conversation and a campaign. In that order and with an interval of a year, twice. In August 2014, Officer Darren Wilson shot dead an unarmed African-American, the 18-year-old Michael Brown, in Ferguson, Missouri. Of all the 'death-by-cop' cases in the past few years, the shooting of Brown, who had been stopped by Wilson for jaywalking and suspected shoplifting, is presumably best stored in public memory as his body was left on public display for hours after Wilson had pulled the trigger. It led to a nationwide uproar that crystallized in the Black Lives Matter movement (BLM henceforth) and revitalized race politics in and beyond the US. However, in November 2014, a grand jury in St. Louis County chose not to indict Wilson. The decision not to charge Wilson was one about which prosecutor Robert P. McCulloch said at a press conference:

> I'm ever mindful that this decision will not be accepted by some and it may cause disappointment for others. But all decisions in the criminal justice system must be determined by the physical and scientific evidence, and the credible testimony corroborated by that evidence. Not in response to public outcry or for political expediency.

Precisely a year after the shooting, Jake Halpern (2015) published an interview with Wilson in *The New Yorker*. Reflecting on what seems to have been a candid conversation, Halpern attempts to 'humanize the police' (Mutsaers, 2018). In the article, we can read how Wilson is suffering from the furore that the shooting had helped to unleash. Living on a 'nondescript dead-end street on the outskirts of St. Louis', Wilson and his wife, Barb, 'rarely linger in the front yard' and have security cameras in front of their house, which are synched to Wilson's phone. After Brown's death, people had threatened to do something to the Wilson's unborn child and when Barb went into labour, Wilson had 'made her check in anonymously'. Although right-wing opinion-makers had lionized Wilson for his response to Brown, Wilson realized that this only made things worse for him: 'It's too hot an issue, so it makes me unemployable', he said. He applied for several police positions, but was considered a liability. In November 2015, a few months after the interview had been published and one year after the grand jury's decision, something else happened. Mercutio Southall, a co-founder of the BLM chapter in Birmingham, Alabama, went to a campaign rally of Donald J. Trump in Birmingham to protest. Video footage shows that Southall was punched and kicked by Trump supporters. The next day, in an interview with *Fox and Friends*, Trump stated that 'maybe he should have been roughed up, because it is absolutely disgusting what he was doing'.

This more or less random take from the countless events related to what can euphemistically be called the current public relations problem of US police departments, leads us to an old question (Quinney, 1972) to which victimologists (Walklate, 2012) have recently returned: 'Who is the victim?' The widely mediatized killing of Brown has pushed the issue of police violence to the forefront of public conversation and, in the process, has brought into existence various publics and counterpublics. These have alternatively depicted Michael Brown yet another victim of police racism but also the epitome of Black criminality. Similarly, Darren Wilson has been rendered a white supremacist who went scot-free as well as an American hero in the war on crime who was cleared by the criminal justice system but has fallen victim to public scandalizing. By the same token, Trump's hedging on the case of BLM foreman Mercutio Southall – should he have been roughed up? – relies on the same rhetoric of victimization: rather than thinking of Southall as a victim of instant punishment he is seen as a saboteur, an uninvited guest, a disturbance, perhaps even a political enemy. And if that is unpalatable, then Trumpian rhetoric at least renders him offender instead of victim. If anyone was harmed, it was Trump for being interrupted in his political discourse. In *Fox and Friends* he could reap the benefits and made no secret that he had a special grudge against Southall.

In this chapter, I will take up this question – 'Who is the victim?' – in the context of BLM. It is not my intention to treat this question as an empirical one that can in any simple way be answered; when it comes to

BLM, the empirics of policing in the US are just too complex for one academic to understand, certainly when that academic operates from a distance, as I am working in the Netherlands. Rather, I mean to approach it as an important social directive that shapes the struggles for victimhood in which BLM, the police and their various (counter)publics are engaging. More specifically, this chapter can be read as an invitation to think about anti-police protests and the concomitant victimhood-claiming as cultural practices that challenge the conventional ways in which victims, offenders and the state are socially constructed in a legal culture. I will argue in the next section that BLM can be understood as a collective effort to challenge the authoritative recognition that is given in the law and legal processes to cultural conceptualizations of the individual as the principal legal entity in the criminal justice system. In the section thereafter, I offer a preliminary analysis of how social media are an aid in this effort to challenge the primacy that the American legal system gives to the individual. I first focus on the 'archival power' of metadata (such as hashtags), more specifically on how the archive can be used to expose police violence against Black Americans as a form of structural violence amounting to state crime, rather than incidents involving individuals. Second, I will argue that digital activism can help to gain recognition for victimhood as a form of collective suffering, because social media do the work of publics. That is to say, they can bring together a multitude of strangers around a public issue and as such forge a shared 'political temporality' in which victims can directly participate as sovereigns, who do not merely suffer from but also subvert the social structures that work to their disadvantage. The final section contains some concluding remarks and suggestions for future research.

The cultural power of law

Anyone who had surfed to the BLM homepage (www.blacklivesmatter. com) in the autumn of 2017 was likely to find a link that redirected readers to an article in the *Washington Post*, entitled 'We say black lives matter: The FBI says that makes us a security threat' (Figure 8.1). In the article, the authors – Shanelle Matthews, director of communications for the BLM Global Network, and Malkia Cyril, executive director of the Center for Media Justice – respond with indignation to the invention by the FBI's Counterterrorism Division of a new category that recently came to light: the 'Black Identity Extremist', or BIE (FBI Intelligence Assessment, 2017). The executive summary of the Intelligence Assessment reads as follows:

> The FBI assesses it is very likely Black Identity Extremist (BIE) perceptions of police brutality against African Americans spurred an increase in premeditated, retaliatory lethal violence against law enforcement and will very likely serve as justification for such violence. The FBI

assess [sic!] it is very likely this increase began following the 9 August 2014 shooting of Michael Brown in Ferguson, Missouri, and the subsequent grand jury November 2014 declination to indict the police officers involved. The FBI assesses it is very likely incidents of alleged police abuse against African Americans since then have continued to feed the resurgence in ideologically motivated, violent criminal activity within the BIE movement. The FBI assesses it is very likely some BIEs are influenced by a mix of anti-authoritarian, Moorish sovereign citizen ideology, and BIE ideology. The FBI has high confidence in these assessments, based on a history of violent incidents attributed to individuals who acted on behalf of their ideological beliefs, documented in FBI investigations and other law enforcement and open source reporting. The FBI makes this judgement with the key assumption the recent incidents are ideologically motivated.

(FBI Intelligence Assessment, 2017, p. 2)

The premeditated, retaliatory lethal violence aginst law enforcement mentioned in the Intelligence Assessment refers to six recent attacks by Black Americans targeting mainly but not only white police officers. Among these are the shooting of 11 law enforcement officers (of which five deceased) by Micah Johnson in downtown Dallas, Texas (July 7, 2016) and the ambush of six officers by Gavin Eugene Long in Baton Rouge, Louisiana (July 17, 2016), which cost the lives of four people, Long included.

The FBI report and the *Washington Post* article that was published as a response to it are interesting for at least three reasons. First and foremost because they tell us something about the battle for victimhood, which is now brought to the next level. While BLM activists like to present themselves as peacemakers who pursue 'healing justice' (BLM homepage) and wish to improve community life (Figure 8.2), the FBI tries to bring across the point that violence, even terrorism, is their reputed trait. Matthews and Cyril (2017) respond to this terrorism-card with furore, arguing that the FBI plays it repeatedly to reverse roles (references to COINTELPRO, Rev. Martin Luther King Jr., and the Black Panthers appear in the article).

But the dispute presented here is worthy of a more detailed look. Second, let us consider the diverging perspectives on the notion of sovereignty. For obvious reasons, I cannot pass judgement on the evidence gathered by the FBI with respect to the assailants' ideological motivations, but stating that 'BIEs' ' identification with Moorish Sovereign Citizen Ideology or other ideologies of Black separatism is reinforced by 'a sense of disenfranchisement from society and a perception that the criminal justice system is unjust' (Matthews & Cyril, 2017, p. 5) is not so strange as it may sound at first. In fact, anthropological studies of policing around the globe indicate that people who have become alienated from the official justice

Figure 8.1 Black Identity Extremists (BIEs).

Source: www.blacklivesmatter.com.

system because they consider its agents a security *threat* instead of a security *provider*, cobble together their own security solutions. Across the world, all kinds of rival forms of policing have emerged that challenge the state as the final arbiter of security (e.g. Albrecht & Kyed, 2015; Denyer Willis, 2015; Goffman, 2014; Goldstein, 2003; Jaffe, 2013; Mutsaers, 2018). Such 'self-help security' initiatives range from benevolent civilian policing groups, social networks, and community watchmen to criminal paramilitaries, gangs, vigilantes, highwaymen and outlaw armies. Some operate in cooperation with public police forces, but others are strongly antagonistic to them and indeed seek to undermine state sovereignty.

However, the FBI talk about Moorish sovereignty is in itself not addressed as an issue in the *Washington Post* article by Matthews and

Black Lives Matter Chicago
27 oktober 2017

Resources the city has money for:

Chicago Public Schools X
Mental Health Clinics X
Affordable longterm housing X
95 MILLION DOLLAR COP ACADEMY √

#NoCopAcademy #DumpRahm #Chicago #Fuck12

http://www.peoplesworld.org/.../chicago-mayor-quietly-pushes.../

Vertaling bekijken

Chicago mayor quietly pushes for $95m police academy

CHICAGO—Despite preliminary budget reports estimating a deficit of $114 million, Chicago Mayor Rahm Emanuel is pushing a proposal to fund a $95 million police and fire training academy.

PEOPLESWORLD.ORG

Figure 8.2 $95m Police Academy.

Source: Facebook Community @blacklivesmatterchi, posted on October 27, 2017.

Cyril. Their concern with sovereignty takes place at a wholly different level. It has little to do with self-governance and segregation but more with the sovereign voices of victims of police violence, who should no longer be thought of (and think of themselves) as mere 'subjects'. In the words of Matthews and Cyril (2017, n.p.): '[W]e must stand up and say that we won't let it happen again. [...] Must we wait for the bodies of today's Black activists to fall before we take unchecked police and vigilante power seriously?' This cry from the heart aligns with Green and Pemberton's (2018) radical manifesto for victimology in which they call on victimologists to

> engage with victims as social actors able to wield agency and shape how they experience victimization rather than just as people who have had things done to them ... A radical victimology starts from the position of the victim as sovereign rather than the victim as subject.

This idea of the sovereign victim, who has agency and can take action against rather than only suffer from police violence, is quintessential to BLM discourses.

Third, as sovereign victims, BLM activists seek to do more than simply take action against incidents of police racism and excessive violence. Their crusade encompasses much more than that. In their article, Matthews and Cyril address the stark contrast that is drawn by the FBI between 'BIEs' as a new *group* of domestic terrorists on the one hand and, on the other hand, police shootings of Black Americans as 'incidents' that are 'perceived' and 'alleged'. They write: '[T]he FBI's report claiming how dangerous Black activism is begins by asserting that violence inflicted on black people at the hands of police is "perceived" or "alleged", not real' (Matthews & Cyril, 2017, n.p.). While Black activists are represented by the FBI as a dangerous group, police shootings of Black Americans are framed as 'incidents' (involving individuals) that are misinterpreted as a consequence of distorted perceptions – and, we may add after prosecutor Robert P. McCulloch, 'public outcry' and 'political expediency'. This individualization of the issue – relegating a public issue to the level of private troubles (Mills, 1959) – reminds us of Maurice Punch's analysis of police deviancy, in which he uses the metaphor of rotten apples. Punch considers this metaphor to be 'part of the rationalization process that beleaguered institutions engage in when defending themselves. What usually cannot be admitted is that deviance had become *systemic* – in some way encouraged, and perhaps even protected, by certain elements in the system' (Punch, 2003, p. 172).

In addition to the question 'Who is the victim?' the question 'Victim of what?' thus becomes an important one. BLM seeks to replace the terminology of 'incidents' and 'perceptions' with a discourse on state crime.[2] On its homepage, we can find out what BLM thinks is at the heart of the movement: 'In many ways, at its essence BLM is a response to the persistent and historical trauma Black people have endured at the hands of the State.' Similarly, Matthews and Cyril (2017, n.p.) write: 'Designating protesters as terrorists makes clear that the Trump administration thinks the government bears no responsibility to end deadly police violence and other *state abuses of power* against everyday Americans' (emphasis added). At its very core, BLM discourse is about reading the police-induced deaths of Black Americans as only a modern-day symptom of a long history of racism in the (criminal) justice system. In *Policing the Black Man*, whose authors declare themselves staunch defenders of Black Lives Matter, we can read that the

> issue of racially motivated police violence or racial disparities in sentencing can't be viewed as a consequence of bad police officers or racially biased judges. There are deep historical forces that have created problems so clearly seen in America's criminal justice system.
>
> (Stevenson, 2017, p. 5)

However, state crime is an accusation that is not readily accepted in modern legal cultures, for at least two reasons. First, crime is typically constructed around concepts of individual responsibility, culpability and capacity. Such a construction obscures the fact that supra-individual actors such as the state have the capacity for wrongdoing as well (Zedner, 2004). Zedner argues that such an individualist construction of crime deliberately resists the labelling of state activities as criminal; it effectively decriminalizes them. As the academic extension of such legal definitions of crime, positivist victimology defines victims in a similar fashion, that is, as individual victims of conventional crime (Walklate, 2012). Other forms of crime, such as lawbreaking by institutional state actors, or collective forms of victimhood remain hidden from view. It is such hiding that advocates of radical and critical victimology courageously resist (e.g. Kauzlarich, Matthews, & Miller, 2002; Quinney, 1972; Spencer & Walklate, 2016; Walklate, 2012).

But resistance is hard for a second reason. Modern legal cultures of the kind that can also be found in the US have theoretically repositioned the state as the victim of crime (Kauzlarich et al., 2002; Spencer & Walklate, 2016). That is to say, 'since the modernization of police agencies and the courts and the displacing of the king (and sovereign power) as the prime arbiter of justice, the state has stood in as victim of crime' (Spencer & Walklate, 2016, pp. xiv–xv).[3] This repositioning has had important effects. It has made it even more difficult to think about the state as a harmful agent in its own right (Spencer & Walklate, 2016) and it has serious complications for people who want to find justice when they are victimized by the criminal justice system that carries out the criminalization process in the name of the state (Kauzlarich et al., 2002).

I have deliberately used the term 'legal cultures' a couple of times because I want to argue that these matters point at the cultural power of law (Merry, 2000). It has long been recognized in the anthropology of law that the law is deeply enmeshed in the work of culture, which 'consists of distinguishing and organizing categories in order that the world make sense and operate as it should' (Rosen, 2006, p. 170). Legal categories and concepts such as blame, wrongdoing, offender, culpability, victim, intent, state, and crime tell us something about how a society orders and gives meaning to relationships (Douglas, 1992). So, rather than thinking about law and its accompanying legal processes and categories only as a vehicle for keeping society functioning, anthropologists prefer to think about it also as a species of social imagination, a framework for ordered relationships, an important force in shaping human behaviour and lending significance to it; in other words, a constructive element within culture (Geertz, 1983; Rosen, 2006, 2017). In addition to a functionalist thinking about law that asks what it does and that is exclusively concerned with the rules that regulate disputes, this 'hermeneutic thinking' also considers law a 'realm in which society and its members envision themselves and their connections to one another' (Rosen, 2006, p. xii).

But in addition to being a system of meaning, the law is of course also an institutional structure backed by the political power of the state (Merry, 2000). If we combine these two aspects, an interesting question arises: which (groups of) members in society have the power to give cultural meanings authoritative recognition in the law and legal processes? The answer to such a question in the here and now will always depend on historical transformations that pre-structure contemporary struggles over which parts of the cultural fabric ought to be vested with legal power. In other words, and returning to our case study, when BLM activists fight to have the state recognize its collective responsibility for 'destroying the Black body', to put in in the words of a famous BLM supporter (Coates, 2015), they fight an uphill battle that is thwarted by a long history of individualism that is still looming large in modern law (Llewellyn & Hoebel, 1941).

Lawrence Rosen (2006) writes in his book *Law as Culture* that studying the Western ideas on how an individual's self and inner state affect legal considerations offers a unique vantage point on the relation of law to cultural history. As our thinking about the self changed with the 'discovery of the individual' in the eleventh and twelfth centuries, European legal systems changed accordingly. It goes without saying that these ideas were not accepted all the time and everywhere, but they 'did start the West down a road with whose repercussions we continue to grapple' (Rosen, 2006, p. 108). One of the repercussions has been the replacement of laws of strict liability – merely concerned with what is done – by more refined categories of crime that reflected a person's actual intent – that is, the spirit in which something is done (Rosen, 2006, p. 108). In itself, such legal innovations have been an important step to prevent people being left to the mercy of circumstance and accident, but they can also leave victims with empty hands when a defendant is set free because it is found that s/he acted without mental fault.

Let there be no doubt about it; my intention is not to question *mens rea* principles. The 'guilty mind' is simply too important a concept in our legal cultures, one that cannot be compromised lest the pursuit of justice becomes a tricky thing. But I do want to entice people to put themselves in the position of Black Americans and imagine their frustrations when yet another police officer is exonerated because s/he had no 'guilty mind' while shooting a Black American, allegedly out of self-defence, while the goal was all along to press charges against a culture of racial violence that dominates so many US police departments and that victimizes, kills and antagonizes Black Americans as a group. These frustrations are a direct result of the fact that there is no place for groups as distinct legal entities in the American system; that is, there is almost no significant political space between the individual and the state (Rosen, 2017). There seems to be one exception these days, terrorism, and that card is used *against* Black Americans, as we saw in the FBI report. I for one need little effort to understand that this only adds to the frustration.

In sum, BLM activists, in their protest against police, are offering resistance against the primacy of the individual in American law, the decriminalization of the state, as well as the political void between the individual and the state. Their fight for the recognition of victimhood as collective suffering and of 'police punishment' (Harkin, 2015) as state crime, is a battle against the cultural power of law and thus a cultural practice that is worth studying in that capacity. Understood as such, BLM is about disrupting the sense of orderliness that arises from the neat unity of legal and cultural systems and the concomitant hegemonic assumptions about criminal justice and the conflicting and overseeing parties involved.

In what follows, I will argue that BLM's online presence can be auxiliary to its cause as described above. Much has been said about online activism (e.g. Gerbaudo, 2012; Juris, 2012) and its use (e.g. in the overthrow of regimes) and uselessness (think, for example, of the hackneyed term 'slacktivism'). I will not hazard a definite answer when it comes to its success in the context of BLM, but I will argue that the power of social media to archive and collectivize is helpful in transcending the level of incidents and individuals. In the long run, this may change the cultural outlook on criminal justice and its legal entities.

Digital activism, archival power and the coming together of strangers

When Officer Darren Wilson shot Michael Brown in Ferguson, Missouri, on August 9, 2014, it only took a minute before a user named 'TheePharoah' published a post on Twitter: 'I just saw someone die OMFG'. In the next week or so, over 3.6 million posts appeared on Twitter that in one way or another had to do with Brown's death, many of them using #Ferguson to relate to the case (Bonilla & Rosa, 2015). These and other kinds of online activities helped to transform an impromptu gathering to protest against Brown's death into a sustained movement across the nation that publically grieves and demands justice for Black victims of police violence. As Brassard and Partis (2015, p. 8) argue in their article 'Standing their ground in #Ferguson',

> the success of digital activism in the case of #Ferguson, stem[med] from the relentless, on-the-ground, minute-by-minute sharing that foreclosed the opportunity for what was happening in Missouri to be drained of political potency and circulate in the daily paper as a depoliticized abstraction.

So, whereas Howard Becker could still pose in 1967 that police and policed are part of a system of ranked groups and that this system allocates to members of the highest group (police) the right to define the situation (i.e. to tell others what 'really' happened), such a position needs serious reconsideration today. The right may still be allocated, but it is also definitely challenged by the ubiquity of 'cameraphones' and online file-sharing (Brown, 2016).[4]

An oft-heard critique of digital activism is that the images and information coming from the grassroots can only ever partly represent what 'really' happened. Some piece of crucial information is always missing because of the angle of the camera or the time it had started or stopped recording, and fictions are easily taken for facts when a critical mass on the internet has accepted a particular storyline. However, biases, misinterpretations and fictions can influence decisions and conclusions everywhere, even in the courtroom. To borrow once more from Lawrence Rosen: 'It is ... important to recall that no legal process can exactly replicate any claimed "fact". In court, one can only approximate what might have been' (Rosen, 2017, p. 28). Turning to the mainstream media to find 'the truth' will certainly not make things better, for these are known to assist in (re)producing hegemonic values and imaginaries. Exemplary is the Fox News coverage in the aftermath of Brown's death, which mainly contained items on 'Black-on-Black' crime, the failure of Black leaders and communities, anti-racism as the 'politics of racial division', and the need for personal responsibility (see also Mills, 2017).

None of these activities – digital activism, litigation, mainstream media coverage – are to be thought of as the ultimate fact-finding or truth-revealing operation. They tell us not so much what happened as what is said to have happened (Trouillot, 1995). However, what makes social media so special is that, for the first time in history, they give ordinary citizens the possibility to store almost everything that is 'said to have happened' into an archive, and to do so collectively, as a group. In other words, they give people archival power. After Trouillot, this can be defined as the power to organize facts and sources and condition what is allowed to exist as a historical statement:

> Archives assemble. Their assembly work is not limited to a more or less passive act of collecting. Rather, it is an active act of production that prepares facts for historical intelligibility. Archives set up both the substantive and formal elements of the narrative. They are the institutionalized sites of mediation between the sociohistorical process and the narratives about that process.
>
> (Trouillot, 1995, p. 52)

Put differently, archives work as indexing systems in the clerical as well as the semiotic sense of the word (Bonilla & Rosa, 2015). Think for example about the role of metadata such as hashtags. In the first sense, these form a quick retrieval system that orders information about a specific theme or topic. However, hashtags additionally work semiotically by marking the intended significance of an utterance. '[They] allow users to not simply "file" their comments but to performatively frame what these comments are "really about", thereby enabling users to indicate a meaning that might not be otherwise apparent' (Bonilla & Rosa, 2015, p. 5). It is important to note that the clerical and semiotic functions are closely integrated. That is to say, a tweet becomes part of a particular frame because it is linked to other tweets in the archive through what Bonilla and Rosa call an 'intertextual chain'. Hashtags have the intertextual potential to link a broad range of tweets, and it is through these links that sense-making occurs.

To clarify, an example may be given that comes from an ongoing ethnographic project on the online activities of the BLM Chapter in Chicago. Spending research time with the Facebook Community @blacklivesmatter-chi, I came across a hashtag I had not been aware of before: #LetUsBreathe (see Figure 8.3). The post in which it was used linked to a Facebook Event, *Transformative Justice 101*, which in turn directed users to another Facebook Community called the #LetUsBreatheCollective (@letusbreathe). On the homepage of this collective (www.letusbreathecollective.com) readers are informed that it is an alliance of artists and activists that imagines a world without prisons and police. It operates the 'Breathing Room' space, which is 'a Black-led liberation headquarters for arts, organizing, and

Black Lives Matter Chicago heeft een evenement van the
#LetUsBreathe Collective gedeeld.
27 juli 2017 · ℮

We talk about justice a lot but what does it actually mean? Come discuss at
#BreathingRoom
https://www.facebook.com/events/118665048771871/?ti=icl

Vertaling bekijken

JUL	F12 presents Transformative Justi...	
31	Ma 16:00 CDT · The #BreathingRoom Spac...	★ Geïnteresseerd
	Goede doelen	

Figure 8.3 The Breathing Room.
Source: Facebook Community @blacklivesmatterchi, posted on July 27, 2017.

healing on Chicago's South Side' and it allies with other activist organizations such as Black Lives Matter Chicago.

Before I started to click on the various links, I initially interpreted the
hashtag solely as a reference to the Eric Garner case. About a month before
the shooting of Michael Brown, Eric Garner had lost his life due to a
chokehold performed by plain-clothes New York Police Department
Officer Daniel Pantaleo. Garner, who was unarmed, was allegedly selling
untaxed cigarettes outside a store on Staten Island, New York. After a
verbal exchange, he was physically handled by Pantaleo and his colleague,
Officer Justin Damico. The tragedy was captured on video, which clearly
shows that Garner gasped that he could not breathe. He said so repeatedly
before losing consciousness and going into cardiac arrest (cf. Fairfax,
2017). Officer Daniel Pantaleo was brought before a grand jury, which
declined to indict. The hashtag #ICantBreathe immediately trended and
many people uploaded photographs of themselves on social media as they

wore a face mask with the same text to express disapproval of the judicial system, which in their eyes had once again done a poor job of protecting and vindicating the rights of Black Americans victimized by police.

#LetUsBreathe does indeed refer to the Garner case, as Kristiana Rae Colón, the co-director of the equally named collective, had initially started the collective to deliver gas masks to protesters in Ferguson and said that she found inspiration in the last words of Eric Garner. To Colón, the throat is a symbol of life (breathing) and liberty (expression), a place 'where all her interests tangle and choke' (Cocozza, 2015). But that is exactly the point: on top of being a protest hashtag, #LetUsBreathe is also about healing and transformation – or 'transformative justice', which is closely related to BLM's earlier mentioned notion of 'healing justice' that features prominently on its website and social media accounts. The archival power of the #LetUsBreatheCollective, BLM and like-minded groups and individuals comes from the fact that they can use hashtags to lasso accompanying texts and their indexical meanings as part of a frame that portrays police as life-taking and Black activists as life-giving. What is more, by linking a variety of 'sociohistorical processes' (Trouillot, 1995) and narratives about these processes (e.g. as they unfolded in Ferguson or Staten Island), hashtags are a powerful tool to point at the structural nature of police violence against Blacks. Every new event is interpreted in relation to hundreds of other events that happened before, and thanks to the indexing systems of social media, these are stored into an everlasting and digitalized public memory. Indeed, as said above in the words of Brassard and Partis, this forecloses the opportunity for these events to be drained of political potency and circulate in the mainstream media as a depoliticized abstraction.

It is important, though, to make it more explicit that the 'structural nature' of police violence against Blacks does not only refer to numbers and frequencies. To argue that such violence is a form of state crime, more needs to be done than counting casualties. Put another way, to make the case that such violence is a public issue rather than a series of private troubles (Mills, 1959) and to effectively counter the earlier mentioned human failure model so often emphasized by police leaders, more needs to be done than claiming that critical mass has been reached to account for the adjective 'structural' in structural violence. Following Paul Farmer (2004, p. 307), we must understand that the notion of structural violence is exactly at odds with our 'moral economy [that is] still geared to pinning praise or blame on individual actors', because it points at 'sinful' social structures that are not the fault of those directly involved in its daily operations. Structural violence is a higher order problem.

Then again, the interesting thing about digital activism is that the intertextual chain constructed by hashtags and other metadata easily allows users to jump scales, that is, to move 'from the individual to the collective, the temporally situated to the trans-temporal, the unique to the common, the token to the type, the specific to the general' (Blommaert, 2010, p. 33). Returning to our earlier remark on hashtags as semiotic indexing systems, we should bear in mind that the connection between scales is exactly what makes them indexical: 'it resides in the ways in which unique instances of communication can be captured indexically as "framed", understandable communication, as pointing towards socially and culturally ordered norms, genres, traditions, expectations – phenomena of a higher scale-level' (Blommaert, 2010, p. 33).

For clarification, we can continue with the #LetUsBreatheCollective. As I wrote earlier, I arrived at the (social) media environment of this collective

Figure 8.4 Black Identity Extremist T-Shirt.

Source: www.letusbreathecollective.com/support.

during fieldwork and I came to understand it as an 'extended field site' that is in the immediate vicinity of BLM Chicago's online world – and is connected to it by many bridges. As I was surfing and observing, I once again stumbled on the term 'Black Identity Extremist', but this time it was 'advertised' on a black T-shirt (see Figure 8.4). Immediately after the FBI report had become public, the hashtag #BlackIdentityExtremist was invented and it did not take long before the collective started mocking the report by means of a T-shirt, which it offers for sale on its website. In itself, this is an interesting act of resistance, one that is best described by what James Scott (1985, 1990) calls the *infrapolitics* of subordinate groups: low-profile forms of resistance that include things such as playing the fool, ridicule and disguised aggression (cf. Mutsaers & Van Nuenen, 2018). These are the 'weapons of the weak'.

But taking it as temporally situated, as instant action, or immediate 'backfire' only, does not do justice to the permanence and higher-order nature of the print. Not only will the T-shirts endure and the hashtags be stored in the digital archive long after the T-shirts are sold out (and thus become trans-temporal), the print also has tremendous indexical power: 'it connects previous utterances with current ones and grants an indexical load to present utterances that have their origins in the existing social order' (Blommaert, 2010, p. 148). As such, it rebels against the report *and* the things it stands for – or, perhaps even more importantly, the things it seeks to legitimize. For instance, following the discussion on #BlackIdentity Extremist, we can immediately notice the concerns people have about the possible intensifying effects of the report on the police practice of racial profiling, which is a serious and well-documented problem in the US (e.g. Epp, Maynard-Moody, & Haider-Markel, 2014; Goffman, 2014). Apart from the content of people's posts on Twitter, these concerns become clear from the fact that many people included hyperlinks in their messages, directing users to a video recording of a hearing in which representative Karen Bass questions Attorney General Jeff Sessions about the FBI report, for which Sessions, as head of the United States Department of Justice, is ultimately responsible. Bass pressed Sessions hard, asking him (a) if he can name one Black *organization* that targets police officers, and (b) if he is aware of the possible damage that the FBI's foregrounding of 'Black Identity Extremists' and simultaneous backgrounding of 'White Identity Extremists' (such as the Ku Klux Klan) can wreak, for instance in terms of intensified police surveillance of Black communities. Sessions avoids most questions and does not provide a single decent answer to the questions without hedging, so the mocking continues on social media (Figure 8.5).

Diverting attention away from the misconduct and racism of individual police officers, these acts of digital activism consistently lock our gaze on the 'sinful' social structures that underpin individual behaviour. By placing new designations such as BIE in a broader context, they become an aid in

Avery Penn heeft het bericht van Doug Mitchell gedeeld met de ···
groep BLACK EXCELLENCE.
15 november 2017 · ⊜

Asked #JeffSessions to name one black identity extremist group.

He couldn't.

Asked him to name ONE white supremacist group that had targeted cops.
... Meer weergeven
Vertaling bekijken

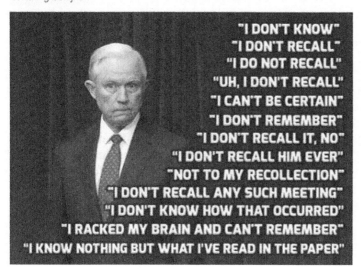

Figure 8.5 Jeff Sessions meme.
Source: Facebook.

rethinking racial profiling, that is, they help us to understand profiling as an organized effort rather than an individual's choice or mistake. Moreover, they also help us to scale up and down and in the process discover what we may call a hidden message, or 'hidden transcript' to quote Scott (1990): the total lack of transparency in the highest political office closely resemblances the mystifying county court system that time and again lets offenders (police officers) off scot-free. People mention this link mostly implicitly, but one can sense that this is what people hint at. Especially because transparency and accountability, or better, their absence across levels of authority, form a recurring theme on the agenda of BLM activists. In short, the hidden message seems to be that the polity is complicit with punitive police behaviour that victimizes Black Americans.

So far, I have mainly addressed the various ways in which BLM activists and their allies have used digital media to expose police aggression against

Black Americans as a form of state crime that exceeds the bounds of individual morality and responsibility. In the last part of this section, I would like to concentrate on how they take issue with the fact that, apart from the class-action lawsuit, there is almost no place for groups as distinct legal entities in the American legal system. How, in such a system, can one gain recognition for victimhood as a form of collective suffering?

In the first place, BLM activists very actively present the movement as a collective of Black and other oppressed groups. For example, in the document 'Celebrating 4 Years Black Lives Matter' (Matthews & Noor, 2017, p. 7) we can read the movement's guiding principles, and some of them are very explicit about BLM being an (expanding) collectivity: 'We see ourselves as part of the global Black family' and 'We disrupt the Western-prescribed nuclear family structure requirement by supporting each other as extended families and "villages" that collectively care for one another...' The self-understanding and presentation of BLM as an (extended) family is a smart thing to do, because the suffering of the family is generally acknowledged to be an important social concern in the context of individuals' legal entanglements (e.g. Harcourt, 2007). This holds true for the misery of a 'death-by-cop' victim's next to kin as well as for the (social) costs that rest on the family of a convicted son, daughter, father or mother. In fact, although the family is not accepted as a legal unit in criminal law, it has long been recognized that

> all legal theory avails nothing to remove from a family the stigma of a convict within it, and today's official law ... relies for its deterrent efficacy quite as much upon this threat to family as upon the threat to the offender.
>
> (Llewellyn & Hoebel, 1941, p. 50)

For an engrossing account of such family-focused deterrence, see Alice Goffman's *On the Run* (2014). Presenting the BLM movement as an extended family thus makes sense when the purpose is to draw attention to suffering beyond the level of the individual.

But the extended BLM family is different from a normal family for a related but different reason than not having a nuclear structure. It is largely a family of strangers rather than of intimates (which does not mean that these strangers can never be intimately related; see below). In the words of Nikita Mitchell, BLM's organizing director: 'A movement is not an individual, an organization, or even a cluster of organizations. A movement is when *the masses*, with different opinions and ideas, engage in collective action towards a common goal' (Mitchell, 2017, p. 8, emphasis added). I would now like to argue that it is one of the strengths of digital media that they can help to forge a 'shared political temporality' (Bonilla & Rosa, 2015) that brings together a diverse mass of strangers around a specific issue and creates 'a public' in the process. In doing so, I draw on Michael Warner's (2002) seminal article in *Public Culture*.

The notion of 'the public' – a multifarious, stochastic and superdiverse composite of social backgrounds, voices and interactions – is critically compounded by the fact that many public expressions nowadays come to rise in online environments such as described above (cf. Mutsaers & Van Nuenen, 2018). Often times, these expressions of grief or frustration by interlinked and 'plugged-in' publics are extensions of offline protests. They differ, however, in that the kind of 'groupness' emerging in these spaces requires neither strong, lasting bonds grounded in shared bodies of knowledge, nor any temporal or spatial co-presence – something that is traditionally conceived of as a prerequisite to 'community' (Blommaert & Varis, 2015). With translocality being the norm in online interaction, it becomes exceedingly difficult to apply traditional understandings of community or kin structure. However, at the same time it is highly problematic to employ terms such as 'the public', exactly because of its multifarious and superdiverse composite. Following Warner, we are advised to use indefinite articles and plurals: 'a public' and 'publics'. 'The public', says Warner, is a kind of social totality, synonymous for the people in general. The various publics and counterpublics that are brought into existence by BLM and similar movements are formed at an intermediate level; they are more abstract than close-knit communities but less so than the people in general.

What, then, is 'a public'? A public, says Warner, is typically a relation among strangers, a relation that comes into being due to the joint attention that people give to texts (of any kind). It is discourse, therefore, that conjures a public into being. Moreover, it exists by virtue of being addressed, that is, it does not need an institutional basis: 'A public organizes itself independently of state institutions, law, formal frameworks of citizenship, or [the] church' (Warner, 2002, p. 51). In contrast to these external frameworks, which function on the basis of formal membership, a public can only produce a sense of belonging if (a minimum level of) attention is secured. One can be an inactive member of a church, but one is not part of a newspaper's public if that newspaper is not read. Warner: 'The cognitive quality of that attention is less important than the mere fact of active uptake' but publics 'commence with the moment of attention, must continually predicate renewed attention, and cease to exist when attention is no longer predicated' (Warner, 2002, p. 61). It is for this reason that no single text can create a public. An ongoing flow of discourse that circulates through time is required to keep a public alive, lest a public dwindles to a group. Finally, although a public appears to be open to indefinite strangers, this is actually not the case. Warner calls a public 'poetic world-making', by which he means that it seeks to specify in advance, in countless ways, the lifeworld of its circulation: through pre-existing forms and channels of circulation, discursive claims, topical concerns, speech genres, idiolects, stylistic markers, address, lexicon, interlocutory protocols, etc. But whatever the poetics, the address of public speech is always both personal and impersonal: 'Public speech can have great urgency and intimate import. Yet we know that it was addressed not exactly to us, but to the stranger we were until the moment we happened to be addressed by it' (Warner, 2002, p. 57).

Keeping in mind these qualifications, it becomes clear that, for instance, a Facebook Community such as @BlackLivesMatter, with its 311,784 followers and 308,769 likes (on December 4, 2017), is actually not a community. Far from it; it meets all the criteria to be called a *public*. First, the open structure allows for the coming together of strangers. People are free to 'follow' and 'like' as they please. All they need is a Facebook account (closed communities are an exception of course). Second, through its emphasis on sharing and aggregating, a page-specific Facebook public provides a constant flow of discourse that, thanks to the archival function, resists the corroding effects of time and can be updated in a split second. Third, although we can never be sure to what extent all these followers pay attention, the participatory framework of social media platforms stimulates uptake – if not voluntarily then forcibly through push notifications and algorithmic intrusion. Fourth, on Facebook and other social media platforms, strangers are typically united by their joint interest in topics rather than shared demographic characteristics (Hayes, 2017). Poetic world-making occurs in the way people talk about these topics, the platforms that they choose and the discursive claims that they make. Finally, social media talk often equals public speech in the sense that we might recognize ourselves as addressees – depending of course on whether or not we fit in the lifeworld that is specified – although the speech may be addressed to more or less indefinite others (see Figure 8.6 for a good example).

In sum, social media increasingly do the work of publics (Hayes, 2017). What's more, they do it according to a logic of aggregation (Juris, 2012, p. 259) that 'involves the assembling of masses of individuals from diverse backgrounds' in both online and offline spaces (e.g. street protests). As such, they are ideal instruments in the hands of activists, who can now bring together a multitude of strangers around a public issue, who would otherwise have been preoccupied with only their private troubles. Although I have promised to keep myself from passing final judgement on the successes of digital activism (and I will stick to that), it is notable that these digital infrastructures do make it possible for people to build a case for collective victimhood. At a minimum, they allow people to share experiences of victimization in a

Black Lives Matter
3 november 2017 · ⊖

When They Call You a Terrorist by Patrisse Khan-Cullors and asha bandele, in stores 1/16/18. Available for preorder.

Her story is our story. #BlackLivesMattermemoir

"This remarkable book reveals what inspired Patrisse's visionary and courageous activism and forces us to face the consequence of the choices our nation made when we criminalized a generation. This book is a must-read for all of us."
— Michelle Alexander

"To call the founders of BLM terrorists is an unconscionable lie. This strikingly beautiful memoir puts the lie to the notion that Black Lives Matter comes from anything other than a place of love-- love of self, community, people, and, ultimately, the very soul of a democratic nation." — Michael Eric Dyson

Figure 8.6 Advertisement for a Black Lives Matter Memoir.

Source: Facebook Community @blacklivesmatter, posted on November 3, 2017.

very targeted way. But they can also give a political temporality to these experiences that is much more efficient than earlier 'public technologies' (television, radio, print), not in the least because they allow for direct participation.

Conclusions

I opened this text with two very similar epigraphs that both strike at the heart of the issue that is central in this chapter, and that issue is best captured by a question: 'Who is the victim?' The second quote reflects Trump's rage, which I briefly addressed in the introduction. The first one is part of a public statement by Nicolas Sarkozy (then Minister of the Interior) during a visit to Argenteuil, one of Paris' *banlieus*, on October 23, 2005. In a (recorded) conversation with a women who was watching from her window, Sarkozy promised that he would 'rid the town of its scum' (Fassin, 2014, p. 107). This bold statement took place in a time of turmoil and urban unrest. Only four days later, the 15-year-old Bouna Traore and the 17-year-old Zyed Benna were electrocuted in a power substation, where they were hiding from police officers who chased them with Flash-Balls – weapons that fire 'non-lethal' rubber ammunition. In response to these events, Sarkozy spoke about 'thieves' and absolved the police of all responsibility, despite the fact that they had seen the boys enter the transformer and had done nothing to prevent electrocution (Fassin, 2014, p. 107). Further investigation proved that Traore and Benna had not been involved in any criminal activity. These events culminated in a period of intense rioting and anti-police protest, affecting hundreds of French towns.

Police legitimacy is far from unequivocal in many places across the world. Images of public outcry against police forces in the UK, the US, Turkey, Brazil, Venezuela, France, the Netherlands, Hong Kong and many other places, are now almost weekly bursting onto our screens (Mutsaers, Karpiak, & Simpson, 2015). In fact, one can randomly point a finger at the atlas and almost anywhere find anti-police protests within close proximity. These 'conflicted contours of policing' (Mutsaers, 2018) give us reason to firmly place anti-police protests on our research agenda. All the more so because we live in a time in which national leaders can permit themselves to make fundamentally unconstitutional statements that encourage the police to become socially divisive and to victimize entire racial groups and classes.

I consider this chapter a modest first step to explore this research agenda. The analysis is preliminary, but I hope it will function as a stepping stone for others interested in the topic. I have basically tried to do three things. First, I have argued that anti-police protests such as those organized by BLM are best understood as a cultural practice, because they essentially question the cultural assumptions of law. One such assumption is that the individual ought to be the only legal entity that is accepted in court. Let there be no mistake: we should be mindful of the fact that this assumption is vital to the protection of individual rights and freedoms. But it also frustrates the actions of people who experience (lethal) police violence as a form of state crime that leads to a collective suffering of those who are targeted and profiled by a state *institution* rather than its individual personnel.[5] Second, I have argued that digital infrastructures can aid activists and victims (these categories often overlap) in their attempts to expose police violence as a form of state crime that goes beyond individual culpability. I have used the notion of 'archival power' to discuss how hashtags and other forms of metadata can be used to link, in an 'intertextual chain', the countless events in which deep mistrust was sown between Black Americans and police departments. Third, I have pointed at the potential of digital activism when it comes to the recognition that is sought for victimhood as a form of collective suffering. Here, I have drawn on Warner's theories of publics and argued that social media increasingly 'do the work of publics'. These publics, as we have seen in the last few years, also organize themselves offline and their coming together as strangers can best be called, after Erving Goffman, a 'focused gathering': 'a set of persons engrossed in a common flow of activity and relating to one another in terms of that flow' (in Geertz, 1973, p. 424). United, these strangers can address very intimate concerns.

Notes

1 I am grateful to Jennie Simpson for her critical reading of and comments on an earlier draft of this text.
3 A useful definition of victims of state crime is given by David Kauzlarich et al. (2002, p. 176): 'Individuals or groups of individuals who have experienced economic, cultural, or physical harm, pain, exclusion, or exploitation because of tacit or explicit state actions or policies which violate law or generally defined human rights.'
4 This happened because, over time, the notion of crime as a dispute between individual parties was overlaid by the notion of crime as a threat to social order (Zedner, 2004); an order that is defended by the state. In this regard, Nils Christie, in a 1976 article in the *British Journal of Criminology*, talks about crimes being 'stolen' by the state, through the apparatus of criminal justice, from their rightful owners: offenders and victims (cf. Zedner, 2004, pp. 8–9).
5 There was no video recording of Brown's death, but many other cases do point at the usefulness of such footage in digital activism.

References

Albrecht, P., & Kyed, H. M. (Eds.). (2015). *Policing and the politics of order-making*. London: Routledge.
Blommaert, J. (2010). *The sociolinguistics of globalization*. Cambridge: Cambridge University Press.

Blommaert, J., & Varis, P. (2015). Conviviality and collectives on social media: Virality, memes and new social structure. *Multilingual Margins*, 2(1), 31–45.

Bonilla, Y., & Rosa, J. (2015). #Ferguson: Digital protest, hashtag ethnography, and the racial politics of social media in the United States. *American Ethnologist*, 42(1), 4–17.

Brassard, L., & Partis, M. (2015). Standing their ground in #Ferguson. *Anthropology News*, 56(1–2), 8–9.

Brown, G. R. (2016). The blue line on thin ice: Police use of force modifications in the era of cameraphones and YouTube. *The British Journal of Criminology*, 56(2), 293–312.

Coates, T.-N. (2015). *Between the world and me*. Melbourne: Text Publishing.

Cocozza, P. (2015, September 7). Kristiana Rae Colón: #LetUsBreathe activist and 'defiant' poet and playwright. *Guardian*. Retrieved from www.theguardian.com/lifeandstyle/2015/sep/07/kristiana-rae-colon-letusbreathe-activist-poet-playwright-nadia-latif-octagon.

Denyer Willis, G. (2015). *The killing consensus: Police, organized crime, and the regulation of life and death in urban Brazil*. Oakland: University of California Press.

Douglas, M. (1992). *Risk and blame: Essays in cultural theory*. London: Routledge.

Epp, C. R., Maynard-Moody, S., & Haider-Markel, D. (2014). *Pulled over: How police stops define race and citizenship*. Chicago: The University of Chicago Press.

Fairfax Jr., R. A. (2017). The grand jury and police violence against black men. In A. J. Davis (Ed.), *Policing the black man* (pp. 209–233). New York: Pantheon Books.

Farmer, P. (2004). An anthropology of structural violence. *Current Anthropology*, 45(3), 305–325.

Fassin, D. (2014). Petty states of exception: The contemporary policing of the urban poor. In M. Maquire, C. Frois, & N. Zurawski (Eds.), *The anthropology of security* (pp. 104–117). London: Pluto Press.

FBI Intelligence Assessment (2017, August 3). *Black Identity Extremists likely motivated to target law enforcement officers*. Retrieved from www.documentcloud.org/documents/4067711-BIE-Redacted.html.

Geertz, C. (1973). *The interpretation of cultures*. New York: Basic Books.

Geertz, C. (1983). *Local knowledge*. London: Fontana Press.

Gerbaudo, P. (2012). *Tweets and the streets: Social media and contemporary activism*. London: Pluto Press.

Goffman, A. (2014). *On the run: Fugitive life in an American city*. Chicago: The University of Chicago Press.

Goldstein, D. (2003). 'In our own hands': Lynching, justice and the law in Bolivia. *American Ethnologist*, 30(1), 22–43.

Green, S., & Pemberton, A. (2018). The impact of crime: Victimisation, harm and resilience. In S. Walklate (Ed.), *Handbook of victims and victimology* (2nd edition). London: Routledge.

Halpern, J. (2015, August 10). The cop. *The New Yorker*. Retrieved from http://newyorker.com/magazine/2015/08/10/the-cop.

Harcourt, B. (2007). *Against prediction: Profiling, policing, and punishment in the actuarial age*. Chicago: The University of Chicago Press.

Harkin, D. M. (2015). The police and punishment: Understanding the pains of policing. *Theoretical Criminology, 19*(1), 42–58.

Hayes, T. J. (2017). #MyNYPD: Transforming Twitter into a public place for protest. *Computers and Composition, 43*, 118–134.

Jaffe, R. (2013). The hybrid state: Crime and citizenship in urban Jamaica. *American Ethnologist, 40*(4), 734–748.

Juris, J. S. (2012). Reflections on #Occupy everywhere: Social media, public space, and emerging logics of aggregation. *American Ethnologist, 39*(2), 259–279.

Kauzlarich, D., Matthews, R. A., & Miller, W. J. (2002). Toward a victimology of state crime. *Critical Criminology, 10*, 173–194.

Llewellyn, K. N., & Hoebel, A. (1941). *The Cheyenne way: Conflict and case law in primitive jurisprudence.* Norman: University of Oklahoma Press.

Matthews, S., & Cyril, M. (2017, October 19). We say black lives matter: The FBI says that makes us a security threat. *Washington Post.* Retrieved from www.washingtonpost.com/news/posteverything/wp/2017/10/19/we-say-black-lives-matter-the-fbi-says-that-makes-us-a-security-threat/?utm_term=.0ae9f95b85da.

Matthews, S., & Noor, M. (2017). *Celebrating 4 years Black Lives Matter.* Retrieved from https://static1.squarespace.com/static/5964e6c3db29d6fe8490b34e/t/59678445 d482e97ec9c94ed5/1499956322766/BLM-4yrs-report.pdf.

Merry, S. E. (2000). *Colonizing Hawai'i: The cultural power of law.* Princeton: Princeton University Press.

Mills, C. E. (2017). Framing Ferguson: Fox News and the construction of US racism. *Race & Class, 58*(4), 39–56.

Mills, C. W. (1959). *The sociological imagination.* Oxford: Oxford University Press.

Mitchell, N. (2017). Why we organize: A letter from our organizing director. In S. Matthews & M. Noor (Eds.), *Celebrating 4 years Black Lives Matter* (pp. 8–9). Retrieved from https://static1.squarespace.com/static/ 5964e6c3db29d6fe8490b34e /t/59678445d482e97ec9c94ed5/1499956322766/BLM-4yrs-report.pdf.

Mutsaers, P. (2018, forthcoming). *Police unlimited: Policing, migrants and the values of bureaucracy.* Oxford: Oxford University Press.

Mutsaers, P., Karpiak, K., & Simpson, J. (2015). The anthropology of police as public anthropology. *American Anthropologist, 117*(4), 786–789.

Mutsaers, P., & Van Nuenen, T. (2018). Protesting police. In W. Garriott & K. Karpiak (Eds.), *The anthropology of police* (pp. 153–171). London: Routledge.

Punch, M. (2003). Rotten orchards: 'Pestilence', police misconduct and system failure. *Policing & Society, 13*(2), 171–196.

Quinney, R. (1972). Who is the victim? *Criminology, November,* 314–323.

Rosen, L. (2006). *Law as culture: An invitation.* Princeton: Princeton University Press.

Rosen, L. (2017). *The judgement of culture: Cultural assumptions in American law.* London: Routledge.

Scott, J. (1985). *Weapons of the weak: Everyday forms of peasant resistance.* New Haven: Yale University Press.

Scott, J. (1990). *Domination and the arts of resistance: Hidden transcripts.* New Haven: Yale University Press.

Spencer, D. C., & Walklate, S. (2016). Introduction: Themes and issues in critical victimology. In D. C. Spencer & S. Walklate (Eds.), *Reconceptualizing critical victimology: Interventions and possibilities* (pp. xi–xvii). Lanham: Lexington Books.

Stevenson, B. (2017). A presumption of guilt: The legacy of America's history of racial injustice. In A. J. Davis (Ed.), *Policing the black man* (pp. 3–30). New York: Pantheon Books.

Trouillot, M.-R. (1995). *Silencing the past: Power and the production of history.* Boston: Beacon Press.

Walklate, S. (2012). Who is the victim of crime? Paying homage to the work of Richard Quinney. *Crime, Media, Culture, 8*(2), 173–184.

Warner, M. (2002). Publics and counterpublics. *Public Culture, 14*(1), 49–90.

Zedner, L. (2004). *Criminal justice.* Oxford: Oxford University Press.

Chapter 9

Online-offline modes of identity and community

Elliot Rodger's twisted world of masculine victimhood

Jan Blommaert[1]

Introduction

Online environments have become an integrated part of social reality; as a new, huge and deeply fragmented infrastructure for social interaction and knowledge circulation, they add substantially to the complexity of social processes, notably those related to identity work and group formation.[2] We see, on the one hand, the emergence of online communities of unprecedented size – think of the population using Facebook, or of the huge numbers of players on some Massively Multiplayer Online Games (MMOG). All of these have long been provoking questions about identity and social impact, often tending towards views of the destabilization of identity and of social cohesion (cf., for example, De Meo, Ferrara, Fiumara, & Provetti, 2014; Lee & Hoadley, 2007). On the other hand we have the online emergence of strongly identity-emphasizing and highly cohesive 'translocal micro-populations' (Maly & Varis, 2015), and practices of online meaning making, control and circulation that betray the presence of at least widely shared systems of normative consensus and conviviality (Georgakopoulou, 2017; LaViolette, 2017; Tagg, Seargeant, & Brown, 2017; Varis & Blommaert, 2015). Given the scope and scale of the online world, it is clear that we have barely started to scratch the surface, and in this chapter I cannot claim to do more than that.

In what follows, I will venture into the less commonly visited fringes of the Web 2.0, in a space called the 'Manosphere' (Nagle, 2017). The Manosphere is a complex of (mostly US-based) websites dedicated to what can alternatively be called 'toxic masculinity' or 'masculine victimhood': men gather to exchange experiences and views on the oppressive role and position of women in their worlds, and often do so by means of ostensibly misogynist, sexist, (often) racist and (sometimes) violent discourse. The intriguing point is that the Manosphere, as an online zone of social activity, and appears to be relatively isolated and enclosed. Large numbers of men are active on these online spaces, but there is no offline equivalent to it: no 'regular' mass movement of angry men organizing big marches, petitions and other forms of offline political campaigning. The Mano-sphere population is very much a group operating in the shadows of the Web (see Beekmans, Sweep, Zheng, & Yu, 2018; Dijsselbloem, Coster, Henskens, & Veeneman, 2018; Peeters, Wijayanti, Van Meer, De Clerck, & Raa, 2018; Schoonen, Fransen, Bastiaense, & Cai, 2018; Smits, Van Gorp, Van der Jagt, Bakx, & Yacoubi, 2018; Vivenzi, Schaffels, De la Vega, & Driessen, 2018).

There are moments, though, of public visibility, and I shall start from one such moment. In May 2014, a young man from California, Elliot Rodger, killed six people and injured 14 others (before taking his own life) around the UCSB (University of California, Santa Barbara) campus at Isla Vista, in what looked like one of many college shooting incidents (Langman, 2016a). Rodger, the son of a Hollywood filmmaker, sent out a long manifesto by email just before his killing spree, entitled 'My Twisted Life: The Story of Elliot Rodger' (see Kling, 2017),[3] as well as several YouTube clips recorded prior to his actions.[4] Since Elliot mentioned Manosphere sites in the text, the manifesto offers us an oppor-tunity to look closer into the ways in which such online infrastructures provide affordances for constructing an – admittedly eccentric – logic of action, strengthening Rodger's sense of victimhood and providing ration-alizations for the murders he committed during what he called his 'Day of Retribution'. More in general, this exercise may lead us to a more precise understanding of the role played by online cultural infrastruc-tures in the construction of contemporary 'outsider' or 'abnormal' iden-tity templates, individual as well as collective ones (cf. Becker, 1963; Foucault, 2003).

Drawing from Rodger's manifesto, I shall first sketch the universe of communication in which he lived, focusing on how his online activities interacted with offline forms of interaction. This will offer us a tentative view of Rodger's 'culture', characterized by a strong affinity with mascu-line victimhood and violence, which he shared with parts of the Mano-sphere. The latter operates, along with several other popular-cultural elements, as a learning environment in and through which a logic of action is constructed, motivating, ultimately, a reversal of roles in which the victim becomes the perpetrator and in which Elliot Rodger himself is morphed from an apprentice to a role model.

I will conclude my contribution with a number of theoretical reflections, aimed at getting a more precise understanding of the specific modes of online interaction in which such a logic of action is constructed. Following Huizinga's (1950) well-known description of the 'ludic' dimensions of culture, I will suggest that we see the online communities of knowledge in which Rodger was engaged as relatively enclosed ('chronotopic') spaces in which 'ludic' learning practices can be organized: highly specific templates of thought and behaviour are being exchanged, shaping and rationalizing 'abnormal' modes of action such as the ones performed by Rodger. Thus, 'light' online communities can have substantial social effects.

Elliot Rodger's twisted world of communication

Herbert Blumer summarized one of the central insights in the tradition of Symbolic Interactionism as follows:

> [...] social interaction is a process that *forms* human conduct instead of being merely a means or a setting for the expression or release of human conduct.
>
> (Blumer, 1969, p. 8, emphasis in original)

With this in mind, let us have a look at how Rodger's manifesto informs us about the kinds of social interactions he maintained.

Born in 1991, Elliot Rodger was 22 when he took his own life and that of six others; he was a digital native, and he had a long history of mental disorder (Langman, 2016b).[5] His parents and acquaintances described him as extremely withdrawn, and Rodger himself in his manifesto frequently described his 'social anxiety' – an incapacity to adequately communicate in collective face-to-face situations, which he invariably experienced as extraordinarily stressful. Here is an example:

> The class I started was a political science class. I figured I would gain some useful knowledge by taking it, though I disliked the teacher because he had the tendency to randomly call on me to answer questions. I was still terrified of speaking in front of the class, even if it was for one sentence. My social anxiety has always made my life so difficult, and no one ever understood it. I hated how everyone else seemed to have no anxiety at all. I was like a cripple compared to them. Their lives must be so much easier. Thankfully, there were no couples in this class, but I still had to see them when I walked through the school. The only thing I could do was keep my head down and pretend they didn't exist. I still cried on the drive home every day.

This communicative disability leads to isolation, and this isolation quickly assumes a very specific shape. As an adolescent, Rodger develops a strong heterosexual desire, but girls do not appear to be attracted to him. Consequently, his problem of loneliness shifts towards something more specific and acute: a problem of involuntary celibacy which he experiences as torture. Since the girls he fancies do connect with young men (in Santa Barbara, especially men described by Rodger as 'hunky'), couples become his object of resentment, and a sense of injustice is piled onto that of unhappiness:

As I spent a lot of time contemplating, I realized that my life was repeating itself in a vicious circle of torment and injustice. Each new semester of college yielded the same lonely celibate life, devoid of girls or any social interaction. It was as if there was a curse of misfortune placed upon me.

This injustice is acute, since Rodger imagines himself as superior to most other men of his age; he describes himself as 'a perfect gentleman', as good-looking, smart and generally attractive – which renders the fact that other men are more successful with girls outrageous:

How could an inferior, ugly black boy be able to get a white girl and not me? I am beautiful, and I am half white myself. I am descended from British aristocracy. He is descended from slaves. I deserve it more. I tried not to believe his foul words, but they were already said, and it was hard to erase from my mind. If this is actually true, if this ugly black filth was able to have sex with a blonde white girl at the age of thirteen while I've had to suffer virginity all my life, then this just proves how ridiculous the female gender is. They would give themselves to this filthy scum, but they reject ME? The injustice!

Rodger attempts to turn this outrageous state of affairs around by material improvements: fashionable and top-of-the range clothing, a BMW car (a present from his worried mother), and dreams of wealth. In order to realize the latter, he spends large sums playing on the Lottery:

This must be it! I was destined to be the winner of the highest lottery jackpot in existence. I knew right then and there that this jackpot was meant for me. Who else deserved such a victory? I had been through so much rejection, suffering, and injustice in my life, and this was to be my salvation. With my whole body filled with feverish hope, I spent $700 dollars on lottery tickets for this drawing. As I spent this money, I imagined all the amazing sex I would have with a beautiful model girlfriend I would have once I become a man of wealth.

When these desperate attempts to acquire a fortune fail, fantasies of violent retribution emerge, always triggered by seeing young couples who 'steal' his happiness and are, in that sense, 'criminals' who deserve to be severely punished:

I wanted to do horrible things to that couple. I wanted to inflict pain on all young couples. It was around this point in my life that I realized I was capable of doing such things. I would happily do such things. I was capable of killing them, and I wanted to. I wanted to kill them slowly, to strip the skins off their flesh. They deserve it. The males deserve it for taking the females away from me, and the females deserve it for choosing those males instead of me.

And a detailed script is constructed for the Day of Retribution:

After I have killed all of the sorority girls at the Alpha Phi House, I will quickly get into the SUV before the police arrive, assuming they would arrive within 3 minutes. I will then make my way to Del Playa, splattering as many of my enemies as I can with the SUV, and shooting anyone I don't splatter. I can only imagine how sweet it will be to ram the SUV into all of those groups of popular young people who I've always witnessed walking right in the middle of the road as if they are better than everyone else. When they are writhing in pain, their bodies broken and dying after I splatter them, they will fully realize their crimes.

What is striking in Rodger's manifesto is the paucity of offline, 'normal' communication he describes. As we have seen, he suffers from communicative anxiety whenever he is facing a group of interlocutors; but even one-on-one communication situations are often described as unsuccessful or unsatisfactory. But, as mentioned earlier, he is a digital native, and frequent reference is made to online interactions in his manifesto. From early on, for instance, he is a dedicated player of the MMOG *World of Warcraft* (WoW), and playing that game provides him a (delicate and fragile) sense of community:

Upon setting up my new laptop, I immediately installed all of my WoW disks. I logged onto my account and took a look at all of my characters that I hadn't touched for a year and a half. Right when I logged onto my main character, I was contacted by James, and he invited me to join an online group with him, Steve, and Mark. They all gave me a warm welcome back.

Changes in the nature of the WoW player community, however, make him decide to quit that game: too many 'normal' people had joined WoW.

The game got bigger with every new expansion that was released, and as it got bigger, it brought in a vast amount of new players. I noticed that more and more 'normal' people who had active and pleasurable social lives were starting to play the game, as the new changes catered to such a crowd. WoW no longer became a sanctuary where I could hide from the evils of the world, because the evils of the world had now followed me there. I saw people bragging online about their sexual experiences with girls … and they used the term 'virgin' as an insult to people who were more immersed in the game than them. The insult stung, because it was true. Us virgins did tend to get more immersed in such things, because our real lives were lacking.

Other interactions with friends also proceed online, or are predicated upon prior online interactions:

During one of my frequent visits home in late Spring, I reunited with my old friends Philip and Addison. I hadn't seen them since the night I emotionally cried in front of them at the Getty museum in the beginning of 2012. This reunion was sparked by the political and philosophic conversations I had been having with Addison over Facebook.

And Facebook also enables Rodger to keep tabs on his offline relations:

In November, my brief friendship with Andy, Stan, and their group faded away. I often saw on Facebook that they did things together without even inviting me, which is the same thing I've had to experience with other groups of friends that I've had in the past. I was always an outcast, even among people I knew. I grew tired of their lack of consideration for me, so I stopped calling them. They weren't even popular anyway, and I wasn't benefitting at all from their friendship. I still continued to meet with Andy at restaurants on occasion, however.

And then, of course, there is the Manosphere. Engaging with websites such as PUAHate.com ('Pick Up Artists Hate', taken down and renamed 'Sluthate' after the Isla Vista killings) reassures Rodger that he is not the only one suffering from the cruelty of women:

The Spring of 2013 was also the time when I came across the website PUAHate.com. It is a forum full of men who are starved of sex, just like me. Many of them have their own theories of what women are attracted to, and many of them share my hatred of women, though unlike me they would be too cowardly to act on it. Reading the posts on that website only confirmed many of the theories I had about how wicked and degenerate women really are. Most of the people on that website have extremely stupid opinions that I found very frustrating, but I found a few to be quite insightful.

The website PUAHate is very depressing. It shows just how bleak and cruel the world is due of the evilness of women. I tried to show it to my parents, to give them some sort dose of reality as to why I am so miserable. They never understood why I am so miserable. They have always had the delusion that everything is going well for me, especially my father. When I sent the link of PUAHate.com to my parents, none of them even bothered to look at the posts on there.

Observe how Rodger describes the website as a place where a *theory* or *worldview* is constructed – an epistemic move towards generalization, from the particular and idiosyncratic to the systemic and common. And note that he considers this an important factor of *understanding*, valuable enough to be communicated to his parents. He had discovered a space where his own feelings, outlook and experiences were *normal*, even *normative*. And he wanted to communicate this to those who, in his eyes, systematically misunderstood him and defined him as an outsider. It is telling that, in the entire manifesto, the above fragment is the only one in which he attempts to *share* a resource for understanding his predicaments, with people from whom he genuinely expects support and sympathy.

Sources and templates: the cultural material

Given what we have seen so far, it is safe to say that Rodger saw websites such as PUAHate.com as formative learning environments, places where he learned how to see his individual predicament fitted into a larger system, and where he learned how to respond to this systemic injustice (cf. Schoonen et al., 2018). But apart from Manosphere sites and the World of Warcraft game he was passionate about, Rodger mentions several other sources of inspiration: he was quite deeply involved in particular forms of popular culture.

Remember that Rodger grew up in the Hollywood movie milieu; in his manifesto, he suggests that stars such as George Lucas were (at least) family acquaintances, and he proudly describes attending several red carpet premières of Hollywood blockbusters. His father was involved as a second unit director in the production of the 2012 hit movie *The Hunger Games*.[6] This genre of violent dystopian fantasy (to which WoW can also be added) clearly belonged to his range of strong interests, and he got addicted to *A Game of Thrones* as soon as he read it:

> For the rest of the summer, I took it easy and played WoW with James, Steve, and Mark; just like old times. I also started reading a new book series called A Song of Ice and Fire, by George R.R. Martin. This medieval fantasy series was spectacular. The first book of the series was A Game of Thrones, and once I read the first chapter I just couldn't put it down. It was like nothing I had ever read before, with a huge array of complex characters, a few of whom I could relate to. I found out that it was going to be adapted into an HBO television series, and I became very excited for that.

> Delving into fantasy stories like WoW and Game of Thrones didn't make me forget about all of my troubles in life, but they did give me a temporary and relieving sense of escape, which I need from time to time. Life would be impossible to handle without those temporary respites.

We can sense the powerful appeal of imagined universes characterized by violence, sex, ruthlessness and brutality in Rodger's words here. Popular culture products such as these provided him with templates by means of which he could organize his experiences and conduct. The latter is made explicit by Rodger with respect to yet another source: a movie called *Alpha Dog*.[7]

> The Santa Barbara plan was formed on that night, but its roots stretch all the way back to when I just turned eighteen. It was all because I watched that movie Alpha Dog. The movie had a profound effect on me, because it depicted lots of good looking young people enjoying pleasurable sex lives. I thought about it for many months afterward, and I constantly read about the story online. I found out that it took place in Santa Barbara, which prompted me to read about college life in Santa Barbara. I found out about Isla Vista, the small town adjacent to UCSB where all of the college students live and have parties. When I found out about all this, I had the desperate hope that if I moved to that town I would be able to live that life too. That was the life I wanted. A life of pleasure and sex.

In other words: the entire scenario of his Day of Retribution is modelled on a template Rodger largely derived from a movie. Popular culture proves to be a learning environment in the most immediate sense here.[8]

Of course, Rodger's manifesto is not a log of his online activities and popular culture interests. The few items he explicitly mentions can be assumed to have particular importance in his constructed world, but there must be far more. There is, for instance, the powerful effect of the dramatic shooting at Columbine High School in 1999, perpetrated by teenagers Eric Harris and Dylan Klebold, which led not only to widespread outrage (voiced, among others, in Michael Moore's award-winning documentary *Bowling for Columbine*),[9] but also to a video game called *Super Columbine Massacre RPG* (based on original surveillance camera images of the shootings),[10] and a number of copycat incidents in which perpetrators declared to be (or were later proven to have been) inspired by Harris and Klebold's example. The Columbine massacre remains perhaps the most dramatic of the American school shootings, also because of its knock-on effects in other, similar incidents. It became, in effect, a template for similar actions.[11]

One such post-Columbine action, bearing striking similarities with that of Elliot Rodger, was the Virginia Tech shooting in 2007. On April 16 of that year, a student called Seung Hui Cho shot and killed 32 people. Interestingly, he, too, had posted videos prior to his actions, and he, too, left a manifesto: a collage of texts and images, articulating a sense of victimhood and a desire for (violent) retribution bearing striking similarities to that of Rodger. Consider the following fragment from Seung Hui Cho's text:[12]

> By destroying we create. We create the feelings in you of what it is like to be the victim, what it is like to be fucked and destroyed. Because of your annihilations, we create and raise new breeds of Children who will show you fuckers what you have done to us. Like Easter, it will be a day of rebirth. It will be a start of a revolution of the Children that you fucked. You have never felt a single ounce of pain your whole life, thus, by destroying you, by giving you pain, we attempt to show you responsibilities and meanings of other people's lives.

Cho, like Rodger, expresses profound pain and bitterness over what he must have experienced as a life destroyed by the agency of others – who, because of that, deserved to die. Cho calls himself a victim, and Rodger concludes his manifesto with exactly the same qualifications:

> All I ever wanted was to love women, and in turn to be loved by them back. Their behavior towards me has only earned my hatred, and rightfully so! I am the true victim in all of this. I am the good guy. Humanity struck at me first by condemning me to experience so much suffering. I didn't ask for this. I didn't want this. I didn't start this war … I wasn't the one who struck first … But I will finish it by striking back. I will punish everyone. And it will be beautiful. Finally, at long last, I can show the world my true worth.

The point to all this is that Rodger, in premeditating, preparing and executing his shooting, could draw on abundantly available cultural material for concrete and specific templates structuring his act. There is, as it were, a carefully elaborated aesthetics to the actions – see his 'it will be beautiful' above. And in elaborating this aesthetics, Rodger draws on examples and models derived from earlier similar incidents as well as from the online and popular culture sources he intensely engaged with. All of this sources provide 'logical' modes of action, patterns of argumentation and rationalizations that Rodger could invoke in designing his own actions.

The aftermath: becoming cultural material

Elliot Rodger, as a digital native, not only consumed online popular culture, but as we have seen, he also created some. His manifesto was electronically circulated hours before his fatal drive into Isla Vista, and I already mentioned that he had uploaded several videos on YouTube as well. Both the manifesto and the videos are remarkable: the text is exceedingly well written and structured, and the videos appear to be well-rehearsed staged performances. Undoubtedly, Rodger's exposure to the Hollywood professional in-crowd was formative.

The Isla Vista shootings were headline news in the US, and several major TV networks controversially broadcast fragments from Rodger's YouTube videos, bringing material from the extreme fringes of the Web into mass circulation, and thus creating the raw materials for what we know as 'memes' – a new and complex online popular culture genre in which (static or moving) image and message are blended in highly productive and diverse ways, often for no other apparent purpose than conveying 'cool' conviviality in online communities (cf. Blommaert, 2015; Varis & Blommaert, 2015). Memes belong to the standard repertoires of online interaction, and they are effective tools for signalling community attachment, flagging its central themes and mobilizing its members into online action (Nagle, 2017).

A particular line from Rodger's Day of Retribution video became emblematic in such memes: 'I am the perfect gentleman'. Figure 9.1 illustrates this.

Other memes poked fun of Rodger's materialism and naiveté in dating girls,[13] and still others simply copied elements from Rodger's manifesto and circulated it as a serious, instructional message, as in Figure 9.2.

There is nothing exceptional to all this: memes can find their sources in nearly all and any event or aspect of life, so choosing a high-profile and heavily publicized incident as the object of memes is self-evident. The point is, however, that Rodger was directly influenced by specific sources and operated within existing templates when he committed his acts; but that he also *became* a format after the act. He and his killings became cultural material either providing legitimacy or rejecting his logic of action. In the present economies of knowledge and information, online infrastructures provide a colossal discursive overlay upon the more conventional news reporting.

Naturally, there was no shortage of uptake of the Isla Vista killings in the Manosphere, and this uptake was ambivalent. In discussions on Manosphere platforms, men condemned Rodger for being a 'loser' while others praised him as a hero, as in Figure 9.3.

The interesting thing, however, is how the figure of Elliot Rodger became entirely absorbed in the ideological structures of the Manosphere. One of these structures is sketched by Angela Nagle as follows:

> One of the dominant and consistent preoccupations running through the forum culture of the Manosphere is the idea of beta and alpha

golden mem

Figure 9.1 Elliot Rodger 'Gentleman' meme.

Source: retrieved from https://me.me/i/th-elliot-rodgers-is-autistic-gentleman-supremacy-e-golden-mem-3683956; accessed November 2017.

males. They discuss how women prefer alpha males and either cynically use or completely ignore beta males, by which they mean low-ranking males in the stark and vicious social hierarchy through which they interpret all human interaction.

(Nagle, 2017, p. 89)

The Manosphere itself is split between alpha- and beta-male camps, and beta-males are usually encouraged either to turn themselves into alpha-males, or altogether reject (and possibly destroy) that world of male–female relationships (cf. Schoonen et al., 2018; Vivenzi et al., 2018). The beta males, obviously, are the victims of a world in which women choose alpha males, and the label is shorthand for an entire system of rationalizations of unhappiness, involuntary celibacy, loneliness and revenge.

Figure 9.2 Elliot Rodger text-quote meme.
Source: retrieved from https://onsizzle.com/t/elliot-rodger; accessed November 2017.

If we now return to Rodger's manifesto using Nagle's description of alpha and beta males, it is overly clear that Rodger self-identified as a beta male, a victim of a society in which women – way too independent and manipulating as they were, in his view – consistently ignored him in favour of more brutal, muscular and rugged types of (alpha) men. The latter, whom Rodger saw as stupid and naïve because they walked into the traps set out for them by women, also became his enemies, and eventually his victims during his Day of Retribution. This act of uncompromising beta-masculine ideological rectitude turned Rodger into some kind of icon of the beta male camp, as we can see in Figure 9.4.

And within the Manosphere, he became a template of such till-death-do-us-part rectitude, important enough to have his acronym 'ER' included in the glossary of Sluthate (the renamed successor of PUAHate.com).[14] Rodger's figure indexes a radical, even extremist position which can be copied (as a template) by others. Smits et al. (2018), for instance, describe the interactions of a man nicknamed 'About2GoER' on Sluthate. The

File: 140103821121.jpg (300 KB, 560x600)

Anonymous (ID: +9vk7osJ) 05/26/14(Mon)01:07:50 No.548081057 ►
>>548081186 >>548081281 >>548081414 >>548081450 >>548081462 >>548081529
>>548081634 >>548082048 >>548082251 >>548083059 >>548083073 >>548083098
>>548083113 >>548083708 >>548084043 >>548084245 >>548084306 >>548084403

He was one of us, /b/.

Normalfags and bitches make fun of him, torture and bullied him. He
was a true gantleman, police, inteligent, the fault that he coundt get laid
it LEFTIST.

Being awkward never was a problem.
Its a problem now in the new world. A world where womens are qual to
man, where faggots have rights.
Thats not this kid fault.

He is my hero.

Anonymous (ID: U+0+9TYi) 05/26/14(Mon)01:09:27 No.548081281 ► >>548081520 >>548084314

>>548081057 (OP)

Kill yourself, he was an absolute creep

Anonymous (ID: ZRPOQAf+) 05/26/14(Mon)01:11:10 No.548081520 ►

>>548081281
> Kill yourself

or just pull a Rodger

Figure 9.3 Screenshot of Manosphere discussion on Elliot Rodger.

Source: retrieved from https://imgur.com/r/4chan/AET4cgb; accessed November 2017.

Figure 9.4 Elliot Rodger the beta male meme.

Source: retrieved from http://knowyourmeme.com/photos/1092353-beta-uprising; accessed November 2017.

name signals intimate identification with 'ER' (Elliot Rodger), and suggests a similar path of future action to that taken by 'ER' ('about to go'). About-2GoER 'states that he rather wants to be with "slayers that are funny" than "faggots that want the world to feel sorry for him"' (Smits et al., 2018) and is aggressive and extravagantly offensive, even by the quite impressive standards of Sluthate.

To sum up and conclude the analysis of the Elliot Rodger case: we have seen how his actions were 'formatted', so to speak, on the basis of sources and templates he had learned and developed in the online-offline world of the Manosphere, games and other forms of popular culture; and we have seen how his line of action, in turn, became part of the cultural material informing and providing action templates for others. Such templates provide a logic of action in which experiences, knowledge, feelings and aspirations are brought in line, so to speak, in a way that plausibly motivates specific lines of action. In the case of Rodger, the templates he had learned and developed converted loneliness and unhappiness into a strong and ideologically structured sense of victimhood – an identity of 'victim' – which in turn, logically, motivated the extremely violent, destructive revenge on those whom he considered to be the perpetrators of the 'crimes' that made him lonely and unhappy. The templates, thus, provide a logic of action in which victims can legitimately become perpetrators, and vice versa.

We see here, in many ways, a classic instance of what Raymond Williams (1977) famously called 'structures of feeling': seemingly incoherent reactions and responses to experienced social realities that gradually become 'structured' by ideological framings provided by similar feelings articulated by others. In the process, we witness the emerging of individual and collective identity categories ('victims', 'beta males') and commonly ratified ('normal') lines of action, which can now be ideologically rationalized as 'the truth'. Rodger, in short, operated within the 'culture' of the beta males – a culture of victimhood and resentment – and he took this cultural logic to its limits.

Reflections: the ludic formatting of online-offline social life

I now must take one step back, away from the concrete (and admittedly harrowing) case of Elliot Rodger, and explain how 'outsiders' such as Rodger can inform us of more widespread social phenomena and processes. And we need to recall Blumer's thesis, quoted earlier: what I have surveyed in the case of Rodger are, in essence, forms and patterns of social interaction forming human conduct, not just reflecting or expressing it. If we add George Herbert Mead's view to this, such forms of interaction also form (not just reflect or express) who we are – our 'minds':

> We must regard mind, then, as arising and developing within the social process, within the empirical matrix of social interactions.
>
> (Mead, 1934, p. 133)

In a slightly overstated rephrasing of Mead's point, we could say that who and what people are is a residue of the totality of social interactions they engaged in over their lives, and specific aspects of who and what people are will be the residue of specific kinds of social interaction. Analytically, then, the crux of the matter is to understand the precise nature of these interactions. And this is where we need to engage with the peculiarities of the new online-offline communicative worlds we presently inhabit.[15]

We know a few things already. We know, for instances, that most online communities – even if they operate as real communities, including forms of leadership and authority, normative behavioural scripts and levels of integration – are open, undemanding and flexible when it comes to membership, and that older conceptions of what it means to be a member impede a precise understanding of the actual forms of attachment developing between individuals and groups. Compared with the robust social formations of classical sociology (family, nation, religion, etc.), they are 'light' communities. The Manosphere is a case in point: even if men can be regular visitors and contributors to Manosphere forums, and attach great importance to interactions on these forums (as did, apparently, Elliot Rodger), the community does not have the robust and perennial structure of, say, a trade union or a sports team. As Smits et al. (2018) showed, outspoken dissidence and even hostility are (even if grudgingly) tolerated, and as Vivenzi et al. (2018) demonstrated, people can enter and leave as they wish.

So how do we imagine the specific forms of social interaction within such 'light' communities? Let us turn to a, perhaps, unexpected and counterintuitive corner of social thought. In his classic *Homo Ludens*, Johan Huizinga emphasized what he saw as an important counterpoint to Weber's rationalization drive in Modernity: the playful character of many social, cultural and political practices. In our tendency to organize societies along rational management patterns, Huizinga insisted, we risked losing sight of the fact that much of what people do is governed by an *irrational* logic, a ludic pattern of action. Even more, much of what we see as the rational organization of societies is grounded, in fact, in play (Huizinga, 1950, p. 5).

Huizinga (1950, pp. 7–14) lists several features of 'play'. I shall select a number of them.

1   Play is *significant*: it is a site of meaning-making in which 'something is at play';

2   it is, at the same time a *voluntary* activity often experienced as a site of personal freedom;

3   it is relatively *unregulated* and unconstrained by established rules and forms of control (distinguishing 'play' from a 'game' such as chess or poker);

4   it is an *authentic* activity in which we observe the unconstrained 'playing out' of the self; it is outside the range of what is commonly seen as 'useful' or 'effective' (it is done 'just for fun');

5   it is *enclosed* in the sense that it often requires a particular spatiotemporal organization different from that of other activities; and, finally,

6   given all the previous characteristics, it is also a *serious* activity demanding focus, intensity and skill, and it has an inevitable aspect of *learning* to it.

Two remarks are in order. One, with respect to the characteristic of authenticity ((4) above), it must be underscored that it is perfectly normal to *play someone else while expressing some essential 'self'*. In fact, forms of play in which roles are assumed by players, masks or other garments are worn or names are being changed for the duration of the event are found everywhere. In the online world it suffices to think of highly developed communities such as those of cosplay and gaming to see the point; but think also of the widespread use of aliases or nicknames on social media platforms. Just as we can distinguish a Foucaultian 'care of the self' in various forms of play, we see a 'care of the selfie' in online play as well (cf. Li & Blommaert, 2017).

Two, with respect to (5) above – Huizinga's requirement of spatiotemporal 'isolation' for play – we can emphasize the chronotopic nature of ludic practices. Play is often reserved for, and reliant upon, restricted and elaborately organized timespace configurations. Think of a 'play room' or a 'play corner', of 'holiday' and 'leisure' as segmented timespace configurations reserved for ludic activities, but also of current expressions such as 'quality time' or 'me time' (a segment of time spent on ludic, non-work activities). Observe, by the way, the strong *moral* ring of such terms: they refer to things we absolutely need and value highly; denial of such things is often perceived as unacceptable. In online activities, the timespace configuration is present as well, and relatively undemanding in addition: we need an individual and an online device, and little more is required. Which is why 'spending time behind your computer' is often perceived as 'asocial' or 'individualistic': we perceive an individual *alone* with his/her device, who is deeply involved, of course, with a community not sharing the physical timespace but very much present and active in the 'virtual' one. In Rodger's case, we saw how perception of offline social awkwardness bypassed his intense engagement with online and popular culture communities 'below the radar', including those of the Manosphere. And we saw the pervasive effect of these forms of separated, enclosed forms of involvement on his 'mind' (to use the Meadian term here).

If we now take Huizinga's characteristics and apply them to the 'light' forms of membership in online communities, we see a potential for application – perhaps not to all forms of online membership but to many of them. We can see how attachment to online groups is not (in a great many instances) conditioned by permanent, heavily ordered, policed and 'total' involvement – one does not have to become an expert in, say, advanced barbecue techniques just by visiting barbecue-focused websites or fora, and one does not have to participate in all events on a cosplay forum in order to be a 'member'.[16] One can also enter and participate on such online platforms without subscribing to the full range of norms, expectations and cultural premises prevailing there, and one can articulate one's participation in terms of very different intentions and desired outcomes from the next person. An online gaming forum is not a school, even if we find organized and tightly observed learning practices on the online gaming forum too. It turns the gaming forum into a ludic learning environment in which different forms of knowledge practice are invited, allowed and ratified. Such practices – precisely – are 'light' ones too – think of 'phatic' expressions of attachments such as the retweet on Twitter and the 'likes' on Facebook: knowledge practices not necessarily experienced as such, and rather more frequently seen as 'just for fun'. And capable, in that sense, of generating 'structures of feeling' shared among participants in the community.

But do note Huizinga's final characteristic: ludic practice is *serious* practice. The relatively 'light', mobile and flexible features of online communities do not prevent intense and profoundly focused forms of attachment. The experience of freedom and authenticity, and the absence of obvious 'normal' forms of usefulness and efficiency might, on the contrary, precisely contribute to the sometimes phenomenal investments made by members in their attachments to such groups. There is a degree of intimacy evolving from ludic practices (including the 'phatic' ones just mentioned): people make friends while playing, because play enables them to show their 'authentic' self, to show the 'truth' about themselves.[17] Here, once more, are the 'structures of feeling': something is genuinely shared and constructed through such ludic forms of practice, and this sharedness is experienced as important and formative.

It is formative of strong normative templates, as we have seen in the case of Rodger. What he learned and developed in his online-offline enclosed communities of knowledge was a strongly normative ('normal') sense of being and of action – a logic of action, as I called it earlier, or a 'culture'. Rodger derived from his engagement in those communities an absolute certainty about his identity as a victim of a world that conspired to steal away his (sexually focused) happiness, and enough of a commitment to take this logic of action to its very end, where the victim becomes the perpetrator. And in so doing, he, in turn, contributed templates of thought, action and identity to other members of that community – his use of available formats contributed to a further solidification of these formats.

This is quite something in the way of social effect. Extreme cases of 'outsiders' such as Elliot Rodger should alert us to the powerful 'cultural' effects of the new online-offline worlds we inhabit, and for which, currently, we only have diminutive terms: 'virtual' or 'light' communities engaging in 'playful' forms of attachment. The very lightness of these terms must encourage us to critically re-examine them, time and time again.

Notes

1 With ICD 2017. ICD 2017 is shorthand for the 2017 class in my 'Individuals and Collectives in the Digital Age' course at Tilburg University, with whom I explored the issues documented in this text. I am deeply grateful to all of the following: Marissa Backx, Ruben Bastiaanse, Inge Beekmans, Norman Cai, Ashna Coster, Dennis de Clerck, Gabriela De la Vega, Jan Dijsselbloem, Lennart Driessen, Hannah Fransen, Boudewijn Henskens, Daria Kholod, Thi Phuong Anh Nguyen, Dianne Parlevliet, Saskia Peters, Jonathan Raa, William Schaffels, Agotha Schnell, Maud Schoonen, Laura Smits, Eva Stein Veeneman, Anne-Marie Sweep, Madelinde van der Jagt, Meauraine van Gorp, Megan van Meer, Laura Vivenzi, Natalia Wijayanti, Noura Yacoubi, Zhifang Yu, Linming Zheng.
2 This is the point of departure of Blommaert (2018), and this paper is part of the larger *Durkheim and the Internet* project. Evidently, the observation is not new, and I let myself be profoundly inspired by, among others, early visionary texts such as those of Castells (1996) and Appadurai (1996).
3 The manifesto is an unnumbered 141-page document; in what follows, consequently, I cannot provide page number for the fragments I shall use. The full text is available in original form on https://medium.com/@benkling/elliot-rodger-male-entitlement-and-pathologization-c394500309b3. As we shall see further below, writing a manifesto is in itself part of a format for such forms of crime. Probably the most famous instance of the format was the 1515-page long *2083: A European Declaration of Independence* by Norwegian mass-murdered Anders Breivik in 2011. See https://publicintelligence.net/anders-behring-breiviks-complete-manifesto-2083-a-european-declaration-of-independence/.
4 Several of these clips can still be viewed on YouTube. His Day of Retribution clip can be viewed (with parental guidance) here: www.youtube.com/watch?v=G-gQ3aAdhIo. See also Rodger's profile on *Criminal Minds Wiki*: http://criminalminds.wikia.com/wiki/Elliot_Rodger.
5 See this excellent article for a detailed account of Elliot Rodger's life: www.nytimes.com/2014/06/02/us/elliot-rodger-killings-in-california-followed-years-of-withdrawal.html.
6 https://en.wikipedia.org/wiki/The_Hunger_Games_(film).
7 https://en.wikipedia.org/wiki/Alpha_Dog.
8 Langman's (2016a) review of half a century of college shootings in the US shows a dramatic increase of such incidents since the turn of the century, an era coinciding with the generalized introduction of the internet as a household commodity. Harris and Klebold, we can note, were both active on online platforms in the peripheries of the Web. We cannot make categorical statements here, of

course, but the Elliot Rodger case shows a direct influence of these new popular-cultural infrastructures on the formatting of his killing spree.

9 https://en.wikipedia.org/wiki/Bowling_for_Columbine.

10 www.columbinegame.com/.

11 See Langman (2009, 2016c) for an analysis of Eric Harris' motives and personality; Langman's remarkable website contains original documents related to school shooters including Harris and Klebold, and it is helpful to look at the similarities across cases after the Columbine incident. A full analysis of these documents is beyond the scope of this paper. For a sober analysis of public multi-victim shootings in the US, one can consult the FBI report examining incidents between 2003 and 2013: file:///C:/Users/c/Downloads/(U)_ActiveShooter021317_17B_WEB.PDF.

12 See https://schoolshooters.info/sites/default/files/cho_manifesto_1.1.pdf. On *Criminal Minds Wiki*, a clear parallel is drawn between Cho's and Rodger's shooting formats: http://criminalminds.wikia.com/wiki/Elliot_Rodger.

13 See for an example www.memecenter.com/fun/3276299/elliot-rodger-aka-jew-rich-boy-dating-simulator-2014.

14 See http://sluthate.com/w/Glossary#ER.

15 What follows is based on Blommaert (2017).

16 Cosplay is a cultural genre in which people gather dressed up, often with meticulous attention to detail, as popular culture characters and play out scenes from popular-cultural sources involving these characters. Hence 'cos(tume) play'. The genre can draw on a large online infrastructure. See for example www.cosplay.com/forum.php.

17 This explains the very widespread genre of 'confession' on social media. Confession, as Foucault (2003) observed, is a *veridictional* genre, a genre of truth-speaking in which an uninhibited self communicates fundamental truths to other uninhibited selves. Elliot Rodger's manifesto and videos are, evidently, veridictional genres. And the density of 'confessions' on the Manosphere is documented in Vivenzi et al. (2018) and Beekmans et al. (2018).

References

Appadurai, A. (1996). *Modernity at large: Cultural consequences of globalization*. Minneapolis: University of Minnesota Press.

Becker, H. (1963). *Outsiders: Studies in the sociology of deviance*. New York: The Free Press.

Beekmans, I., Sweep, A.-M., Zheng, L., & Yu, Z. (2018, forthcoming). Forgive me father, for I hate women. *Diggit Magazine*.

Blommaert, J. (2015). Meaning as a nonlinear effect: The birth of cool. *AILA Review, 28*, 7–27.

Blommaert, J. (2017). Ludic membership and orthopractic mobilization: On slacktivism and all that. *Tilburg Papers in Culture Studies, 193*. Retrieved from www.tilburguniversity.edu/upload/6cfbdfee-2f05–40c6–9617–d6930a811edf_TPCS_193_Blommaert.pdf.

Blommaert, J. (2018). *Durkheim and the Internet: Sociolinguistics and the sociological imagination*. London: Bloomsbury.

Blumer, H. (1969). *Symbolic interactionism: Perspectives and method*. Berkeley: University of California Press.

Castells, M. (1996). *The rise of the network society*. London: Blackwell.

De Meo, P., Ferrara, E., Fiumara, G., & Provetti, A. (2014). On Facebook, most ties are weak. *Communications of the ACM, 57*(11), 78–84.

Dijsselbloem, J., Coster, A., Henskens, B., & Veeneman, E. (2018, forthcoming). Because of patriarchy! *Diggit Magazine.*

Foucault, M. (2003). *Abnormal: Lectures at the Collège de France, 1975–1976.* New York: Picador.

Georgakopoulou, A. (2017). Small stories research: A narrative paradigm for the analysis of social media. In A. Quan-Haase & L. Sloan (Eds.), *The Sage handbook of social media research methods* (pp. 266–281). London: Sage.

Huizinga, J. (1950). *Homo ludens: A study of the play-element in culture.* New York: Roy Publishers.

Kling, B. (2017, May 23). Elliot Rodger, male entitlement, and pathologization. *Medium.* Retrieved from https://medium.com/@benkling/elliot-rodger-male-entitlement-and-pathologization-c394500309b3.

Langman, P. (2009). *Why kids kill: Inside the minds of school shooters.* New York: Macmillan.

Langman, P. (2016a). *Multi-victim school shootings in the United States: A fifty-year review.* Retrieved from https://schoolshooters.info/sites/default/files/fifty_year_review_1.1.pdf.

Langman, P. (2016b). *Elliot Rodger: An analysis.* Retrieved from https://schoolshooters.info/sites/default/files/rodger_analysis_2.0.pdf.

Langman, P. (2016c). *Eric Harris: The search for justification.* Retrieved from https://schoolshooters.info/sites/default/files/harris_search_for_justification_1.3.pdf.

LaViolette, J. (2017). Cyber-metapragmatics and alterity on reddit.com. *Tilburg Papers in Culture Studies, 196.* Retrieved from www.tilburguniversity.edu/upload/6614d6f8–3b03–4c8a-8ac9-b56ecf4b9cb1_TPCS_196_LaViolette.pdf.

Lee, J. J., & Hoadley, C. M. (2007). Leveraging identity to make learning fun: Possible selves and experiential learning in Massively Multiplayer Online Games (MMOGs). *Innovate: Journal of Online Education, 3*(6), Article 5. Retrieved from http://nsuworks.nova.edu/cgi/viewcontent.cgi?article=1081&context=innovate.

Li, K., & J. Blommaert (2017, November 22). The care of the selfie: Ludic chronotopes of *baifumei* in online China. *CRTL+ALT+DEM.* Retrieved from https://alternative-democracy-research.org/2017/11/22/the-care-of-the-selfie/.

Maly, I., & Varis, P. (2015). The 21st-century hipster: On micro-populations in times of superdiversity. *European Journal of Cultural Studies, 19*(6), 1–17.

Mead, G. H. (1934). *Mind, self and society.* Chicago: University of Chicago Press.

Nagle, A. (2017). *Kill all normies: Online culture wars from 4chan and Tumblr to Trump and the alt-right.* London: Zero Books.

Peeters, S., Wijayanti, N., Van Meer, M., De Clerck, D., & Raa, J. (2018, forthcoming). The threat of toxic masculinity: From online Manosphere to toxic masculine public figures. *Diggit Magazine.*

Schoonen, M., Fransen, H., Bastiaense, R., & Cai, N. (2018, forthcoming). The Manosphere as a learning environment. *Diggit Magazine.*

Smits, L., Van Gorp, M., Van der Jagt, M., Bakx, M. & Yacoubi, N. (2018, forthcoming). Extreme abnormals. *Diggit Magazine.*

Tagg, C., Seargeant, P., & Brown, A. (2017). *Taking offense on social media: Conviviality and communication on Facebook.* London: Palgrave Pivot.

Varis, P., & Blommaert, J. (2015). Conviviality and collectives on social media: Virality, memes, and new social structures. *Multilingual Margins*, 2(1), 31–45.

Vivenzi, L., Schaffels, W., De la Vega, G., & Driessen, L. (2018, forthcoming). Infiltrating the Manosphere: An exploration of male-oriented virtual communities from the inside. *Diggit Magazine*.

Williams, R. (1977). *Marxism and literature*. Oxford: Oxford University Press.

Chapter 10

The Cologne translation note

Victims and perpetrators

Sjaak Kroon

Introduction

While having breakfast and reading my newspaper, *de Volkskrant*, one morning in January 2016, I was confronted with a picture of what at first sight seemed to be a snippet of paper with some handwritten words and a sentence in German and Arabic. The note was presented as an illustration accompanying an article that dealt with the wave of sexual assaults that were reported to have taken place on New Year's Eve 2015/16 in the German city of Cologne on the square between Cologne Central Station and the city's magnificent cathedral. Victims of these assaults were hundreds of young German women who celebrated New Year's Eve in Cologne's public space and those allegedly responsible for the sex attacks were refugees, asylum seekers and immigrants of mainly North African or Arab origin. That was at least the main message in most German and foreign newspapers reporting on this incident. In the wake of this news similar stories were reported from other German cities such as Hamburg, Frankfurt, Dortmund, Düsseldorf, Stuttgart and Bielefeld and also from Sweden and Switzerland.

In this contribution I will not go into what exactly happened that night in Cologne and other places and I will not try to explain these happenings against the background of the current refugee crisis in Europe. For an in-depth analysis from a cultural and media perspective respectively, see for example Žižek (2016) and Bergermann (2016), while the papers collected in Pierik (2016) that use 'Caliphate Light' as a subtitle focus on 'the anti-Western resentment of refugees and parts of the migrant community, the failure of governmental institutions and politicians, lying and deceiving and how to proceed', as the back cover text says in Dutch. Here I will deal with the assaults from a somewhat different perspective, i.e. the perspective of the perpetrators.

It goes without saying that the only real victims of the New Year's Eve assaults in Cologne and elsewhere are the 1200 women who, according to the *Independent*,[1] were reportedly sexually harassed, grabbed, robbed and even raped, with 2000 men involved. The focus of this contribution however is not on the victims but on the suspects of these assaults, i.e. men 'from the North African or Arab region', who, when the assaults – after a few days of deliberate silence – were made public by the Cologne authorities and news media, immediately and in very specific ways were framed as perpetrators, guilty of the crimes that had been committed.

In doing so I will focus on three different ways in which these men were discursively constructed or framed as perpetrators. First, I will go into the way they were referred to in German news media. Then I will discuss how these news media presented and discussed a translation note, a piece of paper containing an Arabic-German list of words and expression that was found that night in Cologne. Finally, I will analyse the way in which the media referred to the languages used in the translation note. This includes an analysis of both the German and Arabic writing in the note. Finally, as a postscript, I will briefly refer to the curious case of Kamel Daoud, an Algerian journalist and writer, who as a public intellectual took a position in the Cologne debate in *Le Monde* and found himself heavily criticized by a group of French intellectuals, as a consequence of which he decided to leave the public debate and return to being just a writer.

Who are the perpetrators?

Wikipedia, generally speaking, is not considered the most scientific of all sources one can use to shed light on any phenomenon. After all it is a free encyclopaedia that is collaboratively written by the people who use it. Literally anyone can edit any page. All the changes ever made are, however, recorded in article histories that can be displayed via the Wikipedia 'view history' button. Against this background I will here use Wikipedia as a historical source that directly reflects the public reception of the Cologne assaults and that, as such, can be used as a first line diagnostic of what happened that night and how it was perceived.

The first Wikipedia article on the assaults was created on January 5, 2016 at 11:32 by 'Chemischer Bruder'. It was a rather limited article of just 327 words entitled '*Sexuelle Übergriffe in der Silvesternacht 2015/16*' ('Sexual assaults on New Year's Eve 2015/16').[2] It dealt in about six lines each with what happened (*Ereignisse*), how authorities reacted (*Reaktionen*) and what police investigations resulted in (*Ermittlungen*) and it referred to just three sources (*Einzelnachweise*): *Spiegel Online* (January 4, 2016),[3] *Focus Online* (January 5, 2016),[4] and *Tagesschau.de* (January 5, 2016).[5] Common to the article and its sources is the way they refer to what happened, to the victims and especially to the perpetrators of the assaults. I quote from the Wikipedia article:

> On New Year's Eve 2015/16 there were massive sexual assaults on women, robberies and physical injuries on the forecourt of Cologne's

railway station. The starting point was a group of 1000 men. [...] The assaults occurred between midnight and four o'clock in the morning. So far, 90 women filed a complaint. Several victims stated that groups of 20 to 40 men had surrounded them. Mobile phones, handbags and purses have been stolen. The Cologne police chief Wolfgang Albers said in a first statement one knew of allegedly 80 victims. The estimated number of unreported cases would be higher. The women were groped and robbed in the turmoil. 'There has been a high number of sexual assaults, even in very massive form', said Albers.[6]

The article refers to the perpetrators as follows:

The perpetrators are 'mainly from the North African or Arab region', said police chief Albers. The men should be between 15 and 35 years old. A concrete suspicion against certain persons does not exist so far.[7]

The police statement that the perpetrators are mainly from the North African or Arab region is given an empirical basis where *Focus Online* refers to the fact that witnesses agreed that these men, according to their physical appearance (*dem Aussehen nach*), came from that region. The fact that the German-Arabic translation note, which will be analysed below, was found that night with two men, age 16 and 23, from Morocco and Tunisia respectively, fits the general image of the perpetrators who, right from the start, were framed as criminals and rapists with an immigrant, refugee or asylum seeker background.[8]

Consulting other contemporary sources, i.e. offline and online German news media published on January 8, 2016, we find a more diversified but still rather homogeneous description of the perpetrators.[9] They are in a rather neutral way referred to as 'men' (*Männer*) and 'groups of young men' (*Gruppen junger Männer*), most of them under the influence of alcohol (*alkoholisierte Männer*). They are also called 'suspects' (*Verdächtige, Tatverdächtige*) or even '(presumed) perpetrators' or 'groups of perpetrators' ((*mutmassliche*) *Täter, Tätergruppen*). In most cases a further ethnic or geographic specification is added as in 'men of North African origin' or 'descent' (*Männer nordafrikanischer Herkunft* or *Abstammung*), 'men from Morocco and Tunisia' (*Männer aus Marokko und Tunesien*), North Africans and North African groups of perpetrators (*Nordafrikaner* and *nordafrikanische Tätergruppen*), 'a Moroccan' (*ein Marokkaner*), 'Arab clans' (*Arabische clans*). Also, more general specifications referring to the perpetrators' position in German society are used in, for example, 'men with a migration background' (*Männer mit Migrationshintergrund*), 'asylum seekers' (*Asylbewerber*), 'foreign suspects' (*ausländischen Verdächtige*), 'people with no legal status or stay permit' (*Leute ohne Papiere und Aufenthaltsgenehmigung*), a man 'who lives in a refugee centre' (*der in einer Flüchtlingsunterkunft lebt*) or investigations leading the police 'to refugee centres and their surrounding' (*in Flüchtlings-heime oder deren Umfeld*). In one case 31 known suspects are listed as follows: 'nine Algerian, eight Moroccan, five Iranian, four Syrian, one Iraqi, one Serbian, one US-American and two German citizens. 18 of them presumably asylum seekers' (*neun Algerische, acht marokkanische, fünf iranische, vier syrische, ein irakischer, ein serbischer, ein US-amerikanischer und zwei deutsche Staatsangehörige. 18 von ihnen seien Asylbewerber*).

It is explicitly stated, in for example *Kölner Rundschau*, that so far no sexual crimes could (and should) be related to the asylum seekers who were among the suspects and who did commit, as it is also explicitly stated, physical injuries and theft. The message to the general public however is clear: the perpetrators belong to the large group of people with an migra-tion background, be it recently arrived refugees or asylum seekers from war-struck regions in, for example, Syria, or migrants from a variety of countries in North Africa and the Middle East, who for various reasons came to Germany long before Chancellor Angela Merkel's famous words 'We can do it' (*Wir schaffen das*)[10] referring to the international refugee crisis as a consequence mainly of the war in Syria.

At the time of writing, in the most recent (October 25, 2017) version of the already quoted Wikipedia article[11] – with 11,487 words (versus 327 in 2016) and 175 sources (versus three in 2016), considerably enlarged – we find a summary of the happenings in numbers. There were 1529 female victims and 1000 male perpetrators between 15 and 35 years of age, mainly from the North-African/Arab region; the identity of 71 of them was established by the police. The total number of suspects was 183 of which eight went into inves-tigative custody; 55 suspects were from Morocco, 53 from Algeria, 22 from Iraq, 14 from Syria, 14 from Germany, 73 were asylum seekers, 36 illegal immigrants, 11 had a stay permit and the rest had an unclear legal status. At the end of February 2016, the number of identified perpetrators was 62, mainly refugees, asylum seekers and people with a migration background. Two thirds of the suspects, although they only recently arrived in Germany, where already known by the police. The number of suspects that were actu-ally brought to court was 22, mainly North Africans.

In my understanding, this bombardment of numbers, facts and figures not only contributes to framing the Cologne assaults as a real big crime, which it no doubt was, but also to framing the suspects as perpetrators at a moment when no real proof of their crimes was available. The realism and relativity of this framing becomes clear in an article looking back on the Cologne assaults almost one year after they happened, in *Frankfurter Allgemeine Zeitung*[12] of November 15, 2016. It shows that out of a total of 1205 crime cases that were finally reported to the police, including 509 sexual crimes, only 153 cases were actually brought to court and only six of the men involved were eventually sentenced, mainly for property crimes.

What did they do?

The main topic in all the media attention on the Cologne assaults was a piece of paper that became known in German as *der Übersetzungszettel* ('the translation note'). This translation note, as it was printed in *de Volkskrant*, i.e. how I first saw it, is reproduced in Figure 10.1. The caption of the illustration in *de Volkskrant* was: 'A note with a German-Arabic wordlist that according to the *Kölner Stadt-Anzeiger* would have been found with the suspects.'

The note is yellow, or yellowish, depending on the quality of the picture that one views and plain. The text is handwritten with a blue ballpoint. It shows a wordlist that has three entries. On the first line are two German words, *Große Brüste* ('big breasts'), with next to it a translation in Arabic that as a consequence of a crease in the paper is difficult to read. On the second line is the word *Fucken*, which clearly resembles the German verb *ficken* ('to fuck') without a translation in Arabic. The third line contains a complete German sentence, *Ich will fucken* ('I want to fuck') with a translation in Arabic next to it. Content wise, these three lines obviously belong to the sexual domain: they explicitly refer to female body parts and to (the desire of) having sex. As a consequence, the note in the media led to strong disapproval, horror and outrage. Not only the two men from Morocco and Tunisia[13] with whom the note was found, but also the group they were considered to be part of, i.e. the large number of men with a migration background, asylum seekers, refugees from Syria, North Africa and other places, were simply portrayed or 'framed' (Goffman, 1986) as being sex offenders.

Having a closer look at the various references to the Cologne assaults that could be found on the internet, I was surprised by the number of different fragments of the note that were shown. It turned out that *de Volkskrant* in fact reproduced the smallest fragment of all, only containing the three lines discussed above. A slightly larger version of the note was shown by the

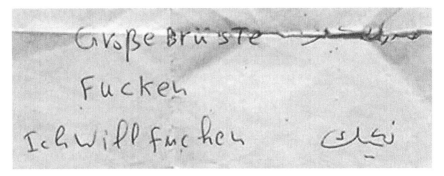

Figure 10.1 Translation note with a German-Arabic wordlist.
Source: *de Volkskrant*, January 14, 2016.

Cologne newspaper *Kölner Stadtanzeiger*.[14] Here, the note had one line more, saying *ich will dich küssen* ('I want to kiss you') with a translation in Arabic. The same fragment was shown by *Zaronews*,[15] *Campogeno*[16] and *Express*.[17] A much more extensive fragment was shown by *Das BlogMagazin*.[18] It has seven more lines with Arabic translations: *ich töte sie ficken* ('I fuck you to death'), *Ich will töte dich küssen* ('I want to kiss you to death'), *Was ist sie?* ('What is she?'), *[i]ch scherze mit ihnen* ('I make fun of you'), *diese* ('this'), *Ich erinne mich* ('I remember') and *Ich scheze* ('I make fun'). Almost the whole note could be found on the *Focus Online*[19] website with two more lines: *ich habe eine überraschungun* ('I have a surprises'; with Arabic on its right side) and *gelegenheit* ('opportunity'). Figure 10.2 shows the full note, which also has been made available on the internet by, among others, WDR[20] and *Kölner Stadtanzeiger*.[21]

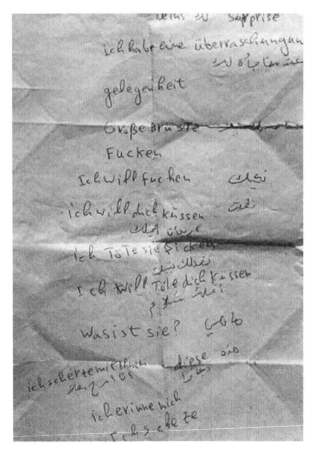

Figure 10.2 The full translation note.
Source: *Kölner Stadt-Anzeiger*, January 8, 2016.

It is remarkable, I think, that in most cases the whole note was not reproduced by the media, just a fragment, and without explicitly indicating that this is the case. All publications refer to the fragment and discuss it without making clear that these are just a few lines taken from the one-page original. The fragments that are reproduced are, generally speaking, chosen in such a way that words and sentences from the sexual domain get central attention. The more or less 'neutral' first three lines, (1) *Deins, surprise*, (2) *ich habe eine überraschungun*, (3) *gelegenheit*, are generally left out. Lines 4 to 9 are reproduced: (4) *Große Brüste*, (5) *Fucken*, (6) *Ich will fucken*, (7) *ich will dich küssen*, (8) *Ich töte sie ficken*, (9) *Ich will tote dich küssen*. And the more or less 'neutral' lines 10 to 14 are often left out again: (10) *Was ist sie*, (11) *ich scherze mit ihnen*, (12) *diese*, (13) *ich erinne mich*, (14) *Ich scheze*.

In this way the men that were involved in the assaults are not only framed as eager for sex but rather as sex offenders, murderous rapists looking for victims that they first would mislead by saying things like 'I have a surprise for you' and then abuse and even kill. In particular, the way in which the sentences *Ich töte sie ficken* and *Ich will töte dich küssen* are generally paraphrased in the media as 'I kill you', is telling in this respect. The translation note that was found with two young migrants became a symbol connected to what 'all those, who are already agitating for weeks against the reception of refugees' refer to as 'associations of "criminal foreigners/Muslims who discriminate women/uncivilized testosterone ruled young men"' (Bergerman, 2016).[22]

What did they say?

De Volkskrant referred to the German newspaper *Kölner Stadt-Anzeiger* as its main source. It will come as no surprise that not only this newspaper but also other offline and online media in Germany and all over the world gave quite some attention to the assaults that happened in Cologne. Most of these articles stated that it was immigrants, refugees or asylum seekers from the Arab or North-African region who assaulted and mugged German women in Cologne and who apparently did so in an organized way. This among other things was concluded from the Arabic-German translation note that the police found that night. The translation note is referred to in the media in a number of different ways that shed an interesting light on the perspective the media took in this matter. The same applies to the headings of the various German articles that I collected online on January 8, 2016,[23] and the way in which they referred to the translation note (see Table 10.1).[24]

In the headings the note is six times simply referred to as *Übersetzungszettel* ('translation note') and once each as *Drohzettel* ('threatening note') and *Zettel* ('note'). In one case the note is specified as *Arabisch* ('Arabic'),

Table 10.1 Selected German media headings and references to the translation note

---

Kölner Stad-Anzeiger (January 8, 2016)
'Ich töte sie' – Polizei findet Übersetzungszettel bei Verdächtigen
- *einen deutsch-arabischen Übersetzungszettel*
- *einen Zettel (…) mit handschriftlichen Übersetzungshilfen in deutsch-arabischer Sprache*
- *einen deutsch-arabischen Übersetzungszettel mit erschreckendem Inhalt*
- *einen Zettel mit kruden Übersetzungen sexistischer Begriffe vom Deutschen ins Arabische*

Kölnische Rundschau (January 8, 2016)
Übersetzungszettel bei Tatverdächtigen
- *ein Übersetzungszettel arabisch-deutsch*

Berliner Zeitung (January 8, 2016)
'Ich töte sie' – Polizei findet Übersetzungszettel bei Verdächtigen
- *einen deutsch-arabischen Übersetzungszettel mit erschreckendem Inhalt*
- *einen Zettel (…) mit handschriftlichen Übersetzungshilfen in deutsch-arabischer Sprache*

Abendzeitung München (January 8, 2016)
Polizei findet Übersetzungszettel: 'Ich will fucken', 'Ich töte Sie'
- *einen erschreckenden Übersetzungszettel*

Focus Online (January 8, 2016)[25]
'Ich töte sie', 'ficken', 'große Brüste' – Skandalnacht von Köln: Das ist der erschreckender Drohzettel, den die Polizei fand
- *der Drohzettel mit den obszönen und erschreckenden Botschaften*

Express (January 8, 2016)[26]
'Große Brüste': Der schlimme Übersetzungszettel der Festgenommenen
- *Hier wurden Übersetzungen von schrecklichen Sätzen notiert*
- *(…) einen Zettel, auf dem 'wichtige' Übersetzungen standen*
- *verdächtiger Zettel*

Metropolico (January 8, 2016)[27]
Polizei findet arabischer uebersetzungszettel
- *deutsch-arabischer Übersetzungszettel*

---

three times it is said to be found with *(Tat)verdächtigen* ('suspects') or *Festgenommenen* ('detainees'). Adjectives that are combined with the note are *erschreckend* ('terrifying') and *schlimm* ('terrible'). Quotes from the note that are used in the headings are: *Ich töte sie* ('I kill you'; five times), *Ich will fucken* ('I want to fuck'; two times), *ficken* ('fuck'; two times), *große Brüste* ('big breasts'; two times). In the articles, a number of specifications of the note are added. It is said to contain rude translations of sexist terms (*kruden Übersetzungen sexistischer Begriffe*), terrifying content (*erschreckendem Inhalt*), obscene and terrifying messages (*obszönen und erschreckenden Botschaften*), terrible sentences (*schrecklichen Sätzen*), 'important' translations (*'wichtige' Übersetzungen*) and it is a suspicious note (*verdächtiger Zettel*). In addition to these January 8 headlines, *Campogeno*[28] (January 9, 2016) refers to the note as *Deutschkurs* ('German lesson') and *Die Welt*[29] (January 22, 2016) says that the suspects had a *Sex-Spickzettel* ('sex cheat sheet') with them – both referring to an 'educational' context in which German is learned in a real life situation, although *Campogeno* adds a further specification, i.e. *mama merkel – grosse brüste – ich wil fucken* ('mama merkel – big breasts – I want to fuck'), and a subtitle that says it all: *die ersten wichtigsten worte auf deutch* ('the first most important words in German') followed by four lines well-known from the note: *Große Brüste – Fucken – Ich will fucken – ich will dich küssen.*

Irrespective of the reference to an educational context for learning the language of the host country, not uncommon to immigrants, the inescapable media message of the way in which the translation note is presented and what is referred to as its main content, is that this wordlist is a way for men from the North African and Arab region to deceive, seduce and abuse German women.

What about their languages?

If we try to imagine the production process of the translation note, the following might be what happened. Two men (at least) come together, one knowing German and (a variety of) Arabic rather well (let's call him the teacher) and the other one (most probably) one knowing only (a variety of) Arabic and wanting to be informed about some German phrases that would be useful for getting into contact with women (let's call him the learner).

The learner might have approached the teacher with a learning need in the semantic field of establishing (sexual) contacts with women in a foreign, i.e. German, language environment in which his own (Arabic) language has no real discursive value. The teacher might have asked the learner what words and phrases he wanted to learn. The learner might have mentioned these in his variety of Arabic. Each of these words and utterances were then first written down by the teacher in German, phrase by phrase, and after that, he or the learner might have added the same words in Arabic – otherwise the learner would not be able to understand and remember what it was all about. The German part was most probably written down first as can be seen from the fact that only where there is enough space after the German words, are the Arabic words put on the same line (written from right to left), whereas in other cases the Arabic is written beneath the German phrase. As a result of this procedure the learner got an overview of the very specific thematic semantic field that he wanted to acquire in a German-Arabic translation.

Already on January 8, 2016, the translation note was uploaded on 'Reddit Translator', 'a social media community for translation requests', by 'ichbindeinfeindbild' with as an accompanying text: 'This note was found on one of the cologne NYE rapists, it does feature some German text, but that makes no sense at all.'[30] This post leads to eight comments, mainly criticizing the content of the note and questioning the quality and correctness of the Arabic as well as the German writing. In his comment, *Malteseraccoon*, after having pointed at what he considers to be mistakes such as missing dots and 'eye-dialect/mis-spelling', concludes: 'I believe whoever wrote this is either non-Arab or an Arab whose native language is not Arabic' and '…they seem to have poor literacy skills in Arabic'. The translation request by ichbeindeinfendbild moved to the *You are not alone* website, 'a recovery subreddit for those who were once followers of Islam'.[31] Here 'Allah-Of-Reddit' gives some translations and adds: 'These are all written in Syrian lingo.' ichbindeinfeindbild then says that '[t]he German translation on that paper makes no sense at all, it is just random words mumbled together' and asks whether some of the phrases are 'tongue-in-cheek … or is this really meant threatening'. Allah-Of-Reddit reacts: 'Tongue in cheek I think, I'm not Syrian but their vulgar linguistics are pretty well known.' Interestingly he also adds: 'As for the German they probably got it from a German speaker, just words put together like when I say "Me sex want"'.

From the above we can conclude that the participants in the discussion are rather critical with respect to the Arabic as well as German phrases on the note that, as they suggest, might be written by someone from Syria as far as the Arabic is concerned and by a German speaker as far as the German is concerned. Let's now have a closer look at the German and Arabic text on the translation note.

German

The German that is used has some remarkable features. First of all it stays rather close to official German orthography by using capital letters in the first word of a sentence (*Ich*, 'I') and in nouns (*Brüste*, 'breasts'). It also uses the German diacritic umlaut with *ü* and *ö* (*Brüste*, 'breasts'; *überraschungun*, 'surprises'; *küssen*, 'kiss'; *Töte*, 'kill'), the combination of *c* and *k* representing /k/ (*fucken* and *ficken*, 'fuck'), the double *ll* representing /l/ (*will*, 'want') and the *ch* representing /g/ (*ich*, 'I'; *mich*, 'me'; *dich*, 'you'). Remarkable is the use of German *eszett* (ß), a sharp s-sound combining the consonants *s* and *z* (*Große*, 'big'). As a consequence of its uniqueness, ß can be considered an iconic feature of German orthography. As a matter of fact, the last German orthography reform that was decided upon in 1998 and became compulsory in 2005 included a change in the rules for using ß. It is now only used for the s-sound after a long vowel (as in *große*) or a diphthong, whereas after a short vowel always *ss* is used (Duden, 2004, p. 81). Although, as a consequence of this change, the appearance of ß in German writing has considerably diminished, this does not necessarily mean that it is more easily mastered by its (native as well as non-native) users.

Apart from these features of correctness following the norm of German orthography, there are also grassroots elements such as the use of capital letter *G* in *Große* ('big') and *F in Fucken* ('fuck'), although one might consider these acceptable since they are at the beginning of a line, *T* in *BrüsTe* ('breasts') and *TöTe* ('kill') and *K* in *FucKen* ('fuck'). In some cases capitals are missing in nouns where they should have been used in German orthography (*überraschungun*, 'surprises'; *gelegenheit*, 'opportunity'). Also, the fact that the sentence in the second line has no dot at the end can be considered an example of grassroots literacy. Finally, there seems to be a kind of hyphenated comma just before the s in *Brü'ste* and we see a number of possibly pronunciation-related writing errors such as a missing *r* in *scheze* (*scherze*, 'make fun'), *erinne* instead of *erinnere* ('remember'), *u* instead of *e* in what seems to be an uncalled for plural *überraschungun* (*überraschungen*, 'surprises'). One of the words on the first line of the note is *surprise*, which looks as if it is changed into *supprise* ('surprise'). This word could be seen as French but the correction suggests that it is meant to be pronounced as English. Grassroots elements in writing are a sign of limited acquisition, proficiency or use of a language. They can often be found in situations where people with limited literacy skills still use a language in writing (Blommaert, 2008). The word *fucken* (as standalone as well as in a sentence) is remarkable in this context. As already indicated, it clearly refers to the German verb *ficken* (meaning among other things 'to fuck', 'having sexual intercourse'). It should be noted here that in the German dictionary by Wahrig (1974, p. 1236) *ficken* is characterized as 'vulgar', as is for that matter 'fuck' in the *Concise Oxford Dictionary* (Sykes, 1976, p. 427). The variant *fucken* seems to be influenced by the English verb 'fuck'. This could either be in the form of simply replacing the first vowel *i* by *u* or by adding the German morpheme *en* indicating a verb, to the English stem 'fuck'.

The combination of iconic German ß and *umlaut ü* and *ö* on the one hand and grassroots features and Anglicized German on the other is remarkable. Although the text is in near-native German, I would suggest it is written by a non-native German speaker, by someone though who knows quite a bit of German as a consequence of having lived in Germany for quite a while but whose proficiency is not stable enough to prevent him from being influenced by English in an admittedly very frequently used word like *fucken* that, as we know, can have all kinds of metaphorical meanings in English as well as in German.[32]

Arabic

Regarding the Arabic writing on the note, the starting point is that the language under consideration here was referred to in all news media as

Arabic, totally in line with the reference to the perpetrators as coming from the North African or Arab region. We have to be aware however, that the concept 'Arabic' can mean a number of different things. It can refer to Classical Arabic, i.e. the language of the Qur'an, to Modern Standard Arabic (MSA) as it is taught at school, or to dialectal varieties of Arabic in North African countries such as Morocco, Algeria, Tunisia and Libya. It can finally also refer to dialectal Arabic used in Middle Eastern countries such as Syria. A second important remark here has to be that it is rather difficult to determine on the basis of writing only, what variety of Arabic the writer had the intention to use. This mainly has to do with the fact that the main features used to distinguish between these varieties are mainly the different ways in which the vowels in a text are pronounced; these vowels however, in whatever form of Arabic, are not written and as a consequence have to be deduced from the context. The analysis below in which I try to identify the version of Arabic that is used on the note is therefore rather speculative. In addition, I don't know any Arabic myself and, as a consequence, had to rely on others.[33]

The analysis of the Arabic writing on the note shows that different 'versions' of Arabic are used. Most of the text is written in Modern Standard Arabic (MSA) and apart from a single spelling mistake, as for example in دعارا (daʿārā, 'prostitution') in which the last letter should have been ö, MSA is generally spelled correctly. A typical MSA feature is the frequent use of glottal stops. Examples are both ʾurid and ʾuqabbilik in the sentence ʾurīd ʾan ʾuqabbilik (أريد أن أقبلك – Ich will dich küssen, 'I want to kiss you'). In particular, the lexical choices made are important here: ʾurīd is MSA versus ʾayez in Egyptian and biddii in Syrian, for instance. The same goes for ʾuqabbilik, as the dialect version would be abuus or buus in Egyptian. Further MSA features are the lexical choice ما هي (mā hiya – Was ist sie, 'What is she') and the structure of this question, which is different from how dialectal Arabic would phrase it; the lexical choice of ʾamzaH in ʾanā ʾamzaH maʿik (أنا أمزح معك – ich scherze mit Ihnen, 'I joke with you'); and the use of هذ (hādhihi – diese, 'this') as a demonstrative.

For some parts of the text it is not clear if it is MSA or dialect since it can be read in both ways. For example, in the first line of the note we infer from the context that ك refers to feminine laki (Deins, 'for you'). It could however also be read as masculine laka or as dialectal līk (masc) or līkī (fem). In Syria ʾilik and in Egypt līkī (not līk) would exclusively refer to feminine and in Moroccan lek could refer to feminine and masculine. From the Arabic writing it cannot be decided whether it is MSA or dialect. The same applies to دعارا (daʿāra – 'prostitution', without a German word), which can be both MSA and dialectal Arabic.

Next to text that is written in MSA there are also words that represent a dialect form of Arabic as used in North African countries such as Morocco or Tunisia. An example is the use of the prefix n(e) (referring to the first person singular) in نكيك (*nkīk(i)* – *Ich will dich Fucken*, 'I fuck you'). In Middle Eastern Arabic *na* would refer to the first person plural (masc and fem). *Nkīk(i)* is a rather rude, insulting and not very frequently occurring use of Arabic for expressing the desire to have sex with a woman in a context of vulgar and rude sexual harassment. It is related to expressions like 'fuck you', 'fuck your mother' and 'son of a bitch' (*ibn el mtnāka*, literally 'the son of the fucked'). Another example is the prefix *ni* in نقتلك نبيك (*naqtulak nibīk* – *ich Töte sie ficken*, 'I kill you fucking'). Since *nibīk* is only used in the dialect, also *naqtulak* is considered dialect, referring to a first person singular and not as in MSA a first person plural (we kill you). Of a totally different nature is MSA نطفت (*naTaft* – 'I gave sperm'), which is a more formal, technically or euphemistically used word that would not be very easily used in an informal conversation and it certainly does not fit the rude expression just discussed. It is derived from *nuTfa* ('sperm') that appears also in the Qur'an.[34]

The combination of such different uses of Arabic (MSA, dialect, rude and formal varieties) in one text suggests that the writer, although originally most probably being a native speaker of (a variety of) Arabic, might have been living outside his original Arabic speaking community for quite some time. This can be concluded from the fact that, although he uses mainly MSA, the consistent use of the prefixes *ni* and *na* for translating German *Ich* (first person singular and, inferring from the context, masculine) points in the direction of someone who is originally from North Africa and who quite some time ago migrated to Germany. In Germany, his proficiency in Modern Standard Arabic, except for the readability of his handwriting, did not really suffer, as is shown from the above analysis, he however combines different 'versions' of Arabic in a way that one would not find in a native speaker with an unbroken language use trajectory. If we assume that the writer of the Arabic and German part of the note is one and the same person – and the handwriting seems to suggest that this is the case – he will most probably be a member of the long-present North African immigrant community in Germany rather than a recently arrived refugee from the Middle East, more specifically Syria – as is (implicitly) suggested by the media.

Conclusions

In this chapter, I discussed the events that happened on New Year's Eve 2015/16 in Cologne, including robbery, theft, groping, sexual harassment and rape. In approaching what happened from different perspectives I identified the initial suggestion that these crimes were committed by men who, judging from their physical appearance and based on the fact that an Arabic-German translation note was found with two of them, were of North African or Arab origin. This suggestion was, however, quickly transformed into an almost general public consensus that the Cologne per-petrators belonged to the community of (mainly) newly arrived refugees and asylum seekers in Germany. As soon as the authorities on January 8, 2016, made public what happened in Cologne and thereby referred to the suspects as being 'mainly from the North African and Arab region' (*über-wiegend aus dem nordafrikanischen beziehungsweise arabischen Raum*) the media immediately started framing these suspects as perpetrators, as criminals guilty of sexually harassing German women. They did so not only by referring to the suspects as perpetrators but also by explicitly con-necting their crimes to their non-German, i.e. North African or Arab origins. An important aspect in framing the suspects was the German-Arabic translation note that was found with two of the suspects. The media mainly showed parts of the note that contained words and phrases that were explicitly related to sexual harassment, and in the way these phrases were translated a connection was made with violent rape and even murder. Moreover, the fact that the language on the note was systemati-cally referred to as Arabic obscured the fact that in addition to Modern Standard Arabic North African dialectal Arabic was also used. This, together with the finding that the German that was used on the note appeared to be rather close to Standard German, might point in the direc-tion of long-present immigrants as writers of the note instead of newly arrived refugees from the Middle East. As a consequence of all this, the men who were celebrating New Year's Eve in Cologne were all lumped together as perpetrators, as thieves and rapists who recently came to Germany from the North African or Arab region. Irrespective of the odd voice that warned against jumping to all-too-easy conclusions with respect to who the suspects were and where they came from, the general public was mainly exposed to the image created by the media of foreigners 'who defiled the pure white woman, who is meant to be protected' (Bergermann, 2016).[35] In this way the alleged perpetrators ended up as nothing more or less than victims, victims of what in Germany is called *gesundes Volksemp-finden*, that is, popular sentiment, created by the media and providing an alternative for an in-depth analysis of the backgrounds and causes of what Žižek (2016) called an 'obscene version of carnival'.

Postscript: one more victim

On January 31, 2016, the Algerian journalist Kamel Daoud, editor and columnist of *Le Quotidien d'Oran*, published an article on the Cologne assaults in *Le Monde*, entitled '*Cologne, lieu des fantasmes*'.[36] Daoud, who was already a respected columnist, had recently become an internationally respected novelist through his well-received prize-winning debut *Meur-sault, contre-enquête* (2013).[37] This book can be seen as a complement to Albert Camus' novel *L'etranger* and, according to Vince (2016), it will become essential reading for those studying Camus, because it evokes – even if it does not neatly describe – the impact of colonialism on the colonised population: the loss of land, the menial jobs, the illiteracy, the fragmented families, and the dispossession of identity.[38]

It is mainly because of this book that 'Daoud's perspective, though it could be politically elusive and knowingly provocative, became a sought-after commodity' as Zerofsky (2016) put it.[39] Daoud's article in *Le Monde* was first published in Italian in *La Repubblica* (January 10, 2016)[40] and as an Op-Ed writer he also contributed an article on this topic in the *New York Times* (January 12, 2016).[41]

In his article in *Le Monde* Daoud reflects on the Cologne assaults and asks himself what had actually happened that night:

> What happened in Cologne on New Year's Eve? It is difficult to know exactly by reading the reports, but we know – at least – what happened in the heads. That of the aggressors, perhaps; that of the Westerners, surely.
>
> Fascinating summary of fantasy games. The 'fact' in itself corresponds to the game of images that the Westerner makes of the 'other', the refugee-immigrant: naïve optimism, terror, reactivation of the fears of ancient barbarian invasions and base of the civilized barbarian binomial. Hosted immigrants attack 'our' women, assault them and rape them. This corresponds to the idea that the right and the extreme right have always built in the speeches against the reception of refugees. The latter are assimilated to the aggressors, even if we do not yet know for sure. Are the culprits long settled immigrants? Recent refugees? Criminal organizations or simple hooligans? We will not wait for the answer to already be consistently out of our minds. The 'fact' has already reactivated the discourse on 'must we welcome or lock ourselves?' against the misery of the world. The fantasy did not wait for the facts.[42]

According to Daoud, the reception of refugees in the West, i.e. saving their bodies, should be combined with efforts to change their souls, especially with regard to the way women are looked upon and treated in the unspecified '*monde arabo-musulman*', i.e. the countries of origin of the Cologne perpetrators (see also Zerofsky, 2016):

> The woman is denied, refused, killed, veiled, shut up, or possessed. This denotes a troubled relationship to the imaginary, to the desire to live, to creation and to freedom. The woman is the reflection of the life that we don't want to admit. She is the incarnation of the necessary desire and is therefore guilty of a terrible crime: life.[43]

Daoud's articles caused quite some international controversy. In *Le Monde* (February 11, 2016) he was strongly attacked by a group of 19 intellectuals who accused him of recycling the most worn-out orientalist clichés.[44] According to them, Daoud's text is based on three logics. First he proposes an obsolete essentialist or culturalist approach in which he 'reduces geographical space that includes more than a billion individuals and occupies several thousand kilometers to a homogenous entity that is solely defined by its relationship to religion, i.e. "the world of Allah"'. Second, he approaches sexual violence in relation to 'the psychological state of the Muslim masses' situating 'the responsibility for sexual violence in the psychology of individuals who are seen as deviant' and thereby portrays a mass of refugees as 'potential sexual predators since they all suffer from the same psychological disease'. Finally, by asking whether the refugee is thus 'a savage' he 'reinforces the idea of absolute otherness' and pleads for a thorough re-education of refugees. According to his critics, in this way he contributes to the growing Islamophobia that can be witnessed across Europe.

Responding to an originally private letter in which Daoud's contributions to *Le Monde* and the *New York Times* were criticized by his friend Adam Schatz, who by his long portrait of Daoud in the *New York Times* (April 1, 2015)[45] 'Stranger still: Kamel Daoud and Algeria, caught between Islamist fervor and cultural flowering' had played an important role in Daoud's international fame as a writer and public intellectual (Heynders, 2016), Daoud drew his conclusions in an open letter to Schatz and his critics:[46]

> Today the writer from the land of Allah finds himself the target of unbearable media solicitations. I can't do much about that, but I can remove myself from it: I had believed I could do so with wisdom, but I can also do it with silence, as I choose to do henceforth.
>
> And so I am turning to literature, and on that point, you're right. I will leave journalism shortly. I am going to listen to trees or to hearts. Read, Recover my confidence and my tranquillity. Explore. Not give up, but go beyond the trends and the media games. I have resolved to pry deeper rather than perform.

The Cologne sexual assaults led to a number of responses. First of all there is the remarkable resemblance between the simple and quick populist voice of the media and the 'heavily literary and allegorical style' (Zerofsky, 2016) with which Kamel Daoud reflected in his article in *Le Monde* on what happened in Cologne. Then there is the *J'accuse* of 19 intellectuals in an open letter to Daoud in, according to Adam Schatz's letter to Daoud, a 'style of public denunciation, which, in its leftist puritanism, reminded me of the Soviet-era excommunications'. From my perspective this shows the difficulty of freely engaging in a discourse that is heavily mortgaged by political correctness and that, as a consequence, can easily lead to victimization of those involved, irrespective of the position they take in their analysis. This might be especially clear in the case of Cologne but it can be observed everywhere and always where issues such as sexual violence against women, immigration, refugees, islamophobia and populism come together in a virulent combination. Proof of this statement can be found in social media around the world literally every day.

Notes

1 See the *Independent* (July 11, 2016) on www.independent.co.uk/news/world/europe/cologne-new-years-eve-mass-sex-attacks-leaked-document-a7130476.html.
2 See https://de.wikipedia.org/w/index.php?title=Sexuelle_%C3%9Cbergriffe_in_der_Silvesternacht_2015/16&oldid=149813567.
3 See www.spiegel.de/panorama/justiz/koeln-60-frauen-erstatten-anzeige-nach-sexuellen-uebergriffen-an-silvester-a-1070418.html.
4 See www.focus.de/regional/koeln/silvesternacht-am-koelner-hauptbahnhof-gruppe-von-1000-maennern-fuer-sexuelle-uebergriffe-verantwortlich_id_5188685.html.
5 See www.tagesschau.de/multimedia/sendung/ts-11963.html.
6 In der Silvesternacht 2015/16 kam es auf dem Bahnhofsvorplatz in Köln massenhaft zu sexuellen Übergriffen auf Frauen, Raubdelikten sowie Körperverletzungen. Ausgangspunkt war eine Gruppe von 1000 Männern. [...] Die Übergriffe ereigneten sich zwischen Mitternacht und vier Uhr. Bislang erstatteten 90 Frauen eine Anzeige. Mehrere Opfer gaben zu Protokoll, Gruppen von 20 bis 40 Männern hätten sie umzingelt. Mobiltelefone, Handtaschen und Geldbörsen seien gestohlen worden. Der Kölner Polizeipräsident Wolfgang Albers verlautbarte in einer erste Stellungnahme, man wisse von mutmaßlich 80 Geschädigten. Die Dunkelziffer sei noch höher. Die Frauen wurden im Getümmel angefasst und bestohlen. 'Es hat dort in sehr hoher Anzahl Sexualdelikte gegeben, auch in sehr massiver Form', so Albers. (My translation.)
7 Die Täter stammen 'überwiegend aus dem nordafrikanischen beziehungsweise arabischen Raum', so Polizeipräsident Albers. Die Männer sollen zwischen 15 und 35 Jahre alt sein. Einen konkreten Tatverdacht gegen bestimmte Personen gibt es bisher nicht. (My translation.)
8 See www.focus.de/politik/videos/ich-toete-sie-grosse-brueste-skandalnacht-von-koeln-das-ist-der-erschreckende-drohzettel-den-die-polizei-fand_id_5198423.html.
9 All citations in this section are taken from the media that I refer to in Table 10.1 and the related endnotes.
10 Chancellor Merkel made this statement at a press conference on August 31, 2015. See www.bundesregierung.de/Content/DE/Mitschrift/Pressekonferenzen/2015/08/2015-08-31-pk-merkel.html.
11 See https://de.wikipedia.org/w/index.php?title=Sexuelle_%C3%9Cbergriffe_in_der_Silvesternacht_2015/16&oldid=170307352.
12 See www.faz.net/aktuell/politik/inland/bisher-wurden-nur-sechs-taeter-der-koelner-silvesternacht-verurteilt-14545141.html.
13 See www.focus.de/politik/videos/ich-toete-sie-grosse-brueste-skandalnacht-von-koeln-das-ist-der-erschreckende-drohzettel-den-die-polizei-fand_id_5198423.html.

14 See www.ksta.de/koeln/sote-deutsch-arabischer-uebersetzungs-zettel,15187530.33 480596.html#plx992025940.

15 See www.zaronews.world/zaronews-presseberichte/ich-toete-sie-polizei-findet-ueber setzungszettel-bei-verdaechtigen/.

16 See https://campogeno.wordpress.com/tag/uebersetzings-zettel/.

17 See www.express.de/koeln/koeln-uebergriffe–grosse-brueste—der-schlimme-ueber setzungs-zettel-der-festgenommenen-23404260.

18 See www.severint.net/2016/01/10/der-silvester-zettel-von-koeln/.

19 See www.focus.de/politik/videos/ich-toete-sie-grosse-brueste-skandalnscht-von -koeln-das-isr-der-erschreckende-drohzettel-den-die-polizei-fand_id_5198423. html.

20 See www1.wdr.de/nachrichten/festnahmen-koeln-102.html with only here a copyright reference to WDR/Hilgers.

21 See www.ksta.de/koeln/sote-deutsch-arabischer-uebersetzungs-zettel,15187530, 33480596.html#plx1996515829.

22 Wie erwartet, haben sofort all diejenigen, die seit Wochen gegen die Aufnahme von Flüchtlingen agitieren, Verbindungen von 'kriminellen Ausländern/ frauendiskriminierenden Muslimen/ unzivilisierten testosterongesteuerten Jungmännern …' ausgerufen […]. (My translation.) See www.zfmedienwissenschaft.de/online/blog/köln-rape-culture.

23 I decided not to include the various dates on which I (repeatedly) accessed all these sources.

24 English translations of all the heading can be found in the text below Table 10.1.

25 See www.focus.de/politik/videos/ich-toete-sie-grosse-brueste-skandalnacht-von-koeln-das-ist-der-erschreckende-drohzettel-den-die-polizei-fand_id_5198423.html.

26 See www.express.de/koeln/koeln-uebergriffe-grosse-brueste-der-schlimme-ueberset zungs-zettel-der-festgenommenen-23404260.

27 See www.metropolico.org/2016/01/08/polizei-findet-arabische-uebersetzungszettel/.

28 See https://campogeno.wordpress.com/tag/uebersetzungs-zettel/.

29 See www.welt.de/150765894.

30 See www.reddit.com/r/translator/comments/402tfk/arabic_english_handwritten_ note_by_cologne_nye/.

31 See https://np.reddit.com/r/exmuslim/comments/402wuf/arabicenglish_translation_ needed_xpost_rtranslator/.

32 See 'How to Use the Word FUCK: 26 Different Uses' (Part I and II) at http:// reallifeglobal.com/how-use-word-fuck/.

33 I could not have done this analysis without the very much appreciated help of my colleagues Jan Jaap de Ruiter (Tilburg University) and Mona Farrag (University of Colorado).

34 See the following chapters and verse numbers in the Qur'an: 16:4; 18:37; 22:5; 23:13; 23:14; 35:11; 36:77; 40:67; 53:46; 75:37; 76:2; 80:19; www.holyquran. net/cgi-bin/qsearch.pl?st=%E4%D8%DD&sc=1&sv=1&ec=114&ev=10&ae= &mw=p&alef=ON.

35 …die die reine Weiße Frau besudelten, welche es zu verteidigen gelte. (My translation.)

36 'Cologne, place of fantasies'; see www.lemonde.fr/idees/article/2016/01/31/ cologne-lieu-de-fantasmes_4856694_3232.html.

37 Kamel Daoud, The Meursault investigation (Great Britain and Australia: One-world Publications, 2015). Translation by John Cullen. Originally published in French as Meursault, contre-enquête (Algiers: Editions Barzakh, 2013).

38 See   http://h-france.net/fffh/maybe-missed/literature-as-post-colonial-reality-kamel-daouds-the-meursault-investigation/.
39 See www.worldpolicy.org/blog/2016/02/26/correspondence-kamel-daoud.
40 'Colonia. Il corpo delle donne e il desiderio di libertà di quegli uomini sradicati dalla loro terra'; see www.repubblica.it/esteri/2016/01/10/news/colonia_molestie_capodanno_un_articolo_dello_scrittore_algerino_daoud-130973948/?refresh_ce.
41 'The Sexual Misery of the Arab World'; see www.nytimes.com/2016/02/14/opinion/sunday/the-sexual-misery-of-the-arab-world.html?_r=0.
42 Que s'est-il passé à Cologne la nuit de la Saint-Sylvestre? On peine à le savoir avec exactitude en lisant les comptes rendus, mais on sait – au moins – ce qui s'est passé dans les têtes. Celle des agresseurs, peut-être; celle des Occidentaux, sûrement. Fascinant résumé des jeux de fantasmes. Le 'fait' en lui-même correspond on ne peut mieux au jeu d'images que l'Occidental se fait de l''autre', le réfugié-immigré: angélisme, terreur, réactivation des peurs d'invasions barbares anciennes et base du binôme barbare-civilisé. Des immigrés accueillis s'attaquent à 'nos' femmes, les agressent et les violent. Cela correspond à l'idée que la droite et l'extrême droite ont toujours construite dans les discours contre l'accueil des réfugiés. Ces derniers sont assimilés aux agresseurs, même si l'on ne le sait pas encore avec certitude. Les coupables sont-ils des immigrés installés depuis longtemps? Des réfugiés récents? Des organisations criminelles ou de simples hooligans? On n'attendra pas la réponse pour, déjà, délirer avec cohérence. Le 'fait' a déjà réactivé le discours sur 'doit-on accueillir ou s'enfermer?' face à la misère du monde. Le fantasme n'a pas attendu les faits. (My translation.)
43 La femme est niée, refusée, tuée, voilée, enfermée ou poussédeé. Cela dénote un rapport trouble à l'imaginaire, au désir de vivre, à la création et à la liberté. La femme est le reflet de la vie que l'on ne veut pas admettre. Elle est l'incarnation du désir nécessaire et est donc coupable d'une crime affreux: la vie. (My translation.)
44 www.lemonde.fr/idees/article/2016/02/11/les-fantasmes-de-kamel-daoud_4863096_3232.html. In what follows I refer to the English translation of this article by Muriam Haleh Davies published in the Arab Studies Institute's independent ezine Jadaliyya, see www.jadaliyya.com/pages/index/23841/the-fantasies-of-kamel-daoud.
45 See www.nytimes.com/2015/04/05/magazine/stranger-still.html?_r=1.
46 See 'Lettre à un amie étranger' in *Le Quotidien d'Oran* (February 17, 2016), www.lequotidien-oran.com/?news=5224963. This letter and the letter by Adam Schatz are published in English by Elisabeth Zerofsky on www.worldpolicy.org/blog/2016/02/26/correspondence-kamel-daoud. That's the version I quote here.

References

Bergermann, U. (2016, January 10). Köln/Rape Culture. *Online Blog Zeitschrift für Medienwissenschaft*. Retrieved from www.zfmedienwissenschaft/online/blog/köln-rape-culture.
Blommaert, J. (2008). *Grassroots literacy: Writing, identity and voice in Central Africa*. London: Routledge.
Duden (2004). *Die deutsche Rechtschreibung: Duden Band, 1*(23). Völlig neu bearbeitete und erweiterte Auflage. Herausgegeben von der Dudenredaktion. Auf der Grundlage der neuen amtlichen Rechtschreibregeln. Mannheim: Dudenverlag.
Goffman, E. (1986). *Frame analysis. An essay on the organization of experience*. Boston: Northeastern University Press.

Heynders, O. (2016). *Writers as public intellectuals: Literature, celebrity, democracy*. Basingstoke: Palgrave Macmillan.

Pierik, P. (Ed.). (2016). *Keulen: Kalifaat Light en de Fallout van een conflict*. Soesterberg: Uitgeverij Aspekt.

Sykes, J. B. (Ed.). (1976). *Concise Oxford Dictionary* (6th edition). Oxford: Clarendon Press.

Vince, N. (2016). Literature as post-colonial reality? Kamel Daoud's 'The Meursault Investigation'. *Fiction and Film for French Historians: A Cultural Bulletin*, 6(4). Retrieved from http://h-france.net/fffh/maybe-missed/literature-as-post-colonial-reality-kamel-daouds-the-meursault-investigation/.

Wahrig, G. (1974). *Deutsches Wörterbuch*. Herausgegeben in Zusammenarbeit mit zahlreichen Wissenschaftlern und anderen Fachleuten. Gütersloh: Bertelsmann Lexikon-Verlag.

Zerofsky, E. (2016, February 26). The correspondence of Kamel Daoud. *World Policy Blog*. Retrieved from www.worldpolicy.org/blog/2016/02/26/correspondence-kamel-daoud.

Žižek, S. (2016, January 13). The Cologne attacks were an obscene version of carnival. *New Statesman*. Retrieved from www.newstatesman.com/world/europe/2016/01/slavoj-zizek-cologne-attacks.

Epilogue

Imagining cultural victimology

Antony Pemberton

Introduction

Victimology has shown a remarkable growth in the past few decades, mimicking the rising stature of the plight of victims in policy and practice (e.g. Groenhuijsen, 2014). The notion that victims are no longer the 'forgotten party' of criminal justice has become widespread and the same can be said of the attention to them in academic research.

However, the rise of victimology has been skewed geographically, methodologically and topically (e.g. McGarry & Walklate, 2015). Empirical research concerning the experience of victimization, analysis of victimization as a social phenomenon and the historical development of victims' rights has largely concentrated on the experience in the Anglo-Saxon world and a small group of countries in the north-west of Europe. Empirical research into basic victimological phenomena is not available for large areas of Europe, let alone the rest of the globe.

Furthermore, current victimological knowledge is mostly based on analysis of large quantitative datasets (see an overview in Van Dijk, 2007). This has offered important insights, such as the discovery of the phenomena of repeat and secondary victimization, as well as the large 'dark number' of victims who do not report their crimes to the authorities. However, the data are too abstract and general to map the specific features of victim groups in varying contexts, to query the mechanisms underlying key phenomena and/or to fully comprehend victims' own perspectives on their needs and experiences (Green & Pemberton, 2018). It also tends to unreflectively adopt definitions of behaviour culled from criminal legislation. In doing so, lumping a large variety of experience under categories not fit for purpose, while reinforcing divisions unhelpful and unsuited for gaining understanding of victimological experience. A prominent example of the latter is the moral binary between victims and offenders: an unwarranted act of essentialism that obscures the overlap in victimization and offending behaviour within groups and even within the same individuals. Indeed, some of the most intriguing and important victimological phenomena concern the connection between victimization experience and offending, including crime, political violence and even genocide.

Finally, research has concentrated on a small number of subjects: the prevalence of victimization, mental health effects and the experience with certain features of justice processes, such as victim impact statements or victim-offender mediation. The attention given to these phenomena is well-deserved, but is in urgent need of being complemented by research that embeds victimological phenomena in the relevant societal, historical, religious, institutional and political context. How victimization is experienced first-hand, the victimological reactions that are deemed appropriate and the manner in which wider society understands and views victims are culturally embedded and constructed: the portability of constructs and findings from one context to the next needs to be ascertained, not assumed.

At the most general level, victimology is in urgent need of examining and re-evaluating the manner in which it approaches research into the experience of victimization. In his landmark publication Theodore Sarbin (1986) drew upon Pepper's (1942) classification of 'root metaphors' for metaphysical systems to make a similar argument for psychology. The most relevant distinction is that between mechanism and contextualism. Sarbin (1986, p. 6) finds that the former

> sees events in nature as the products of the transmittal of forces. Modern science has taken this world view as its metaphysical foundation – a view that supports the scientist's search for causes. Efficient causality description is the goal for scientists working with one or another paradigm within the mechanist world view.

The root metaphor for contextualism by contrast is the historical event: rather than a focus on distilling universal and context-independent causes and effects, the metaphor elicits an imagery 'of an ongoing texture of multiple elaborated events, each leading to others, each being influenced by collateral episodes, and by the efforts of multiple agents who engage in actions to satisfy their needs and meet their obligations' (Sarbin, 1986, p. 8).

These opening remarks only seek to reinforce what should be readily apparent from the previous chapters, which have offered a compelling and sometimes fascinating showcase of what a *cultural victimology* could look like. Like its counterpart, cultural criminology, it entails placing victimization and the reaction to victimization in the context of culture, i.e. seeing victimization and the reaction to victimization as at least partly cultural products (McGarry & Walklate, 2015; Mythen, 2007). The chapters display the wide variety in manners in which culture – loosely grouped under ritual, art and media – interacts with, defines, includes and excludes concepts, understandings and interpretations of victimhood, by those suffering themselves, but by wider society as well. In the midst of all this diversity, the common refrain concerns the importance of practice, which informs and transforms the manner in which victimhood comes to express itself.

As a victimologist, following on from colleagues mostly working in various areas of cultural studies, it perhaps falls on me to consider the importance of such a cultural victimology for developments in research, policy and practice concerning victims. I will do so by a no means encompassing survey of various areas of current victimological concern to which cultural victimology has a vital contribution to make: the implementation of the EU Victims directive; the mental health effects of victimization and the work on restorative and transitional justice.

The latter two domains of inquiry and activity can serve to highlight the emancipatory and empowering potential of cultural victimology, given the esteem they already afford those directly afflicted in their theories and processes. But they also reveal the difficulty in achieving and maintaining this potential. The introduction of this volume emphasized the blind spots and weaknesses attributed to an all too positivist victimology (see also Green & Pemberton, 2018). Partly as an analysis of why this has been the case and partly as a cautionary tale I would like to advance two possible explanations for this.

Finally, I would like to take up the challenge Hoondert, Mutsaers and Arfman propose in their introduction, by doing something in the way of 'a Wright Mills' (1959) and (sociologically) imagine in what other ways culture and victimology can usefully interact. Where the subjects in this book have hewed closely to the view of cultural victimology as examining victimological phenomena as products of culture, some sketches of a partly reverse connection are in order. This takes up the invitation of a 'victimological turn in culture studies' to which Hoondert and colleagues allude in the introduction. To what extent are elements of culture rooted in victimology? And to what extent can we understand (elements of) culture as at least partially victimological products?

The empowering potential of cultural victimology

In the past few years, the European Union has staked a claim to being a pre-eminent force in the protection and empowerment of victims of crime (e.g. Biffi et al., 2016). Acknowledging the magnitude of the social consequences of victimization, with 90 million inhabitants of the EU becoming victims of crime annually, observing the large disparities in the manner in which member states of the European Union treat victims and asserting the contradiction this poses to the fundamental freedom of travel between member states, the Treaty of Lisbon explicitly considered victims of crime to belong to the competencies of the EU and its agencies (see Groenhuijsen, 2014; Pemberton & Groenhuijsen, 2012). Ensuring that sufficient support and aid is available, as well as the tools to navigate the intricacies of the justice processes that follow victimization, is part of the 'EU victims directive', or the 'Directive 2012/29/EU of the European Parliament and of the Council of 25 October 2012 establishing minimum standards on the rights, support and protection of victims of crime' in full (EU Victims Directive, 2012). This is a development that undoubtedly should curry favour with a victimologist. However, even the first hurdle of EU legislation, the transposal of the Directive into national legislation, has proved insurmountable (Biffi et al., 2016). It is lacking in most jurisdictions two years after the 2015 due date. Where the national law does meet muster, its translation into the lived experience of victims is often no more than a faint echo of the directive's aspirations. This applies to the extent to which available provisions are sufficiently armed and enforced, the level of organizational and financial support for required services and even the availability of basic information allowing victims to know what rights and services are available: victims might not be forgotten any longer, but in many European jurisdictions that remains the only positive assessment warranted (e.g. Pemberton & Van Eck-Aarten, 2017).

A key variable missing in the European legislative equation concerning victims of crime is that of culture. This applies to the diversity in cultures of national compliance to EU law, cultures of legislative enforcement and administrative prowess, and to police and magistratorial culture (Biffi et al., 2016; Pemberton & Groenhuijsen, 2012). In addition, it concerns cultural variation in the perception of victimization, of particular groups of victims, of the stance towards organizations that might provide support, protection or services to victims. Integration through law is the hallmark of the EU project. But it runs into fundamental difficulties when it supposes other fields of public policy to be simply and unproblematically analogous to the single market (see Lavenex, 2007). Victim policy serves to bring these issues into sharp relief. Cultural victimology can offer the perspectives that actors working in the practice of victimology can use to navigate the distance and – at least to a degree – close the gap between the supranational, top-down aspirations of the Brussels behemoth and the lived reality across the 27 member states. In doing so, it would not only provide a much needed corrective in the field of victim policy, but will offer vital insights into the unprecedented administrative experiment that is the European Union.

The largest body of empirical research in the area of victimology circles the orbit of post-traumatic stress disorder. The volume of studies concerning PTSD or traumatic stress outnumbers research under the banner of victimology by ten to one. In the best-seller *Crazy Like Us*, Ethan Watters (2011) had already singled out PTSD as an example of the more general transplantation of Western and in particular American diagnoses of psychological ailment to other areas and situations around the globe. Even on its own terms, PTSD is defined by a particular event and the interpretation of that event by the person experiencing it (e.g. Kilpatrick, Resnick, & Acierno, 2009). It is in fact the only diagnosis in DSM to which this observation applies. But trauma psychology is only recently waking up to the importance of the interpersonal and cultural environment of the victim in question that this implies (Hinton & Good, 2016).

PTSD has already had its fair share of criticism. Most often this amounts to opposing its medicalization *tout corte* for its recasting of the social, moral and political processes and sequelae of victimization as a health issue, over which the spectre of the pharmaceutical industry casts a long shadow. Doing so is then viewed as disempowering in and of itself, and dismissed on these counts. Fully doing so strikes me as being an overreaction. Anyone who has witnessed and/or experienced the symptoms of full-blown PTSD (Ehlers & Clark, 2000; Herman, 1992) knows that attempts to dismiss it as a mere social construction are better viewed as a fluke of postmodernism than as an avenue for empowerment of those suffering from trauma. In her philosophical analysis of her own rape, Susan Brison (2002, p. 75) says it well:

> Unlike others [...] who consider the medical diagnoses of victims of sexual violence to be dismissive (and even destructive) of the survivor's agency, I felt enormous relief when I realized I had all the symptoms of PTSD and when I learned that there was evidence that it was a neurological condition, treatable by drugs. There's hope I thought. It's chemical!

But that does not make PTSD the be all and end all, the 'paradigm' of our understanding of the aftermath of victimization. As Brison (2002, p. 76) explained: 'So for me medication was a necessary but not sufficient for recovery.' That is true given the other aspects of victimization, but also on its own turf. The nosology of psychotrauma is in urgent need of an *emic* perspective, embedding it in a wider socio-cultural context, in which the particular experiences of victims are crucial (Hinton & Good, 2016). To mention just one example: the work of Sotheara Chhim, whose research into the Cambodian traumatic stress reaction to the Khmer Rouge genocide, uncovered the experience of Cambodian victims as being more accurately described as '*Baksbat*' ('broken courage') than as posttraumatic stress disorder (see Chhim, 2012). As Chhim (2012) explains: 'People with baksbat feel *reang-charl*; they sense that they will not or dare not do something ever again.' Part is traceable to longstanding, cultural traditions, for instance the role of *reasey* ('bad luck, fortune, or supernatural luck') in Khmer culture (Hinton et al. 2009). Part is due to the particular features of the Khmer Rouge regime: the ways in which silence and submission were enforced (see also Hinton, 1998); the breakdown of family life, in forced marriage and child replacement; the barring of cultural practices and forced displacement to other new and unfamiliar localities, as so-called cultural bereavement areas (Eisenbruch, 1991). As Hinton and Good (2016) conclude:

> All these traumas and somatic states mark the space-time of the Pol Pot period, constitute a somatic chronotope for the Cambodian refugee survivor. Teasing out the chronotope for victims of different stripes is an endeavour to which cultural victimology will prove vital.

Finally two phenomena that already seem to embrace features of cultural victimology are transitional (Teitel, 2000) and restorative justice (Johnstone, 2013). Both are already featured in various chapters in this volume (e.g. Hoondert, Clarke, and Varona), so I will presume the reader is familiar with them. Both have emerged as a critique of formal criminal justice, in the manner in which it ignores those directly affected, including prominently victims of crime; in its lack of attention to local and historical context; and the manner in which it paves over the immediate experiences with conflict and crime.

Cultural victimology: some words of caution

Both restorative justice and transitional justice have also displayed a tendency to backslide in the direction of the phenomena that they criticize. The contextualist potential that seems inherent to them might not effectively emerge. For instance, the United Nations has defined four pillars of transitional justice: truth, justice, reparations and guarantees of non-recurrence, that apply irrespective of context. The issue is not so much that each one of these 'pillars' can be criticized. The guarantees of non-recurrence depend upon the unfolding power structure (Kennedy, 2016). Reparations are framed in fundamentally aspirational language (Letschert & Parmentier, 2014). Justice is not a neutral and necessarily benign force in the processes of transition (Pemberton & Letschert, 2017). And it is questionable whether truth is indeed the necessary first step towards reconciliation and/ or whether it does not often need to take a backseat against imagination or artistic representation. The issue is more generally that these features of transitional justice are asserted a priori, rather than left to the interpretation of those living through their situations.

Restorative justice increasingly comes equipped with its own set of how-tos and best practices, even down to the pre-scripted version of conferencing that the International Institute for Restorative Practices (IIRP) touts as 'real justice' (Wachtel, O'Connell, & Wachtel, 2010). It is visible in the manner in which restorative justice is examined and theorized, with an influential group of scholars emphasizing the importance of randomized controlled trials of restorative justice (Sherman & Strang, 2007) and in the application of the same mechanistic terms in use in formal processes of justice to the working of restorative processes (e.g. Rossner, 2018). This is not to condemn this type of work. Given that I have been involved in various attempts to do the same (e.g. Cleven, Lens, & Pemberton, 2015; Pemberton & Vanfraechem, 2015) that would be very hypocritical. It does seek to stress that transformative co-option, to which restorative justice scholars and practitioners have been very much alive when it comes to inclusion of restorative practices in criminal justice, can also occur by more subtle means (e.g. Karstedt, 2011).

This brings me to the points of caution I want to make in this section. The notion that something so deeply moral, personal, identity-laden, idiosyncratic, emotional and embodied as victimization (e.g. Pemberton, 2015) could be fully shoehorned into a positivist research agenda seems to be difficult to square with reality. It therefore calls for an explanation. That is all the more so given that this is not a novel observation. The issue has been raised since the research domain of victimology achieved any academic maturity (e.g. Mawby & Walklate, 1994; Quinney, 1972). The arguments also apply to other domains of social inquiry, and can be marshalled to critique social science generally (e.g. Flyvbjerg, 2001). For victimology, they can come with the added sting of reinforcing the de-individuation, disempowering and de-humanizing impact of the victimization act itself. The criticism of positivist victimology, beyond its epistemological blind spots, resides in the manner in which it talks down to victims: claiming an understanding of victims' situation, that they themselves lack; viewing them as a repository of causal mechanisms that would have applied equally to others in the same situation, thereby denying their individuality; and prescribing the ends that victims should pursue and the roles by which they can achieve these ends, thereby denying victims autonomy and abilities to act in line with this autonomy.

That this is so, I think, is first a carry-over from victimology's bigger sister – criminology – and can at least in part be explained by the distrust with which she views her research subjects (Presser, 2016). As noted in the introduction to this volume, victimology emerged as a counterpart, or as some might have it 'a wayward sub-discipline' of criminology (Rock, 2007), and criminology has been similarly slow to adapt to the cultural turn. Jock Young (2011) lamented that 'mainstream criminology is guilty of an over-reliance on statistically driven research that abstracts the experi-ence of crime and bloats the criminological lexicon to the detriment of its own creativity'. In a discussion of the difficulties facing the similar 'narrative turn', Lois Presser notes:

[...] our ultimate referent is the wily offender. In the criminal justice system offenders face demonstrable institutional incentives for portraying themselves in particular, not-necessarily-true ways. Offenders' stories are taken as devices meant for manipulation. A perspective tied too closely to their stories would likely seem suspect.

(Presser, 2016, p. 146)

This not only influences the approach to research but also determines the topics of study: the larger the volume of a particular behaviour, and the greater ease there is to track this behaviour with 'hard' data, the more likely it is to become a topic of criminological inquiry.

These observations also hold for victimology. It has spent large efforts on relatively high volume but low impact forms of victimization, in areas of the world that are at peace, while paying little to no attention to areas of the world in which norm-transgressive behaviour is endemic, and victimization is an everyday occurrence (McGarry & Walklate, 2015). In the past ten years scholars could legitimately claim to have re-discovered a so-called 'supranational' victimology given the dearth of research into gross human rights violations, war and genocide under these banners (e.g. Letschert, Haveman, De Brouwer, & Pemberton, 2011). I venture that a similar suspicion towards victims is at work here: perhaps as no more than a sense of equality of arms with the offender. By a sort of analogy with the criminal justice process: if the latter's story is to be viewed with suspicion, the opposing tale is so as well.

This scientific mark of Abel (Van Dijk, 2006) is difficult to overcome. The features of victimization experience – personal, identity-laden, idiosyncratic, emotional and embodied – are difficult to square with the requirements of an 'objective' social science. As a result, victims' first-person take on their own experience is not taken seriously. This is reinforced by an – often implicit – liberal or deontological stance that any destructive emotions, thoughts and behaviours on the part of victims are the result of mistaken, faulty and ineffective interpretations of their own situation. The almost total dearth of research into the phenomenon of revenge is an important case in point (Jacoby, 1983). Revenge is one of the most important themes in world literature, and has obvious victimological significance. But before any serious inquiry into revenge gets underway, it is already dismissed on moral and instrumental grounds and subsequently pathologized (e.g. Kaufman, 2013; Zaibert, 2006). It can either be overcome in one way or another by our faculties of reason and/or by treatment of the pathology. Along with other examples of similar phenomena this means that the extent to which victims' experiences are seen as fully authentic and legitimate, is narrowly constricted (see also Bosma, Mulder, & Pemberton, 2018). Of course a cultural victimology could illuminate the extent and variation of such idealized and stereotypical framing of victims' ordeal. Nevertheless, the track-record of practice and theory in restorative and transitional justice suggests that the more difficult facets of victimolog-ical experience are in danger of being airbrushed out of the picture. Most of the interesting questions in victimology arise precisely where there is no real possibility, even no real conception, of what restoration actually entails, and reside in the reality that transition and restoration on the one hand and justice on the other can and will conflict with each other (Pemberton, 2015). Invoking seemingly benign concepts such as human rights or reconciliation is no solution, often these run roughshod over victims' own perspectives and needs and thereby become tools in stealth oppression and denial of victimological experience.

I have a firm belief that cultural victimology has an empowering and emancipatory potential. The extent to which it lives up this promise, in my view, depends upon the extent to which it can set aside suspicions of victims' first-person perspectives and does not mistakenly sweep key ele-ments of victims' experiences under a liberal carpet.

Victimology of culture

Beyond the importance of viewing victimization at least partially as a product of culture, the cross-fertilization might also include the reverse connection: the role of victimological phenomena in (elements) of culture. In this final section I want to mention some examples that could be con-strued to fall under this heading. Of course the space of one section does not allow more than a cursory and superficial examination, and I cannot claim much specific expertise on some of the topics I will discuss. With this disclaimer though, I have at least found it worthwhile, when considering the relationship between (interpretations of) victimization and cultural explanations for its interpretations, to keep on open mind on the co-creation of these explanations. To do so, I marshal a hodgepodge of theor-etical and philosophical perspectives, including Vamik Volkan's work on chosen traumas (Volkan, 1997), David Graeber's analysis of the emergence of money and value (Graeber, 2011), and even Nietzsche's *Genealogy of Morality* (1967 [1887]), which I have already put to use in my *Victimology with a Hammer* (Pemberton, 2015). They signify the importance of victi-mological phenomena in national identity, morality and value.

Tales of group victimization can foster violent extremism, incite polit-ical violence and even full-scale conflict and war (e.g. McCauley & Moskalenko, 2010; Waller, 2002). They can offer a sense of moral entitle-ment culminating in acts of vicarious revenge against members of an opposing group (Waller, 2002). In turn, this can be taken to mean that such group victim narratives are a barrier to post-war reconstruction of peace and order.

There is probably a good deal of wisdom to this, but the issue is compli-cated by the role victimization narratives seem to play in the creation of group identities. Vamik Volkan (1997) developed the view that such narratives of victimization, what he calls *chosen traumas*, are a key element of such large-scale group identity, even more powerfully so than shared stories of triumph, *chosen glories*. The notion that they are *chosen* concerns the fact that the historical narratives in use at any given time can co-vary with political circumstances. This applies both to the choice for a particular historical episode and its interpretation. The latter also means that the historical narrative can be more akin to a myth than to an actual historical occurrence. The narratives in turn play a role in determining the content and boundaries of group membership.

The reason that victimization narratives can do this is exactly because of their moral quality. Unresolved injustice at the group level at once gives a reason to act in the present as well as a means to bind individuals into the sense of being a member of a group. Volkan presents a vast array of cases to make his point. One of the most poignant ones is the tale of the defeat of the Serbian Tsar Lazar by the Ottoman Empire at the battle of the Field of the Blackbirds in 1389. It has been a recurring theme in Serbian identity in history and was re-appropriated by Milosevic exactly 600 years later in a speech at that spot. It is that speech that set in motion the events leading to Balkan wars of the 1990s and the demise of Yugoslavia.

The role of victimization in shared morality in post-modern times was explicitly explored by Dutch theorist and criminologist Hans Boutellier (1993, 2002). He followed Richard Rorty's (1989) line of thinking that the secularization and the state's retreat from any say in people's private views on normativity have reduced a shared morality to a bottom-line, summarized in the question 'Are you suffering?' and the rejection of suffering and cruelty. This makes the victim the central figure of our moral system. Indeed, Boutellier argued that much of the current interest in victims and victimization can be traced to this feature of post-modernity.

I can follow this line of thought, but have suggested that the role of victimization is more fundamental to morality (Pemberton, 2015). Nietzsche's (1967 [1887]) work on the *Genealogy of Morality* has led me to the belief that victimization can be understood to be key to the development of morality itself. Nietzsche positioned suffering, and the complexities or even impossibilities of finding meaning in suffering as among the most fundamental forces in social life. In Nietzsche's view, morality – or as he sometimes disparaging calls it 'slave morality' – seeks to offer society's losers – those suffering without possibility to impose themselves on the world, with nothing to look forward to except their demise, without ever making their mark – a means to turn the tables on the strong. It does so first by labelling the strong's oppressive actions evil, and the weak's actions good. And subsequently proposes *an ascetic ideal* that as Ridley (1998) neatly summarizes makes the 'slaves' apply the 'evil' side of their new distinction to *everything* temporal, immanent, this-worldly, and the 'good' side of it to whatever lacks these qualities – to the 'beyond', to God, to heaven. The ascetic ideal then makes life bearable, gives suffering meaning, by demonizing life itself. All good things come from heaven, all value transcends life.

(Ridley, 1998, p. 9)

The cause of our suffering is life itself, to be overcome by those values that go beyond life. This view is central to Nietzsche's claim to be an immoralist: not because of his opposition to ethical systems or his disdain of (the importance of) suffering, but because the system of morality that aspires to the ascetic ideal does not offer any real contribution to countering this suffering.

Nietzsche also crops up in David Graeber's (2011) *Debt: The First 5,000 Years* (see p. 76). An important work for victimologists because of the insights it provides into the vexing issue of compensation for suffering. For many forms of victimization, affording a monetary value can lead to a feeling of unease, captured by Fiske and Tetlock's (1997) notion of a *taboo trade-off*. Before reading Graeber I often thought that this was something fairly specific to the experience of victimization, but I now understand that it is but one example of the more general problem of attaching a numeric value to human experience, particularly in means used for exchange. Like most people who have had some basic training in economics, I thought that such quantification was an autonomous 'invisible hand' by-product of the move from bartering goods to money and subsequently to systems of debt and credit. People exchanged goods for goods, and to solve 'the problem of the double coincidence of wants' money with its numerical value was invented. In that way people could buy goods at one time, and sell them at another, and similarly buy them from one person and sell them to another. In these exchanges the laws of supply and demand determine the numerical value of goods. And the unease I might feel then should result from my perception of a difference between the spheres of goods and the spheres of human suffering.

The issue is, however, that as Humphrey (1985, p. 48) stated: 'No example of a barter economy, pure and simple, has ever been described, let alone the emergence from it of money; all available ethnography suggests that there has never been such a thing.' Graeber reveals that from Adam Smith's *The Wealth of Nations* (1776) onward the 'myth of barter' never depicted any recognizable historical reality, but merely set up a foundation story of the discipline of economics. Rather than the steps from barter, to money, to credit, Graeber points out that the evidence suggests exactly the opposite sequence, while rather than emerging in free exchange, money is as creature of the state.

Without the availability of the invisible hand of the free market as an explanation it calls into question how numerical value become affixed to human affairs. Graeber's explanation is victimological, and worth quoting at some length:

> On the other hand, if Joshua's pig just destroyed Henry's garden, and especially, if that led to a fight in which Henry lost a toe, and Henry's family is now hauling Joshua in front of the victim assembly – this is precisely the context where people are most likely to become petty and legalistic and express outrage if they feel they have received one groat less than was their rightful due. That means exact mathematical specificity: for instance, the capacity to measure the exact value of a two-year-old pregnant sow. What's more, the levying of penalties must have constantly required the calculation of equivalences. Say the fine is in marten pelts but the culprit's clan doesn't have any martens. How many squirrel skins will do? Or pieces of silver jewelry? [...] This would help explain why, for instance medieval Welsh law codes can contain detailed breakdowns [...] of the monetary value of every object likely to be found in an ordinary homestead [...] despite the fact that there seems no reason to believe that most such items could even be purchased on the open market at the time.
>
> (Graeber, 2011, pp. 61–62)

Rather than victimization being forced to be an odd and uneasy bedfellow of monetary value, it turns out that situations of victimization are the well-spring of the type of quantification that states eventually parlayed into money itself.

Given that I find this to be one of the most fascinating findings of which I am aware, I will leave it at that. I very much look forward to the foray into the unknown upon which cultural victimology is set to embark, and hope and even expect that this endeavour will lead to more such remarkable discoveries.

References

Biffi, E., Mulder, E., Pemberton A., Santos, M., Valério, M., Vanfraechem, I., & Van der Vorm, B. (2016). *IVOR report: Implementing victim-oriented reform of the criminal justice system in the European Union*. Lisbon: APAV.

Bosma A. K., Mulder, E., & Pemberton, A. (2018, forthcoming). The ideal victim through other(s') eyes. In: M. Duggan (Ed.), *Revisiting the 'ideal victim': Developments in critical victimology*. Bristol: Policy Press.

Boutellier, H. (1993). *Solidariteit en slachtofferschap: De morele betekenis van criminaliteit in een postmoderne cultuur*. Nijmegen: SUN.

Boutellier, H. (2002). *De veiligheidsutopie: Hedendaags onbehagen en verlangen rond misdaad en straf*. The Hague: Boom Juridische uitgevers.

Brison S. J. (2002). *Aftermath: Violence and the remaking of a self*. Princeton: Princeton University Press.

Chhim, S. (2012). Baksbat (broken courage): The development and validation of the inventory to measure Baksbat, a Cambodian trauma-based cultural syndrome. *Culture, Medicine and Psychiatry, 36*(4), 640–659.

Cleven, I., Lens, K. M. E., & Pemberton, A. (2015). *De rol van herstelbemiddeling in het strafrecht: Eindrapportage onderzoek pilots Herstelbemiddeling.* Tilburg: INTERVICT.

Ehlers, A., & Clark, D. M. (2000). A cognitive model of posttraumatic stress disorder. *Behaviour Research and Therapy, 38*(4), 319–345.

Eisenbruch, M. (1991). From post-traumatic stress disorder to cultural bereavement: Diagnosis of Southeast Asian refugees. *Social Science and Medicine, 33*(6), 673–680.

EU Victims Directive (2012). Directive 2012/29/EU of the European Parliament and of the Council. *Official Journal of the European Union*, November 14, 2012, 57–73.

Fiske, A. P, & Tetlock, P. E. (1997). Taboo trade-offs: Reactions to transactions that transgress the spheres of justice. *Political Psychology, 18*(2), 255–297.

Flyvbjerg, B. (2001). *Making social science matter: Why social inquiry fails and how it can succeed again.* Cambridge: Cambridge University Press.

Graeber, D. (2011). *Debt: The first 5,000 years.* New York: Melville.

Green, S., & Pemberton, A. (2018). The impact of crime: Victimisation, harm and resilience. In S. Walklate (Ed.), *Handbook of victims and victimology* (2nd edition, pp. 77–101). London: Routledge.

Groenhuijsen, M. (2014). The development of international policy in relation to victims of crime. *International Review of Victimology, 20*(1), 31–48.

Herman, J. L. (1992). *Trauma and recovery.* New York: Basic Books.

Hinton, A. L. (1998). A head for an eye: Revenge in the Cambodian Genocide. *American Ethnologist, 25*(3), 352–377.

Hinton D. E. & Good. B. J. (2016). *Culture and PTSD: Trauma in global and historical perspective.* Philadelphia: University of Pennsylvania Press.

Hinton, D. E., Hinton, A. L., Pich, V., Loeum, J. R., & Pollack, M. H. (2009). Nightmares among Cambodian refugees: The breaching of concentric ontological security. *Culture, Medicine and Psychiatry, 33*(2), 219–265.

Humphrey, C. (1985). Barter and economic disintegration. *Man, 20*(1), 48–72.

Jacoby, S. (1983). *Wild justice: The evolution of revenge.* New York: Harper.

Johnstone, G. (2013). *Restorative justice: Ideas, values, debates.* London: Routledge.

Karstedt, S. (2011). Handle with care: Emotions, crime and justice. In S. Karstedt, I. Loader, & H. Strang (Eds.), *Emotions, crime and justice* (pp. 1–19). Oxford, UK: Hart Publishing.

Kaufman, W. (2013). *Honor and revenge: A theory of punishment.* Dordrecht: Springer.

Kennedy, D. (2016). *A world of struggle.* Princeton: Princeton University Press.

Kilpatrick, D. G., Resnick, H. G., & Acierno, R. (2009). Should PTSD criterion A be retained? *Journal of Traumatic Stress, 22*(5), 374–383.

Lavenex, S. (2007). Mutual recognition and the monopoly of force: Limits of the single market analogy. *Journal of European Public Policy, 14*(5), 762–779.

Letschert, R., Haveman, R., De Brouwer, A-M., & Pemberton, A. (Eds.). (2011). *Victimological approaches to international crimes: Africa.* Antwerp: Intersentia.

Letschert, R., & Parmentier, S. (2014). Repairing the impossible: Victimological approaches to international crimes. In I. Vanfraechem, A. Pemberton, & F. M. Ndahinda (Eds.), *Justice for victims: Perspectives on rights, transition and reconciliation* (pp. 210–228). London: Routledge.

Mawby, R., & Walklate, S. (1994). *Critical victimology: International perspectives*. London: Sage.

McCauley, C., & Moskalenko, S. (2010). *Friction: How radicalization happens to them and us*. Oxford: Oxford University Press.

McGarry, R., & Walklate, S. (2015). *Victims: Trauma, testimony and justice*. London: Routledge.

Mythen, G. (2007). Cultural victimology: Are we all victims now? In S. Walklate (Ed.), *Handbook of victims and victimology* (pp. 464–483). Cullompton, UK: Willan.

Nietzsche, F. (1967 [1887]). *On the genealogy of morals* (W. Kaufmann & R. J. Hollingdale, Trans.). New York: Random House.

Pemberton, A. (2015). *Victimology with a hammer: The challenge of victimology*. Tilburg: Prismaprint.

Pemberton, A., & Groenhuijsen, M. (2012). Developing victim's rights within the European Union: Past, present and future. In H. Morosawa, J., Dussich, & G. Kirchhoff (Eds.), *Victimology and human security: New horizons*. Nijmegen: Wolf Legal Publishers.

Pemberton, A., & Letschert, R. (2017). Justice as the art of muddling through: The importance of *nyaya* in the aftermath of international crimes. In C. Brants & S. Karstedt (Eds.), *Transitional justice and the public spheres: Engagement, legitimacy and contestation*. Oxford: Hart Publishers.

Pemberton, A., & Van Eck-Aarten, P. (2017). A radical in disguise: Judith Shklar's victimology and restorative justice. In I. Aertsen & B. Pali (Eds.), *Critical restorative justice* (pp. 315–330). Oxford: Hart Publishers.

Pemberton, A., & Vanfraechem, I. (2015). Victims' victimization experience and their need for justice. In D. Bolivar, I. Vanfraechem, & I. Aertsen (Eds.), *Victims and restorative justice* (pp. 15–47). London: Routledge.

Pepper, S. (1942). *World hypotheses*. Berkeley: University of California Press.

Presser, L. (2016). Criminology and the narrative turn. *Crime Media Culture*, *12*(2), 137–151.

Quinney, R. (1972). Who is the victim? *Criminology*, *10*(3), 314–323.

Ridley, A. (1998). *Nietzsche's conscience: Six character studies from the 'genealogy'*. New York: Cornell University Press.

Rock, P. (2007). Theoretical perspectives on victimisation. In S. Walklate (Ed.), *Handbook of victims and victimology* (pp. 37–61). Cullompton, UK: Willan.

Rorty, R. (1989). *Contingency, irony, and solidarity*. Cambridge: Cambridge University Press.

Rossner, M. (2018). Restorative justice and victims of crime: Directions and developments. In S. Walklate (Ed.), *Handbook of victims and victimology* (2nd edition, pp. 229–246). London: Routledge.

Sarbin, T. R. (1986). The narrative as a root metaphor for psychology. In T. R. Sarbin (Ed.), *Narrative psychology: The storied nature of human conduct* (pp. 3–21). New York: Praeger.

Sherman, L., & Strang, H. (2007). *Restorative justice: The evidence*. London: The Smith Institute.

Smith, A. (1776). *An inquiry into the nature and causes of the wealth of nations*. Oxford: Clarendon.

Teitel, R. (2000). *Transitional justice*. Oxford: Oxford University Press.

Van Dijk, J. J. M. (2006). *The mark of Abel: Reflections on the social labelling of victims of crime* (Inaugural Lecture). Tilburg University, Tilburg.

Van Dijk, J. J. M. (2007). *The world of crime: Breaking the silence on problems of security, justice and development across the world*. Thousand Oaks, CA: Sage.

Volkan, V. (1997). *Bloodlines: From ethnic pride to ethnic terrorism*. New York: Basic Books.

Wachtel, T., O'Connell, T., & Wachtel, B. (2010). *Restorative justice conferencing: Real justice and the conferencing handbook*. Bethlehem, PA: IIRP.

Waller, J. (2002). *Becoming evil: How ordinary people commit genocide and mass killing*. Oxford: Oxford University Press.

Watters, E. (2011). *Crazy like us: The globalization of the American psyche*. New York: Free Press.

Wright Mills, C. (1959). *The sociological imagination*. New York: Oxford University Press.

Young, J. (2011). *The criminological imagination*. Cambridge: Polity Press.

Zaibert, L. (2006). Punishment and revenge. *Law and Philosophy*, *25*, 81–118.

About the authors

William Arfman has a background in the archaeology and anthropology of Central America, as well as in the comparative study of religion. Currently, he is a postdoctoral associate and lecturer in the field of ritual studies at Tilburg University (the Netherlands). Favouring an interdisciplinary approach, his main research interests are late modern ritual dynamics, ritual innovation and traditionality, ritual and (community) art, and ritual commemoration. In the past he explored these interests through topics such as contemporary Mexican ancestor veneration and the emergence of a ritual field of collective commemoration in the Netherlands. Currently his research focuses on the ritual negotiation of victimhood in the so-called European refugee crisis.

Jan Blommaert is Professor of Language, Culture and Globalization and Director of the Babylon Center at Tilburg University, the Netherlands, and Professor of African Linguistics and Sociolinguistics at Ghent University, Belgium. Publications include *Ethnography, Superdiversity and Linguistic Landscapes: Chronicles of Complexity* (Multilingual Matters, 2013), *The Sociolinguistics of Globalization* (Cambridge University Press, 2010), *Ethnographic Fieldwork: A Beginner's Guide* (Multilingual Matters, 2010), *Grassroots Literacy* (Routledge, 2008), *Discourse: A Critical Introduction* (Cambridge University Press, 2005), and *Language Ideological Debates* (Mouton de Gruyter, 1999).

David Clarke is a senior lecturer in the Department of Politics, Languages and International Studies at the University of Bath. His research interests include the politics of memory and cultural memory. He is co-editor (with Ute Wölfel) of *Remembering the German Democratic Republic: Divided Memory in a United Germany* (2011) and is the author of recent articles on memory politics in *Memory Studies, History and Memory, Central Europe* and *German Politics*.

Odile Heynders is Full Professor of Comparative Literature at the School of Humanities and Digital Science at Tilburg University. Her current research focuses on European contemporary literature and politics. She recently published *Writers as Public Intellectuals: Literature, Celebrity, Democracy* (Palgrave Macmillan, 2016). She is now working on the book *Experiences of Migration, Literature as Social Knowledge*.

Martin Hoondert studied musicology and theology and is specialized in music and rituals. Since 2007 he is (Assistant) Professor of Music, Religion & Ritual at the Department of Culture Studies of Tilburg University (the Netherlands). His research focuses on 'music and death' and 'practices of memorialization'. His research topics include: the contemporary requiem, musical repertories of funeral rites, commemoration and music, music and grief/bereavement, music and consolation, music and the First and Second World Wars, practices of memorialization regarding genocide (especially Rwanda and Srebrenica).

Sjaak Kroon is Professor of Multilingualism in the Multicultural Society. He is a member of the Department of Culture Studies and Babylon, Center for the Study of Superdiversity at Tilburg University, the Netherlands. His main focus in research and teaching is on linguistic and cultural diversity, language policy, literacy and education in the context of globalization.

Paul Mutsaers studied cultural anthropology at Utrecht University and works as a police anthropologist for the Department of Culture Studies, Tilburg University, where he is employed as a postdoctoral researcher. He has previously worked at the Police Academy of the Netherlands, where he carried out his PhD research on police discrimination. His research has been published in journals such as *American Anthropologist*, *The British Journal of Criminology*, *Critique of Anthropology*, *Anthropology of Work Review*, *Social Anthropology* and *Theoretical Criminology*. He has a book contract with Oxford University Press to publish his manuscript 'Police Unlimited: Policing, Migrants and the Values of Bureaucracy' (in the Clarendon Studies in Criminology).

Antony Pemberton is Professor of Victimology and Director of INTERVICT, the International Victimology Institute Tilburg at Tilburg University in the Netherlands. He is a political scientist and a criminologist. His research interests concern the broad topic of Victims and Society, including victims' perspectives on justice, societal reactions to victims and processes of victimization, cultural victimology, narrative victimology and the ethics of victimology. He has published over 80 articles, book chapters and books on the subject of victimology. Most of his current ideas are reflected in his inaugural address in Tilburg, *Victimology with a Hammer: The Challenge of Victimology* (2015).

Paul Post studied theology and liturgical studies in Utrecht and Christian art and archaeology in Rome. He is Professor of Ritual Studies at Tilburg University (the Netherlands, School of Humanities and Digital Science, Department of Culture Studies). His main interests are in the field of liturgy, popular religion and Christian art, and (post)modern developments in ritual, on which he has published books and articles. In recent years the focus of his research has been on ritual space and place, pilgrimage and tourism, and cyberritual. He is now coordinating two book projects: one on 'absent ritual', and one on 'disaster ritual'.

Gema Varona is a lecturer in Victimology and Criminal Policy at the University of the Basque Country and senior researcher at the Basque Institute of Criminology (Donostia/San Sebastian, Spain). In 1998 she was honoured with the Junior Scholar Competition Award of the International Society of Criminology for her research comparing restorative justice in gypsy and non-gypsy communities. Coordinator of the degree in criminology and Co-director of the Master in Victimology of that University, she has authored books on migration and human rights, restorative justice, juries and the construction of juridical truth, women's local safety audits, victims of terrorism, and victims of sexual abuse.

Lieke Wijnia lectures on Art History at University College Tilburg and is a postdoctoral fellow of the Centre for Religion and Heritage at the University of Groningen. Her research focuses on artistic practices at the intersection of religion, heritage, and politics. She has published in *The Burlington Magazine* and *Material Religion*. She is co-editor of the volume *The Bible and Global Tourism* (Bloomsbury), author of *Post-Secular Art* in the series *Research Perspectives in Religion and the Arts* (Brill), and is reworking her dissertation for publication in the series *Religion & Society* (De Gruyter).

Index

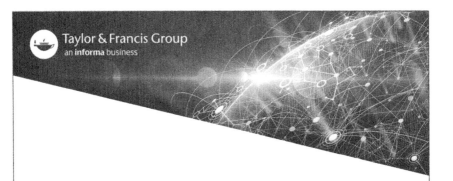